Hiking Waterfalls Southern California

A Guide to the Region's Best Waterfall Hikes

Liz Thomas and Justin Lichter

FALCONGUIDES

GUILFORD, CONNECTICUT

An imprint of The Rowman & Littlefield Publishing Group, Inc.
4501 Forbes Blvd., Ste. 200
Lanham, MD 20706
www.rowman.com

Falcon and FalconGuides are registered trademarks and Make Adventure Your Story is a trademark of The Rowman & Littlefield Publishing Group, Inc.

Distributed by NATIONAL BOOK NETWORK

Copyright © 2019 by The Rowman & Littlefield Publishing Group, Inc.
Maps by The Rowman & Littlefield Publishing Group, Inc.

Photos by Liz Thomas unless otherwise noted

British Library Cataloguing in Publication Information available

Library of Congress Cataloging-in-Publication Data available
Names: Thomas, Elizabeth, author. | Lichter, Justin, author. | FalconGuides (Publisher) | Rowman and Littlefield, Inc.
Title: Hiking waterfalls Southern California : a guide to the region's best waterfall hikes / Elizabeth Thomas and Justin Lichter.
Other titles: Falcon guide.
Description: First Edition. | Guilford, Connecticut : FalconGuides, [2019] | Series: A Falcon guide | "Distributed by NATIONAL BOOK NETWORK"—T.p. verso.
Identifiers: LCCN 2019021027 | ISBN 9781493037247 (paperback : alk. paper) | ISBN 9781493037254 (ebook)
Subjects: LCSH: Hiking—California, Southern—Guidebooks. | Waterfalls—California, Southern—Guidebooks. | Day hiking—California, Southern—Guidebooks. | Hiking for children—California, Southern—Guidebooks. | Hiking with dogs—California, Southern—Guidebooks. | Walking—California, Southern—Guidebooks. | Rock climbing—California, Southern—Guidebooks. | Bouldering—California, Southern—Guidebooks. | Mountaineering—California, Southern—Guidebooks. | Backpacking—California, Southern—Guidebooks. | Camping—California, Southern—Guidebooks. | Mountain biking—California, Southern—Guidebooks. | Cycling—California, Southern—Guidebooks. | Trails—California, Southern—Guidebooks. | Outdoor recreation—California, Southern—Guidebooks. | Natural history—California, Southern—Guidebooks. | California, Southern—Description and travel. | California, Southern—Guidebooks.
Classification: LCC GV199.42.C22 T56 2019 | DDC 796.5109794/9—dc23
LC record available at https://lccn.loc.gov/2019021027

Contents

Acknowledgments viii
Introduction ix
How to Use This Guide x
Hiking Gear and Essentials xv
Risks and Dangers of Hiking Waterfalls xvi
How to Be a Good Hiker.. xxiii
Map Legend xxvi

Angeles National Forest 1
  1. San Antonio Falls 3
  2. Soldier Creek Falls (Lewis Falls) 6
  3. Fish Canyon Falls 10
  4. Monrovia Canyon Falls 14
  5. Hermit Falls 18
  6. Sturtevant Falls 22
  7. Eaton Canyon Falls 25
  8. Millard Falls 30
  9. Switzer Falls 34
 10. Colby Canyon Falls 38
 11. Cooper Falls 39
 12. Upper Buckhorn Falls 43
 13. Lower Buckhorn Falls 45
 14. Trail Canyon Falls 48
 15. Placerita Canyon Falls 53

Pacific Coast and Santa Monica Mountains 56
 16. Paradise Falls (Wildwood Falls) 58
 17. La Jolla Canyon Falls 63
 18. Escondido Falls 67
 19. Newton and Zuma Falls... 70
 20. Santa Ynez Falls 74
 21. Temescal Canyon Falls 78

Orange County... 82
 22. Holy Jim Falls 83
 23. Hidden Falls (Trabuco Canyon Falls/Falls Canyon Falls)... 87
 24. San Juan Falls 89
 25. Chiquito Falls 92
 26. Ortega Falls... 95
 27. Tenaja Falls... 98

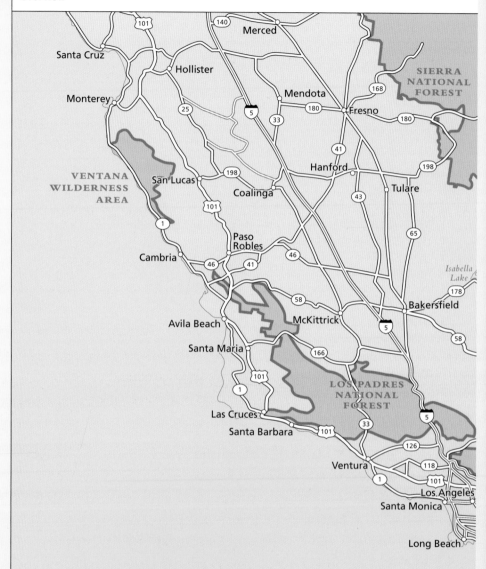

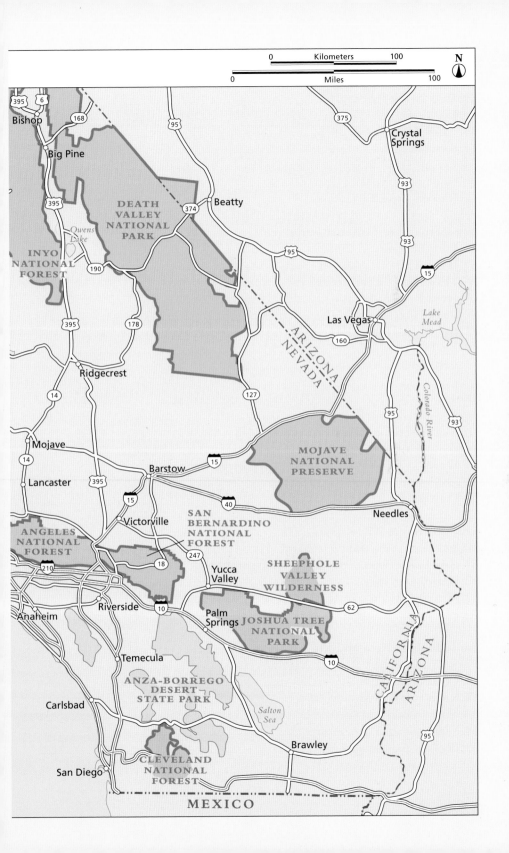

San Diego County 102
28. Cedar Creek Falls.. 104
29. Three Sisters Falls Trail 109
30. Jack Creek Falls... 114
31. Los Peñasquitos Falls 118
32. Sweetwater Falls... 122
33. Green Valley Falls Trail... 126
34. Cottonwood Creek Falls 130
35. Kitchen Creek Falls... 134

San Bernardino National Forest 138
36. Etiwanda Falls 139
37. Bonita Falls 143
38. Middle Fork of Lytle Creek Falls (Third Crossing Falls) 146
39. Heart Rock Falls.. 151
40. Aztec Falls 154
41. Cold Creek Falls 158
42. Big Falls 161
43. Fuller Mill Creek Falls 165

Desert 168
44. Tahquitz Canyon Falls 169
45. Murray Canyon Falls.. 174
46. West Fork Falls 178
47. Borrego Canyon Falls (Borrego Palm Canyon Trail) 181
48. Maidenhair Falls.. 185
49. Darwin Falls... 189

Ojai and Sespe Wilderness 193
50. Santa Paula Falls and Punchbowl... 194
51. Rose Valley Falls.. 198
52. Potrero John Falls.. 201
53. Matilija Falls.. 205
54. Piru Falls.. 209

Santa Barbara Area and the Central Coast.......................... 214
55. San Ysidro Falls 215
56. Cold Springs Falls (Tangerine) 219
57. Seven Falls (and Mission Falls).. 224
58. Nojoqui Falls 228
59. Little Falls 231
60. Big Falls and Middle Falls 235

Big Sur 239
61. Black Swift Falls (Ragged Point Falls) 240
62. Salmon Creek Falls 244
63. Limekiln Falls... 247
64. McWay Falls 251
65. Canyon Falls 254
66. Pfeiffer Falls 256

Sequoia, Kings Canyon, and Southern Yosemite 259
67. Grizzly Falls 260
68. Roaring River Falls... 263
69. Mist Falls 267
70. Tokopah Falls 271
71. Chilnualna Falls.. 274

Mammoth and the Eastern Sierra 278
72. Lone Pine Falls 279
73. Twin Falls 283
74. Rainbow Falls and Lower Falls.. 286
75. Minaret Falls 291
76. Horsetail Falls 293
77. Tuolumne Falls and White Cascade Falls................................... 296
78. California, LeConte, and Waterwheel Falls................................. 301
79. Lundy Canyon Falls 304
80. Horse Creek Falls 307
81. Leavitt Falls.. 311
82. Sardine Falls... 314
83. Falls of Emigrant Wilderness 318

Resources.. 322
About the Authors.. 325

Acknowledgments

This book is but the beginning of your lifetime of waterfall searching. May it lead to new discoveries and take you to adventures and explorations off the beaten path.

In my search for those places, I thank the guidebook and web writers who have come before me. Anyone interested in expanding their waterfall and hiking experiences beyond this guidebook should consult their works, which are listed in the Resources section. While the authors before me deserve their own round of applause, I'd specifically like to thank my hiking partner and local guidebook author David Harris, whose insight and experience—not to mention weekly 5 a.m. hiking get-togethers—have been an inspiration and model as I wrote this book.

I also thank my editor David Legere and the production and mapping staff at FalconGuides/Rowman & Littlefield for their patience, guidance, and vision.

Anyone who enjoys spending time in or looking at undeveloped landscapes in Southern California must recognize the conservationists with the foresight to keep open space wild.

To truly understand the history of where we hike, we should also acknowledge those who lived on this land before us and the history of the land we hike on today. When possible, I include natural and cultural history in my hike and regional descriptions, but I encourage you to explore https://native-land.ca/ before you explore each trail.

Additionally, thanks to the land managers and trail builders and maintainers who care for these places. California and its trails have been (and will be again) hard hit by wildfires, floods, and debris flow. Hikers who value public lands should support leaders who value restoring and protecting the land. You should also consider volunteering for one of the trail organizations listed in the appendix. It's actually fun.

I owe this book to Brian Davidson for his research, patience, support, and company while scouting. Thanks also to my hiking and business partner Naomi Hudetz, who took up the slack at Treeline Review while I finished this manuscript. I appreciate the company of my hiking partners, whose faces are featured in the photos in this book, including Werner Zorman, Duncan Cheung, Shawnté Salabert, Mike Unger, and Whitney LaRuffa. Lastly, I dedicate this book to my parents, Bruce and Masako, for taking me hiking and camping as a kid, despite what I may have written earlier on the topic. May my readers show the same love you did by exposing young people to the beauty of nature.

Introduction

"People will hike four times as far as they normally would if there's a waterfall at the end." Years ago, a friend told me this to explain the number of hikers on a waterfall trail in the LA area.

Like climbing a peak, reaching a waterfall as a reward after a day of hiking provides motivation to keep moving. Be it waterfalls or mountains, when we set a goal in the outdoors, we take ourselves to natural places we otherwise wouldn't visit, and to views and experiences we otherwise might not see. Consequently we learn (cliché as it is) that hiking is about the journey more than the destination.

Like chasing mountains, standing below a waterfall makes us aware of how small we are against the forces of nature. Standing above a waterfall, we have a metaphor for life's unpredictability: Often water moves from a peaceful slow river to a sudden, dramatic drop, only to go back to a calm river again. Most waterfall hikes route us up rivers where we witness firsthand water's destructive power and contemplate our powerlessness compared to the natural environment.

Over the course of writing this book, Southern California experienced a multi-year drought and its largest wildfire in state history, followed by landslides and debris flows that took out homes, lives, and trails. After a summer and fall of more wildfires, we experienced the longest government shutdown in US history, followed by monumental rain, flooding, and more landslides.

We Californians know natural forces are part of life here. But we also understand as the climate and weather patterns change, every beautiful waterfall we visit today may be different (or washed away) next time we visit. The impermanence and seasonality is what makes each hike in the book precious.

In choosing which hikes to include in this age of social media, we were hypersensitive to the push-and-pull of public access versus the fragileness of this landscape. This book guides you to eighty-three waterfalls, from those named on maps and quite popular to those off-the-beaten path and graced by my own naming convention. Waterfalls are to be enjoyed by everyone—whether you're looking for a wheelchair-friendly route or an off-trail backpacking trip. The type of people who read guidebooks tend to be the most responsible of trail users. We ask you lead by example and teach others to respect this land and support the protection and management of it for future generations.

Once you start chasing waterfalls, you'll begin looking for them everywhere. When driving past dry gullies, you'll wonder, "Will there be a waterfall here when the rain falls?" Every time we see the waterfall symbol on a map, we get giddy—especially if it's unnamed.

May this book be but the beginning of a lifetime of curiosity for you.

How to Use This Guide

Distance

Mileages and elevation were recorded using GPS technology. They do not always correspond to mileages on maps and signs (differences are noted).

Elevation Gain

We include cumulative elevation gain and loss (when significantly different) for a one-way hike. We believe when you travel along a mostly flat ridgetop, your legs feel every bump. Some trips are reverse hikes, meaning that, like the Grand Canyon, most of the elevation gain is on the return trip. In these cases, pace yourself and save energy for the climb out.

Beauty Rating

It's hard for us to rate the beauty of a hike or waterfall. Every time we dreaded visiting a certain falls because we had read in another guidebook that it "wasn't as scenic," we found ourselves in awe of how magical it really was. For those with an open mind, any hike can be beautiful.

As any Southern California waterfall chaser knows, a falls' beauty depends a lot on the season you're there. But a hike can be beautiful not just for the flow and height of the waterfall at the end, but for the surrounding vegetation (e.g., trees and ferns), the grotto of rock surrounding it, and a reflective plunge pool.

Maidenhair ferns along the Maidenhair Fern falls hike.

It seems unfair to judge nature—who has no control over how the elements may affect her beauty—based on our human standards. But we realize we're in the minority, so we have attempted to describe beauty relative to a waterfall's relationship with humans:

- Graffiti and trash: This isn't on nature—this is on humans. It's unfair to judge nature's beauty based on what humans have done to it. But graffiti can mar an otherwise inspiring sight.
- Access: Just because a falls is beautiful doesn't mean the walk to get there is pleasant. Escondido Falls, for example, is one of the finest falls in the book, but private property restrictions require you to walk a mile on pavement to reach the trailhead. It's well worth it—and the human mind has great capacity for forgetting the more unpleasant memories of a hike. This is another hike where human decisions on access and trail routing impact the overall beauty of the hike.

Difficulty Rating

When we first started chasing waterfalls, as a category we thought they were mostly easy hikes. But chasing waterfalls can be as hard as climbing mountains. They require research, dedication, discipline, and patience to reach your destination. But the skills for waterfalls can at times feel more intense—bushwhacking, scrambling, slippery rocks, steep loose terrain, and, of course, being cold and wet. While mountain trails can last years, trails following streams attract vegetation that can cause trails to become overgrown. Floods can wash out a trail. So for the falls described, you need to work as hard almost to get to a waterfall as to a mountain peak.

Almost all the hikes in the book are less than 10 miles round-trip. Difficulty ratings take into account distance and elevation gain and loss (after all, when you go down to a waterfall, you have to come back up). We also account for the roughness of the terrain, and note when off-trail navigation is required. None of the routes described in the book require rock climbing (Class 5) moves or canyoneering equipment, although there are fine waterfall trips in Southern California available to those with that skillset.

Trail-routing and maintenance/quality: Trails aren't part of nature. They are designed and constructed by humans. Humans make decisions about where trails go. For example, trails can be routed around private property, even if it is not the most scenic way to get to a waterfall (see Access above). Humans, usually at the US Forest Service, decide which trails are defined and marked and how well they will be defined and marked. In recent years, the Forest Service has been forced to spend much of their budget on fighting wildfires—a constant threat in California. New legislation passed in 2018 may change this, but we have yet to see whether this means more trail maintenance. Nonetheless, we note when a trail is overgrown and cross our fingers that it changes in the future.

Route Finding

The majority of the hikes in the book are well marked and maintained on clear trails. We note when this is not the case in the difficulty ratings and route description. Often, to access the base of a falls, a hiker must diverge from a well-marked trail via a rough use trail for usually no more than 0.5 mile. Some routes are on use trails or require bushwhacking or scrambling for longer distances, although we usually opted not to include these routes if on-trail options exist nearby. Always read the route description prior to starting a hike.

Best Seasons

With the exception of the hikes in the Sierra, most of the hikes in this book are best enjoyed between December and April, the best hiking months in Southern California. While waterfalls may run year-round, visiting in the summer can sometimes be unpleasant (or deadly) and in winter, hikes may be inaccessible or require specialized skillsets or gear to appreciate (or be deadly).

California is one of five ecological hot spots in the world with a Mediterranean climate making up less than 0.2 percent of the world's landmass. Southern California has a distinct rainy winter season and summer where six months without rain is not uncommon. Choose your waterfalls by season—some are dry in summer or fall. But relish these falls—much like the plants along the hike—they change by season.

Permits and Passes

You are required to display an Adventure Pass at sixty-six "improved" recreation sites in Angeles National Forest and elsewhere in Cleveland National Forest, Los Padres National Forest, and San Bernardino National Forest. Recent federal court cases mandated fee sites to offer a fee-free parking area within 0.5 mile of the fee-required trailhead.

Adventure Passes are $5 per day or $30 for an annual pass. They are available at small mountain town stores close to trailheads and ranger stations as well as outdoor gear stores like REI. You can also display the America the Beautiful Annual Inter-agency Pass ($80), which gets you into all the national parks for a year. If you have a fourth grader in your family, the Every Kid in a Park Pass is free to your family and works like the America the Beautiful Pass.

The hikes in national and state parks require entrance fees. National park fees are good for one week. State park entrance fees are good for one day, but are accepted across the entire park system (so you can hit up another state park the same day if you'd like; this is a useful tip for visiting the Big Sur region).

Permits are required for a handful of hikes in this book. Two dayhikes require permits: the fee permit for Cedar Creek Falls and the free permit for Middle Fork of Lytle Creek (because it enters the quota region of the Sheep Wilderness). All backpacking trips described in this book also require a permit.

Maps

We list USGS topo maps for most of the hikes, though prefer to reference the high-quality, hiker-specific maps designed by Tom Harrison (https://tomharrison maps.com) or Bryan Conant (https://bryanconant.com) when they are available for a region. Some local or California State Parks provide a free brochure map (also available as a pdf). While basic, these maps are easy-to-read and adequate for most of the hikes where applicable. USGS Topo maps can be purchased online or downloaded and printed for free from https://viewer.nationalmap.gov.

How the Hikes Were Chosen

Despite what naysayers from out-of-state may think, there are many falls in Southern California. We used the following criteria to choose which of the hundreds of falls to include in the book:

1. beauty of the falls and the route to reach it;
2. reliability of the flow (at least during winter and spring);
3. the fun factor of the hike separate of the destination; and
4. accessibility of the trailhead and the route to get to the falls (relative to other falls in the area).

The falls in this book include classic Southern California day hikes, roadside tourist destinations, and unnamed or harder-to-reach falls. Almost all the routes are 10 miles or less round-trip, with the exception of three that are described as backpacking trips.

We seek to share a diversity of hikes for folks of different ability levels, skills, energy levels, and time commitments. Specifically, we note when hikes are wheelchair friendly or appropriate for folks with limited mobility. We also note when hikes are well suited for kids or dogs, as well as when hikes require off-trail travel or scrambling. However, we chose not to include routes requiring any rock climbing moves (Class 5) or canyoneering equipment.

The majority of the hikes are within an easy 2-hour drive of Los Angeles, Orange County, Santa Barbara, or San Diego. We also include hikes in popular road trip destinations including Big Sur, the western Sierra national parks (Sequoia, Kings Canyon, and southern Yosemite), and Mammoth and the Eastern Sierra (an area that is an easy, albeit long, drive from the greater LA area).

Waterfalls abound on both the east and west sides of the Sierra. We mention the major must-see highlights. For those heading into the Sierra or farther north and to Yosemite Valley, those falls are expertly documented by Tracy Salcedo-Chourré in the companion to this guide, *Hiking Waterfalls in Northern California*, and *Hiking Waterfalls Yosemite National Park* by Suzanne Swedo. The exception is we include falls along the Sonora Pass corridor in the north, which are not included in Tracy's guide and are surprisingly easy to access from Southern California.

Trailheads

All the trails in the book are accessible via two-wheel-drive vehicles, though occasionally you'll need to drive on dirt roads. Depending on the season, roads can be muddy, flooded, snowy, closed, blocked by landslide, or inaccessible. Since we learned the hard way, we advise that you check CALTRANS for paved road conditions at www.dot.ca.gov. Additionally, always call ahead or check the Forest Service's website to make sure the last few miles of dirt access roads to your trailhead are open.

We have spent significant time researching and documenting mileage. However, we realize the way most folks get to trailheads is via the Google Maps smartphone app. For each hike, we offer the *correct* Google Maps search term to get to the trailhead you need to start the hike. Often the app directs you to the hike itself via cross-country routes and is not helpful on wheels or foot. For more obscure unsigned trailheads, we include the numbers found on highway mileage marker signs along the road.

All the hikes in this book were visited by one of us, with the exception of those closed during the scouting time. In the case of the closed hikes, we chose to include them in the book because they have long been considered classic Southern California hikes and we would be remiss not to include them. They remain in this book because authorities say there are plans to reopen those trails by 2020, if not sooner.

How to Use the Maps

Overview map: This map shows the location of each hike in the area by hike number.

Route map: This is your primary guide to each hike. It shows the waterfalls, all the accessible roads and trails, points of interest, water, landmarks, and geographical features. It also distinguishes trails from roads, and paved roads from unpaved roads. The selected route is highlighted, and directional arrows point the way.

Hiking Gear and Essentials

No matter how much gear you carry, the stuff you carry in your head and your attitude are worth more. Check conditions before you go, be willing to postpone your trip, and have a backup hike in mind.

For more on hiking and backpacking gear and skills, see the Resources section.

Weather and conditions can change rapidly while chasing waterfalls. Bring the Ten Essentials and know how to use each of the items. In particular, Southern California hikers will want to bring plenty of water, sunscreen, sunglasses, and a brimmed hat.

Bring a paper map and compass and know how to use them for navigation. Follow along where you are on the map as you hike. It can be fun and also reduces the chances you'll become lost.

You may consider bolstering (but not replacing) your navigation system with a GPS or phone app. We like the Gaia app. Don't expect cell reception to be available on any of these hikes or even at the trailhead. Download maps and GPX tracks of your hike prior to leaving home.

Hiking with a partner or two may help in case of an emergency, and, more importantly, can make your hike more fun. Whether going solo or in a group, leave your hiking itinerary with a reliable person who is staying home before you head into the wilds. Check in with them when you're back. Consider carrying a two-way satellite GPS messenger with an SOS button. Even if you have a GPS messenger, also carry backcountry essentials like an emergency blanket and whistle in case you become lost or otherwise can't return to the trailhead.

Waterfall hikes are notorious for flash floods or high water levels. Check the weather forecast before leaving home. Check in with the applicable ranger district about water levels before you go. High-altitude hikes are liable to snowstorms. Watch cloud formations and be ready to come back another day if weather looks iffy.

Before leaving for your hike, find out current conditions and hazards of your route. Call the ranger district. Their job is to help you make safe decisions in the backcountry.

Risks and Dangers of Hiking Waterfalls

Hiking is generally a very safe hobby on the spectrum of outdoor activities. But learning about dangers and how to avoid them before you go can help you make smart, informed decisions when problems arise.

Slips and Falls

Waterfall hikes, perhaps because they attract a higher number of participants, seem to result in more injury than the typical hike. To reach the falls in this book, you often cross slippery rocks and uneven surfaces. You may find yourself on cliffs near gorges. These all put you at risk for twisted ankles, falls, injuries, and even death. It's your responsibility to make safe decisions while visiting falls.

Cliff diving from waterfalls or into plunge pools below waterfalls is a major cause of injuries and fatalities associated with waterfalls in Southern California. These kinds of casualties have been well documented in places like Hermit and Cedar Creek Falls. In addition, canyoneering or climbing in an attempt to get better views of waterfalls has resulted in numerous well-publicized casualties in places like Switzer and Eaton Falls. Alcohol and drugs may have been involved. More influential than those substances, however, is the appeal of a photo or video to post on social media; such atempts can result in injury or death. For your own safety, cliff diving or scrambling off-route is not advised. Don't put yourself or others in danger to get a cool video for social media.

As guidebook writers, we can't alert you to all the dangers of a particular area and the dangers specific to your party and to the conditions when you're visiting. Use your best judgment and assume responsibility for your own safety.

Stream Crossings

Most of the stream crossings described in this book can be achieved via rock-hops (dry crossings on stepping-stones or logs) for most of the hiking season. Occasionally, you may need to wade across a creek. Search for the widest part of a stream with shallow water and a slower current. We find we have better traction on crossings if we keep our hiking shoes on. However, this results in wet feet. If water looks deep or swift and you can't find a log or rock crossing or safe wading point, turn around and choose to come back another day.

Wildlife

The trails and wildlands in Southern California are home to creatures that have been here far longer than humans. Respect them and give them space.

Do not feed any wild animal. The cute ones sometimes beg. Squirrels, chipmunks, and marmots in national parks are particularly bothersome. Human food is not healthy for them, or for bears or any other wildlife. Feeding wildlife also reduces their chances for survival when winter comes, as they become less skilled in foraging. Becoming accustomed to human food makes wildlife more likely to think it's ok to take human food even when they aren't being fed—like chewing open your backpack or breaking the window of your car (both of which have happened to me).

Keep your distance from wildlife. This reduces chances you may be bitten or attacked. It also reduces anxiety levels of the animals.

Bears

You may see black bears while on Sierra Nevada hikes. They're uncommon but also exist in the San Gabriel and San Bernardino Mountains, though you're more likely to see scat than the actual animal. They can be encountered in almost all the regions described in this book, but are rare.

Always obey signs if areas have been closed due to bear activity.

Experts recommend keeping at least 300 feet from black bears.

If you do see a black bear, make noise and look big. Traveling with a group is helpful. Pick up children without bending over. Don't run or turn your back. Slowly back away while speaking calmly. Never get between a mother and her cub.

If attacked, defend yourself and try to remain standing. Playing dead doesn't work on black bears. Report the attack to officials, and do not disturb the site of the attack.

Always follow local regulations, notably for food storage. Never leave a backpack or anything containing food unattended, especially in the Sierra. Aside from reduction of habitat, food is the main reason bear-human conflict happens. Save a bear. Use bear-proof cans or boxes.

Mountain Lions

Sightings are rare and attacks even rarer. But mountain lions consider most of the places mentioned in this book to be their home, including the seemingly more urban areas like the Santa Monica Mountains. To stay safe:

- Travel with others and stay together as a group. Keep small children nearby.
- Mountain lions are most active during dusk and dawn. If you are worried about mountain lions, avoid hiking at those times.
- If you see a mountain lion more than 50 yards away, back away slowly, keeping the animal in your peripheral vision. Don't bend over, but look for rocks or sticks to use as a weapon, or be prepared with hiking poles or bear spray. Keep young children close.
- Most of the time, lions are curious. Be prepared to abandon your hike and come back another day.
- If you see a mountain lion less than 50 yards away, slowly back away and maintain eye contact. Do not run or turn your back. Make continuous loud noises and try to look big by raising arms and/or a jacket above your head and making a steady waving motion. Pick up kids without bending over.

- If attacked, fight back and try to remain standing. Playing dead doesn't work on mountain lions. Use rocks, sticks, hiking poles, or bear spray.

Rattlesnakes

Much more common than bears and lions, rattlesnakes live in most of the ecosystems described in this book. Snakes usually don't attack humans. We're too big to be food. But we may be viewed as a predator. Perhaps it's telling that the most common demographic for snakebites are young men 18 to 24—the demographic who are most likely to attempt picking up a snake. Leave snakes alone and chances are they won't bother you.

Always watch where you sit, where you put your feet on the trail, and where you put your hands and feet when stepping over logs and rocks. Snakes sometimes attack if they are surprised.

If you see a snake, give it room. It'll slither off or you can go around it.

Ticks

By far the most common dangerous animal on your hike, ticks can transmit Lyme and other diseases that can have permanent negative impacts on your health and life. While we associate Lyme disease and ticks with the East Coast, the disease has spread to California.

Waterfall season is tick season. Wear light-colored long pants and shirts. Treat hiking clothing fabric with Permethrin before you leave home. On the day of your hike, use tick repellent. When you get home, have a trusted friend or family member check your body for ticks. They like warm areas like the armpits and groin.

If you find a tick, remove it immediately, using tweezers to remove the entire body including the head. Save the tick and call your doctor to have it tested. Don't wait for a bull's-eye rash to appear. It may be too late by then, and the rash doesn't appear in many cases of Lyme. Your doctor may prescribe a round of antibiotics. With tick bites, time is of the essence, so take care of tick-related issues as soon as you spot them.

Poison Oak

Waterfall hikers in particular are more likely to encounter poison oak than the traditional hiker. Poison oak loves water, shady canyons, and riparian woodlands—all ecosystems you are likely to visit on your hike. Avoid shiny leaves of three. In the autumn they can be colorful, and in winter they may drop their leaves completely (making identification much more difficult). Wear long pants and long-sleeved shirts. After your hike, use a soap like Technu and calamine lotion. Poison oak oils can spread and stay on your clothing, gear, and pets, so give them all a wash, too.

If you've got a poison oak rash, avoid scratching if you can. Bacteria under your nails can cause infection. There's an easy and effective topical steroid to help most poison oak rashes, but it requires a prescription from a doctor. Seek medical attention.

The author next to metal bent by the force of flooded water and debris flow at San Ysidro Falls.

Poodle-dog Bush

Also known as Turricula, this native, fire-following plant has tiny hairs that can irritate skin enough to require hospitalization, as happened to a good friend of ours. Six feet tall with leaves looking like a poodle's fur and a dank smell reminiscent of another plant recently legal in California, the purple-flowered poodle-dog is hard to miss.

Poodle-dog bush was common in the 2009 Station Fire burn area, but as other plants grow back, the noxious bush has become less common. Over-the-counter creams and antihistamines can make the rash worse. Avoid touching the plant, wear long sleeves and long pants, and seek medical attention if you notice symptoms.

Stinging Nettles

Stinging nettles (*Urtica dioica*) have a hollow stinging hair called a trichome, which injects histamines into your body when you come into contact. Skin may feel inflamed, itchy, or irritated, usually lasting 15 minutes to 24 hours. They are perennial plants common in moist areas in the spring—precisely the time and location when most waterfalls hikers are about—but are dormant in winter. The plants grow 3 to 7 feet tall on a wiry main stem and have deeply serrated green leaves 1 to 6 inches long that are heart shaped on the base with distinctive bristly hairs. Wear long pants and long-sleeved shirts and avoid contact. If you do have contact, over-the-counter anti-itch drugs can help. If itching continues, seek medical attention.

Weather-Related Conditions

We can experience any kind of weather in Southern California. Check forecasts before you go and postpone trips if the weather or water levels look less than ideal. For more on clothing and layering for changing weather, see the Resources section of this book.

Our best advice is to take a wilderness first-aid course prior to seriously undertaking any hiking in Southern California. While medical dangers are highly unlikely, having the knowledge and habits to know what to do in case of an emergency puts you and those in your party at a clear advantage if something were to happen. Classes are available locally through the Red Cross, at REI stores, and through the Sierra Club Angeles chapter and its Wilderness Trail Course.

Heat-Related Illness

Heat-related illness is possibly the greatest danger of the hikes described in this book. Heat can claim lives and it has done so most commonly at Cedar Creek Falls, Three Sisters Falls, and Borrego Canyon Falls. Heatstroke has claimed the lives of countless dogs who have been unwillingly dragged on waterfall hikes by their owners.

Many hikes described in this book are exposed—with little or no shade for portions of the hike. If attempting the hike in any season, Southern California hikes can get hot enough to kill.

To avoid heat cramps, exhaustion, and stroke:

- Avoid hiking during the hottest parts of the year. Most of the falls in this book aside from those in the Sierra run best in winter and spring.
- Avoid hiking during the hottest parts of the day regardless of what season you hike.
- Stay hydrated and carry electrolytes and/or salty foods to help balance your water intake. You may want to bring frozen water bottles or top off your water with ice cubes. Do not drink alcoholic or caffeinated beverages, which can contribute to dehydration.
- Opt for loose-fitting clothing like sun shirts, which are designed to allow perspiration to evaporate to cool your skin. Light colors are best. Also wear a thick-brimmed hat and use sunscreen on any part of your body not covered by clothing.

Symptoms of heat exhaustion and heatstroke include nausea, vomiting, headache, light-headedness, fainting, weakness, fatigue, lack of coordination or concentration, and flushed skin. You should watch for sunburns, which can be a painful early symptom.

If you or anyone in your party is showing these symptoms, find shade (or make it with clothing and objects). Have them rest on their back with their legs elevated.

Immerse victims in water, mist their skin, fan them off, and use cold or ice packs. Loosen their clothing.

If they're conscious, have them drink cool non-alcoholic fluids. If you're at a waterfall or a stream, have them get into the water (only if you are confident they can do so safely).

Call for emergency help by using a two-way transmitter, a cell phone to call 911 if you have reception, or send someone for help (be sure to also leave someone with the victim).

If after returning to the car the victim doesn't feel better within an hour, call urgent or emergency care. An IV may be needed.

Pets and Heatstroke

Every year, rescuers retrieve the bodies of dogs from Southern California hiking trails. If you have to ask whether a trail is too hot for your dog, you should leave your best friend at home.

The ground temperature in Southern California frequently is 30°F warmer than the air temperature. It can burn canine feet. Dog owners should be able to read signs of heat illness on their dog and be willing to turn around if their dog isn't up for a hike. Your dog will follow you to the ends of the earth. Don't have its loyalty lead to its demise.

Signs your dog has had enough include staggering, collapsing, weakness, fatigue, unwillingness to walk, seizures, excessive rapid, loud panting, dark or bright red tongue, sticky or dry tongue and gums, and a rapid heartbeat.

Short-nosed breeds of dogs like pugs and bulldogs are most susceptible to heat, as are large, heavy-coated breeds. Think twice about bringing overweight dogs or those with heart or respiratory illness.

As with a human, if your dog shows symptoms of overheating, seek shade, get out of the heat, and pour cool but not ice water on your pet (ice water can constrict blood vessels, which slows the cooling process). Place cool wet clothing on your pet's feet and around its head and neck.

If your dog shows symptoms, *carry your animal* back to the trailhead and immediately contact an emergency veterinarian.

Hypothermia

Hypothermia happens when your body's internal temperature drops well below 95°F. It happens with exposure to cold, but is most common at 30 to 50 degrees (and can happen at much warmer temperatures, too). Getting wet and wearing wet clothing—which often happens on a waterfall hike—make hypothermia more likely. Wind, cold, rain, snow, and moist feet and clothing can all contribute to hypothermia.

The best bet against hypothermia is to stay dry. Check weather forecasts and creek and river levels before you go on your trip. Be willing to postpone your trip and go on a backup trail instead. Carry rain and wind gear and enough clothing layers to cover your head, torso, and legs.

The most frustrating thing about hypothermia is you can't always trust the victims. They may deny they have an issue. Symptoms begin with fumbling—including difficulty with fine motor skills and numb extremities. This progresses to stumbles and mumbles: sluggish thinking and slower, less controlled walking. They may show violent uncontrollable shivering and slurred or difficult speaking. It can progress to a life-threatening situation where they cannot get up, stop shivering, become incoherent, and then become drowsy.

If you or a hiking partner notice these symptoms, stop, get out of the wind and rain, strip off wet clothing, and change to warm, dry clothing. Provide warm drinks. If victims are able to get off the trail to safety, move them and seek immediate medical attention. If not, use an emergency transmitter or send someone for help (but also leave someone with the victim).

(De-)Hydration

Hydrate before, after, and during your hike. We always take drinks in the car and guzzle at the trailhead before the hike and then as a reward when we get back to the car.

While hiking, a rule of thumb is to carry 1 liter of water for every hour you plan to be hiking. You may bring more or less depending on heat, conditions, and the distance and elevation gain of a hike. For example, rangers checking your permit for Cedar Creek Falls require you to carry a minimum of 1 gallon of water and will send you home if you can't prove you have enough.

For most of the hikes in this book, we carried 2 liters of water minimum plus a water filter to get water along the way. For hiking in Southern California, we highly recommend a hydration bladder with a hose. With water bottles, hikers notoriously never stop enough to drink water. We've seen dehydrated hikers return to the trailhead with almost full water bottles. A hose and bladder system makes it much easier to continuously sip, treating the hose like an IV constantly hydrating your body at a rate at which it can process water. The body can usually only process 1 liter of water per hour before wanting to pee it out. In our experience, the body prefers to get water slowly via a tube rather than guzzling in one go at a once-every-2-hour snack break. If you use a bladder system, check for leaks before you go and always carry a backup water bottle. While the bladders tend to be sturdy, spiky Southern California vegetation is unforgiving.

How to Be a Good Hiker

Guidebook writer Casey Schreiner includes this idea in his LA-specific book, and we can't think of a better way to describe the motivation for learning hiker etiquette. Guidebook readers tend to be more responsible and nature-loving than most. For this reason, we know you'll take time to learn about the Leave No Trace outdoor philosophy and inform others in your party (or those you meet along your hike) about LNT. Lead by example and instruct children and friends you introduce to hiking about the "rules" of our hobby.

Southern California is particularly susceptible to human impact on the land, perhaps because of its high population with proximity to nature. A waterfall hike to

This is what happens when hikers do not respect Leave No Trace Principles. Leave waterfall hikes better than you found them. Bonita Falls.

Bonita, Hermit, or Aztec Falls is all you need to learn about how humans can impact nature. No matter what hike you're on, we encourage you to bring a trash bag and volunteer with organizations that do graffiti and trash clean-up.

Any trash you create on your hike—including banana or orange peels, apple cores, or avocado pits—needs to come back to the trailhead with you. Many trailheads have trash cans. These items aren't natural and can't biodegrade quickly in our dry climate. This goes for beer cans and cigarette butts, too. Wildlife dig up and eat and choke on food scraps while becoming more dependent on human handouts. Glass bottles break and can make hiking in certain areas dangerous. Trash is unsightly and gross.

Do a favor for the next hiker. If you had the energy to bring an item in on your hike, you have the energy to bring it back to the car, too. This goes for camp chairs, coolers, and any other item you bring to enhance your hiking, swimming, and water-fall enjoying experience. While it may seem like other hikers could benefit from the camp chair you left behind, it often washes downriver and becomes degraded in the sun, ultimately becoming garbage no one wants to use.

Stay on the trail as much as possible. When a trail has switchbacks, avoid cutting them. It leads to erosion, damages vegetation, and is an absolute pain for volunteers to rebuild.

Respect private property. Close gates when you find them across the trail. This helps keep livestock in certain areas and away from eating plants they aren't supposed to.

Don't use speakers to listen to music while hiking or hanging out by swimming holes. Many people hike to get peace and quiet. Loud sounds make wildlife anxious. If you must listen to music, please use headphones.

Most trailheads have privies. If you use the toilet in the outdoors, carry a trowel. Bury human waste 6 to 8 inches deep. Pack out used toilet paper in a plastic bag. Carry out dog waste as well.

While it may seem like you're helping other hikers by spray-painting trail markers or building rock piles (called rock cairns or "ducks"), it takes away from the wild feel of natural areas. Certain hikes in this book are well marked with official signs specifically for folks who prefer a hike with good signage. Other hikes purposely have not been marked to cultivate a wild feel. If you choose to hike the latter, please respect the intention of land managers who deliberately chose not to sign the hike. Adding a rock sign or spray paint to a trail is like going to someone else's house and rearranging their furniture. They likely had a reason for why they chose to decorate the way they did. If land managers want to sign an area, they'll let local volunteers know and we encourage you to help.

Go to www.lnt.org and read up on how to be the best hiker you can be.

Never get too close to the lip or base of a waterfall. This warning sign at Rainbow Falls tells of hikers who have fallen.

Map Legend

Municipal

≈⟨5⟩≈ Interstate Highway

≈⟨101⟩≈ US Highway

≈⟨1⟩≈ State Road

════ Local/County Road

= = = = Gravel Road

= = = = Unpaved Road

— · — · — State Boundary

— · · — County Boundary

• — • — • Power Line

Trails

- - - - - - Featured Trail

- - - - - - Trail

———— Paved Trail

Water Features

Body of Water

Marsh

River/Creek

Intermittent Stream

Spring

Waterfall

Symbols

⌣ Bridge

■ Building/Point of Interest

▲ Campground

∩ Cave

🍴 Food

⬤ Gate

🛏 Lodging

🅿 Parking

⟩⟨ Pass

▲ Peak/Elevation

📞 Phone

🎪 Picnic Area

🏠 Ranger Station/Park Office

🚻 Restroom

📷 Scenic View

🐎 Stables

○ Town

① Trailhead

❓ Visitor/Information Center

💧 Water

♿ Wheelchair Accessible

Land Management

National Park/Forest

National Monument/Wilderness

State/County Park

Indian Reservation

Angeles National Forest

Waterfalls abound in proximity to people here in Angeles National Forest. Established in 1892, the national forest is among the oldest in the country. At almost 700,000 acres—346,000 of which are in the San Gabriel Mountains National Monument—it encompasses the San Gabriel and Santa Clarita Mountains and Antelope Valley. With more than 3.5 million visitors per year, this forest has five federally protected wildernesses. It covers mountains from 1,200 feet to more than 10,000 feet in elevation.

The land managed within Angeles National Forest is the ancestral home of five native nations: Gabrieleno/Tongva, Chumash, Fernandeno/Tataviam, Kitanemuk and Serrano. They established the first trail system through these mountains as trade routes with other tribes across the range. Thousands of people walked these trails annually. You can learn more from a Native American ranger or guest host at the nearby Haramokngna American Indian Cultural Center on Red Box Saddle (Highway 2). When the Spanish arrived, Native populations were decimated after being forced into the mission system and exposed to disease. In the late 1800s the mountains became home to prospectors and the lower frontcountry went to rancheros. During the "Great Hiking Era" (1895–1938), canyons in Angeles National Forest became home to mountain trail resorts, many of which were/are near waterfalls.

The San Andreas fault runs to the north with the San Gabriel and Sierra Madre faults to the south and Soledad fault to the west. Much of California is composed of exotic rock (terranes) and the Southern California batholith, igneous rock crystalized 100 million years ago beneath tropical volcanic rock. Streams cut out deep Vs in canyons. The US Forest Service protects these water sources today for use by the cities below (and manages them to prevent flooding). Between the faults and erosion from the water, the mountains of Angeles National Forest are geologically mixed. You may find limestone, schist, quartz, or granite in creek beds on your way to waterfalls.

The San Gabriels are part of the Transverse Ranges that run east–west instead of north–south like most mountain ranges in the state. The higher altitudes are found inland with the front-range canyons in the south being home to most of the waterfalls in this book.

Honorable Mention: For those further interested in falls in the area, the Royal Gorge, Allison Gulch, and Devils Canyon waterfalls are well worth the trip for those willing to hike more than 10 miles and who have the skills, experience, and patience to travel extended mileage off-trail. In rainy years, Rubio and Bailey Canyon may hold water, but they're rather unreliable compared to other frontcountry falls close by. This book is but an introduction to the most accessible of the numerous falls here. Canyoneers and those willing to travel even farther off the beaten path have found amazing things in these mountains. Grab a topo map and explore.

You are required to display an Adventure Pass on your dashboard at most Angeles National Forest trailheads described in this book. See How to Use This Guide for more about this fee.

1 San Antonio Falls

This paved, family-friendly, dog-friendly hike leads to a three-tiered 100-plus-foot falls that usually runs year-round.

Height: 75–80 feet over at least 3 tiers
Beauty rating: ★★★★★
Distance: 1.2 miles out and back
Elevation gain: 275 feet
Difficulty: Easy, paved, and dog-friendly; option to scramble at end
Best season: Winter, spring, fall, summer
County: Los Angeles
Trailhead amenities: About 75 parking spots, dog-friendly, open to hikers, horses, and mountain bikers

Land status: Angeles National Forest/San Gabriel Mountains National Monument
Maps: Tom Harrison Mt. Baldy and Cucamonga Wilderness; USGS Mt. San Antonio
Trail contact: Mount Baldy Visitor Center, Mount Baldy Road, Mount Baldy 91759; (909) 982-2829; www.fs.usda.gov/main/angeles/home
Fees and permits: Display Adventure Pass

Finding the trailhead: Google Maps: Manker Flats Trailhead. From I-210 East in Claremont, take the Baseline Avenue exit. Turn left, heading north, then turn right on Padua Avenue. After 1.8 miles turn right on Mount Baldy Road, heading up the mountain through two tunnels and through Mount Baldy Village over the next 11 miles. Continue 0.3 mile past the Manker Flats Campground. Parking is at a dirt lot near the gated trailhead road or along the road. If you find yourself at ski lift parking at the end of the road, you've gone too far.
GPS: N34 15.561' / W117 37.516'

The Hike

This family-friendly, paved path is the beginning of one of the most popular climbs up Mount San Antonio, aka Mount Baldy. The tallest mountain in Los Angeles County (but depending on how you count, #22 or #24 by height in Southern California), this 10,064-foot peak is one of the most climbed in the Southland. Its south-facing eponymous bald top, visible throughout the county and beyond, is distinctive looking when covered in snow.

San Antonio Creek (home to this falls) was named by padres of the Mission San Gabriel in 1794 after the miracle-working Franciscan friar Saint Anthony of Padua, Italy. The peak was then named in 1884 after the creek. It's one of three "saint-named" mountains in the Southland (the others being San Jacinto and San Gorgonio). Prospectors in the 1870s renamed it "Old Baldy."

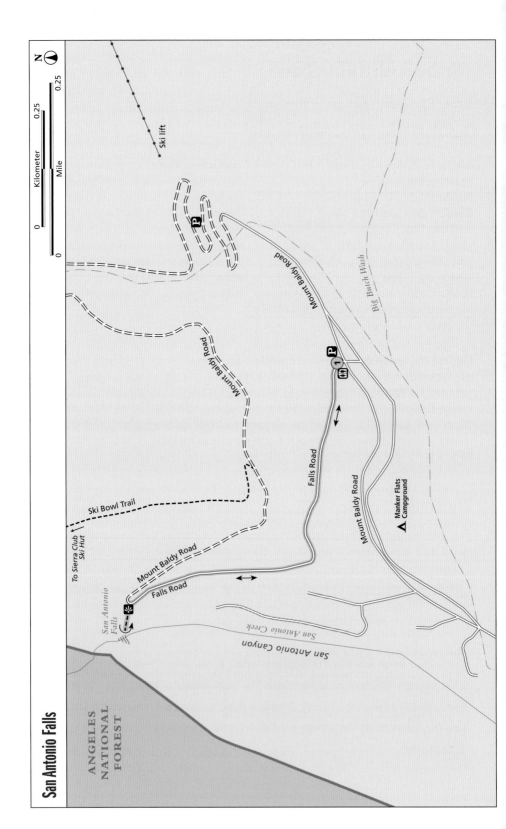

San Antonio Falls

ANGELES
NATIONAL
FOREST

San Antonio Falls

To Sierra Club
Ski Hut

Ski Bowl Trail

Mount Baldy Road

Falls Road

Falls Road

Mount Baldy Road

Mount Baldy Road

Mount Baldy Road

San Antonio Canyon

San Antonio Creek

Manker Flats
Campground

Big Butch Wash

Ski lift

N

Kilometer
0   0.25

Mile
0   0.25

From the overviewpoint, you can see multiple tiers of the tall San Antonio Falls. After a storm or in a big snowmelt, a waterwheel forms at the bottom.

From the Manker Flats parking area, take the gated, paved fire road past the outhouse, info signs, and uphill. To your left are private cabins, so don't accidentally end up in someone's driveway. Climb through Jeffrey and Ponderosa pine forest.

At a hairpin turn where the road turns right, you'll reach a stone wall reinforcement, which is the Falls overlook. From here, you can see all three tiers of the falls. San Antonio Creek flows below. The creek is fed by springs near Baldy Bowl, including the one near the ski hut. In winter and early spring, a snowbank may hold out across the ravine (though you can see it, you usually won't have to walk on snow). There is a path that scrambles down 0.1 mile to the base, but the Forest Service warns the loose rock and rough trail above the ravine can "cause tragedy." Certainly, scrambling on the rock or dirt cliffs along the side of the falls has led to injuries.

I've visited the falls a couple dozen times over as many years and it seems to at least trickle year-round, though winter and spring are the best time for viewing. After a good snowmelt the bottom tier can form a waterwheel—where the sheer force of the flow throws water upward after it hits a rock or pothole (if you think that's neat, see Waterwheel Falls).

Miles and Directions

0.0 Start at the trailhead by the privy and the gate.

0.6 Viewing point for base of falls. (**Option:** Continue 0.1 mile to base of falls.) Return the way you came.

1.2 Arrive back at the trailhead.

2 Soldier Creek Falls (Lewis Falls)

This shaded, dog-friendly hike leads to a three-tiered 30- to 50-foot falls that usually runs year-round and is free of crowds.

Height: 30-50 feet over at least 3 tiers

Beauty rating: ★★★★★

Distance: 1 mile out and back

Elevation gain: 425 feet

Difficulty: Easy to moderate (due to last 0.1 mile of scrambling)

Best season: Spring, fall, summer, winter

County: Los Angeles

Trailhead amenities: About 4 parking spots, dog-friendly

Land status: Angeles National Forest/San Gabriel Mountains National Monument

Maps: Tom Harrison Angeles High Country; USGS Crystal Lake

Trail contact: Angeles National Forest/San Gabriel Mountains National Monument, San Gabriel River Ranger District; 110 N. Wabash Ave., Glendora 91741; (626) 335-1251; www .fs.usda.gov/main/angeles/home

Fees and permits: None

Finding the trailhead: Google Maps: Falling Springs, CA (Lewis Falls will get you close, but doesn't show parking; it's the hairpin to the southwest of the falls). From I-210 in Azusa, take exit 40 (Azusa Avenue/CA 39). Continue for 20.3 miles as it turns into Crystal Lake Road. Pass the turnoff to East Fork Road and continue north toward Coldbrook Campground. Set your odometer. In 2 miles look for mining equipment on a dirt pullout on the left side of the road. Continue climbing for 0.3 mile to a hairpin turn left as you enter the trees on both sides of the road. This is where Soldier Creek goes under CA 39. There's unmarked trailhead parking along the right side of the road right before mile marker 34.83.
GPS: N34 18.046' / W117 50.175'

The Hike

The Crystal Lake Recreation Area is one of the most accessible ways for Southlanders to experience the high central San Gabriel Mountains. This hike takes you through the shaded, former mountain resort community of Falling Springs (aka La Cienega). There are privately leased cabins and the remains of others along this hike. The area near the Crystal Springs Recreation Area and road burned in the 2002 Curve Fire and was closed until 2011. Now reopened, you can drive to 6,000 feet and experience clean air, pine and cedar forests, and this fine waterfall.

The most difficult part of this hike is finding the right trailhead. From the pullout, take the good trail up the right (east) side of Soldier Creek. It joins another creek to become the North Fork of the San Gabriel River downhill near Coldbrook Campground, which you passed on the drive up. Soldier Creek Falls is sometimes called "Lewis Falls" after the former Mount Baldy district ranger Anselmo Lewis, who once patrolled here.

The author at Lewis Falls on an autumn-like December day.

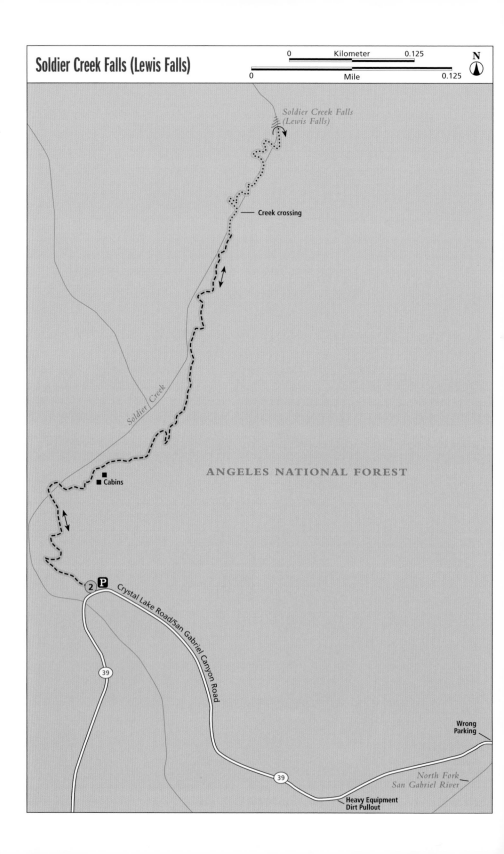

Soldier Creek Falls (Lewis Falls)

Kilometer
0   0.125

0   Mile   0.125

N

Soldier Creek Falls
(Lewis Falls)

Creek crossing

Soldier Creek

ANGELES NATIONAL FOREST

■ Cabins

2 P Crystal Lake Road/San Gabriel Canyon Road

39

39

Wrong
Parking

North Fork
San Gabriel River

Heavy Equipment
Dirt Pullout

As you climb, you'll pass several cabins, now foundations after the Curve Fire. You may find swarms of ladybugs in the late autumn. While this area had broken glass and graffiti in the past, most of it has been cleaned up and it's relatively pristine.

A tributary joins from the hillside on the right 0.3 mile in. The trail may get muddy and flooded here, but keep heading north high on the right bank. You may notice several cascades in the creek below among giant boulders.

When you get to a large cabin foundation, the trail appears to end at a wooden fence "overlook" on the bank high above the water. Follow the fenceline to a rough path leading steeply down to Soldier Creek. In low water, cross the creek and follow a path on the left (west) side of the creek to the end of the canyon 0.1 mile later. In higher water, parts may be underwater and require wading. Whichever way you take upstream, expect to get wet, scramble on rocks, and bushwhack through branches. (During high water you may want to turn around and come back another day.) At the end of the canyon, you'll find solitude and peace at this 50-foot falls.

Miles and Directions

1.0 Start at the trailhead.

0.3 Creek joins from the right.

0.4 Abandoned cabin foundation with fenceline leads to rough path down to creek.

0.5 Base of falls. Return the way you came.

1.0 Arrive back at the trailhead.

3 Fish Canyon Falls

The trail to the 90-foot three-tiered falls is a testament to the importance of public access to open land and what is possible with the cooperation of three land managers: federal, local, and private.

Height: About 90 feet
Beauty rating: ★★★★★
Distance: 4.8 miles out and back
Elevation gain: 830 feet
Difficulty: Moderate
Best season: Winter, spring
County: Los Angeles
Trailhead amenities: Dogs allowed on weekends only. No bikes or equestrians.
Land status: Vulcan Materials Azusa Rock Company (private), Angeles National Forest, City of Duarte
Maps: Tom Harrison Angeles High Country; USGS Azusa

Trail contact: Angeles National Forest, San Gabriel River Ranger District; 110 N. Wabash Ave., Glendora 91741; (626) 335-1251; www.fs.usda.gov/main/angeles/home
Fees and permits: Adventure Pass not required as of 2016, but check current regulations. As of the last time the trail was open to the public, hours were daily 7 a.m. to 7 p.m. April through September and 7 a.m. to 5 p.m. October through March. Gates are closed at all other hours, and remaining cars are towed at owners' expense.

Finding the trailhead: Google Maps: 3901 Fish Canyon Road, Azusa 91702. From I-210 in Duarte, take Foothill Boulevard. Turn left onto Encanto Parkway until it turns into Fish Canyon Road, which becomes gravel road on Vulcan Materials property. Enter through the Access Trail gate. The City of Duarte used to a free shuttle to the trailhead from the Duarte Gold Line Station. **GPS:** N34 09.257' / W117 55.258'

The Hike

Note: Fish Canyon burned in the San Gabriel Complex Fire/Fish Fire of June 2016. The hike has three entities controlling it: Angeles National Forest/San Gabriel Mountains National Monument, the City of Duarte, and the private quarry Vulcan Materials. Check www.azusarock.com or http://accessduarte.com/howdoi/find/fish.htm to determine whether it's open before going. The trail description below is based on 2016 conditions. It is included in this book because it's considered one of the most classic waterfall hikes in the region, and its reopening is highly anticipated.

After a multiyear process involving litigation, in June 2014 Vulcan Materials allowed a 0.8-mile trail across their operations to allow hikers access to Fish Canyon. Outdated guide books mention visiting via the 9-mile, 2,400 feet of elevation gain Van Tassel

The multi-tiered elusive Fish Canyon Falls is a favorite spot for photography. ɪsтоcк ▶

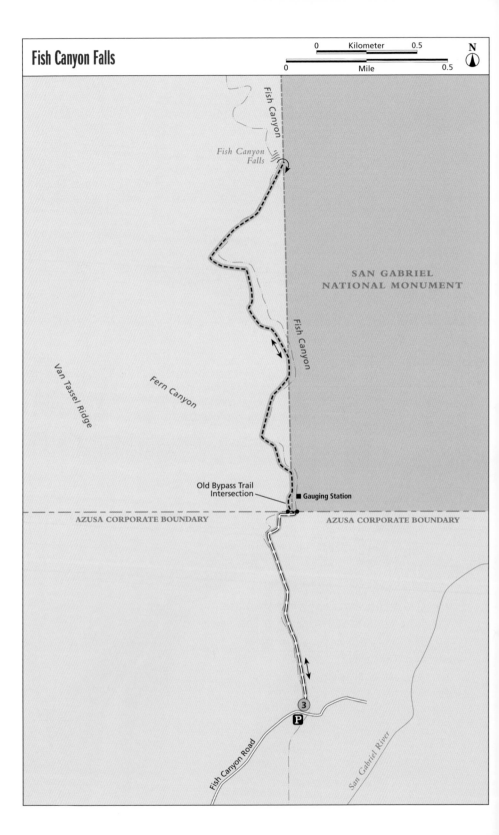

Fish Canyon Falls

Fish Canyon

Fish Canyon
Falls

SAN GABRIEL
NATIONAL MONUMENT

Fish Canyon

Van Tassel Ridge

Fern Canyon

Old Bypass Trail
Intersection

Gauging Station

AZUSA CORPORATE BOUNDARY

AZUSA CORPORATE BOUNDARY

3

P

Fish Canyon Road

San Gabriel River

Ridge Trail (now closed and considered trespassing). The new trail cuts those numbers down to a more reasonable size and was built with grant funding from LA County.

In the "Great Hiking Era" (1895–1938), Fish Canyon was one of the most popular places in these mountains. It once held almost fifty cabins. A 1958 wildfire and subsequent debris flows in 1959 took most of them out, but you may see invasive plants, relics of their gardens.

The new hiking route starts on a flat, fenced-off trail at the edge of Vulcan Materials' operation, paralleling their gravel road. The fence protects you from industrial activity. When visiting on a weekday, you can watch (and hear) the quarry in action, including passing under a conveyor belt.

After 0.5 mile you parallel Fish Canyon Creek. Signs inform you of Vulcan's work on ecological restoration here done in conjunction with the Wildlife Habitat Council. It's part of their lease agreement to work here. Resist the temptation to go down to the creek or off-trail, as it is protected habitat.

After 0.7 mile, leave Vulcan property through a fence and cross a gate. The trail starts feeling more like wilderness with oaks along a riparian corridor and even colonies of cacti. You reconnect to the old 9-Mile Van Tassel Ridge trail here.

The seasonal Fern Creek crosses the trail from the canyon on the left at 1.2 miles, before you make a relatively steep ascent high above Fish Canyon. This section was sunny and exposed in 2016, and the fire probably didn't help the situation. Be sure to drink plenty of water.

At 1.9 miles, descend toward the creek, ignoring a side canyon, which may be running. In 0.1 mile, rock-hop across the water. Watch for poison oak. Due to the history of erosion and landslides in this canyon, use caution on the narrow trail.

As you ascend the canyon, you'll get your first views of the falls. Descend toward the creek.

Fish Canyon Falls has three tiers—each with a pool below in winter and spring. It's long been a favorite destination for photographers, though is less of a sight to behold in late summer after the falls have dried.

Miles and Directions

0.0 Start at the trailhead inside Vulcan Materials' fence.

0.7 Leave the Vulcan area through fence and cross bridge.

1.2 Seasonal Fern Creek crosses the trail.

2.0 Cross Fish Creek.

2.4 Base of falls. Return the way you came.

4.8 Arrive back at the trailhead.

4 Monrovia Canyon Falls

This shady, well-marked hike is dog- and family-friendly. Walk up a shady, cascade-filled creek bed to a beautiful falls. It tends to be slightly less crowded than other nearby falls and feels more pristine.

Height: 30–40 feet
Beauty rating: ★★★★★
Distance: 1.6 miles out and back
Elevation gain: 290 feet gain there/30 feet gain way back
Difficulty: Easy
Best season: Winter, spring, fall, summer
County: Los Angeles
Trailhead amenities: 40 parking spots near a nature center, flush toilets and running water, trash/recycle bins, Little Free Library
Land status: Monrovia Canyon Park

Maps: Tom Harrison Angeles High Country; USGS Azusa
Trail contact: Monrovia Canyon Park; 1200 N. Canyon Blvd., Monrovia 91016; (626) 256-8282; www.cityofmonrovia .org/Home/Components/FacilityDirectory/ FacilityDirectory/28/787
Fees and permits: Cash entrance fee at the self-registration center. If you need to pay by card, park at the station and a human will help you.

Finding the trailhead: Google Maps: Monrovia Canyon Park Nature Center, but cell carriers don't have coverage at the nature center itself. From I-210, take exit 32 in Arcadia. Head north on Santa Anita Boulevard for 0.2 mile. Turn right onto Foothill Boulevard and follow it for 2 miles. Turn left on Canyon Boulevard, passing a house from the movie Bird Box. After 0.7 mile, take a right to continue on Canyon Boulevard. After self-paying at the entry station kiosk, continue uphill on the road, passing a scout camp on the right, following signs for the nature center. The park is open 8 a.m. to 5 p.m. weekdays except Tuesday and 7 a.m. to 5 p.m. on weekends.
GPS: N34 10.299' / W117 59.138' W

The Hike

Walk a pristine, shady, well-defined trail and follow a creek bed up a geologically and ecologically interesting canyon to end at a waterfall. Small cascades at check dams give you bonus beauty, even if they are human-made.

The hike starts at the nature center, a great educational addition to your hike where you can learn about flora, fauna, and history, and view the cities and valleys below. During the Great Hiking Era, Ben Overturff built a resort lodge at nearby Deer Park. Now there's a trail here named for him. By the Nature Center is a redwood carving of a black bear named Sampson, who allegedly hung out in a hot tub near here. He ate a plastic bag and couldn't be released to the wild; Monrovia residents raised money so he wouldn't be euthanized. Sampson moved to the Orange County zoo (with a hot tub in his exhibit) until he died in 2001.

Monrovia Canyon Falls is a gentle, family-friendly hike.

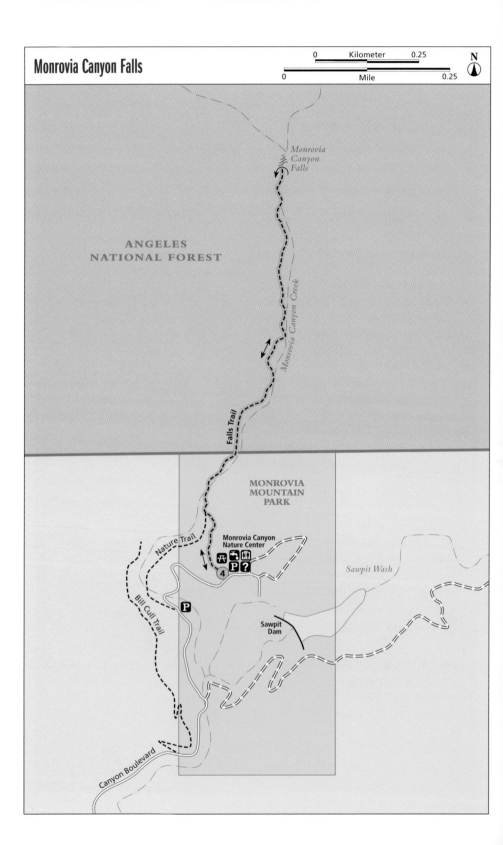

Take the path from the info sign near the toilets toward the back of the nature center through the oak- and pine-shaded picnic area. After 0.1 mile, go through a gate. Dogs are required to be on-leash here. Free dog waste bags are available. Sometimes there is a free paper nature trail guide.

Descend toward the creek. In 0.1 mile you reach a T junction. Turn right and uphill toward a "check dam," which looks like a cement fence. You'll pass about six of these as you ascend the canyon. In high water each can become its own mini-waterfall (so if your party isn't feeling the energy to make it to the end, there are plenty of cascades to satisfy your itch).

A quarter mile from the picnic area, ford a small creek (there are stepping-stones, so unless the water is high, you won't have to get your feet wet). Gently climb upstream along the left bank of the creek.

Ferns, maples, sycamores, white alders, fragrant bay laurels, and coast live oaks provide shady spots to sit trailside. When you look across the creek at the steep and crumbly canyon wall on the other side, you can appreciate the skill of the trail designers who made this pristine trail.

Continue to climb, occasionally ascending on steps. There's a short section where the 3- to 4-foot-wide trail hugs the rocky canyon wall. The drop-off on the right may feel exposed.

There are several side trails that take you down to the creek. You may see salamanders in the water or near the riparian vegetation. At the end of the canyon, cross the creek near a sign here asking not to climb the walls around the waterfall. Soon you reach a grotto and the two-tiered falls surrounded by small boulders.

Miles and Directions

0.0 Start at the info sign by the nature center.

0.1 Gate past picnic area.

0.2 T junction; turn right and uphill toward check dam.

0.25 Cross creek to left side.

0.4 Climb steps above check dam #3.

0.8 Base of falls. Return the way you came.

1.6 Arrive back at nature center.

Option: Extend this hike by starting on the Bill Cull trailhead near the entrance station. It's about 6 miles long. The main gate is locked at 5 p.m., so be back to your car before then.

5 Hermit Falls

Although it starts at the same trailhead as Sturtevant Falls, the smaller, more remote-feeling Hermit Falls has become a popular (and sometimes dangerous) place for swimming.

Height: About 25 feet
Beauty rating: ★★★
Distance: 2.8 miles out and back
Elevation gain: 675 feet (on the way back)
Difficulty: Easy to moderate
Best season: Fall, winter, spring, summer
County: Los Angeles
Trailhead amenities: 100+ parking spots on a terraced lot, Adams' Pack Station sells Adventure Passes and other goods when open (usually weekends), trash/recycle bins, picnic area, barbecues, outhouses. Dogs on-leash allowed but not recommended if headed to the base of Hermit Falls. This is a very busy trailhead. Overflow parking on road

Land status: Angeles National Forest
Maps: Tom Harrison Angeles Front Country; USGS Mount Wilson
Trail contact: Angeles National Forest/San Gabriel Mountains National Monument, San Gabriel River Ranger District; 110 N. Wabash Ave., Glendora 91741; (626) 335-1251; www .fs.usda.gov/main/angeles/home
Fees and permits: Display Adventure Pass. Nearby Adams' Pack Station has overflow parking for an extra fee (not covered by your Adventure Pass). Adventure Pass required everywhere else. Gates locked from 8 PM to 6 AM.

Finding the trailhead: Google Maps: Chantry Flat Picnic Area. From I-210, take exit 32 in Arcadia. Head north on Santa Anita Avenue, which turns into Chantry Flat Road—a two-lane mountain road that ends 4.9 miles later. The road is subject to landslides; call to make sure it's open. The parking lot is notoriously crowded on weekends. Gate to road locked from 8 PM to 6 AM.
GPS: N34 11.463' / W118 01.217'

The Hike

Although this is the shorter of the two waterfall hikes from Chantry Flat, it's the more adventurous. It requires deeper creek crossings and climbing high on a narrow trail above a steep canyon. The falls themselves are only partially visible from the trail and require that you have skills and are comfortable walking on smooth rock slabs to get close enough to take in a full view. In summer this is a popular place for swimming and jumping in the water. Be aware of water levels and flow before doing either. Chasing videos for social media and cliff diving here have resulted in double-digit rescues annually, including highly publicized helicopter rescues and fatalities. Enjoy the falls, but don't become a statistic.

Despite some human impact, the beauty, polished granite, and swimming holes at Hermit Falls make it worth a visit.

▶

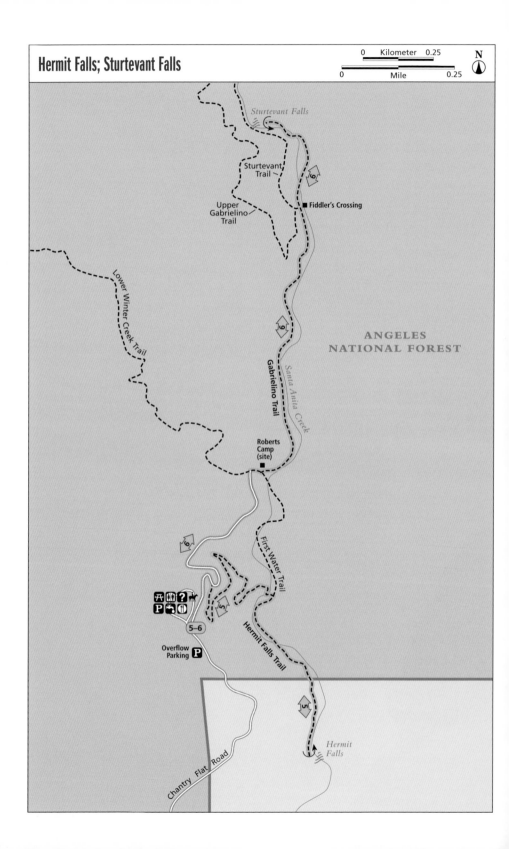

0   Kilometer   0.25

0   Mile   0.25

N

Sturtevant Falls

Sturtevant Trail

Upper Gabrielino Trail

■ Fiddler's Crossing

Lower Winter Creek Trail

ANGELES NATIONAL FOREST

Gabrielino Trail

Santa Anita Creek

Roberts Camp (site) ■

First Water Trail

Hermit Falls Trail

Overflow Parking **P**

5–6

5

6

5

6

9

Chantry Flat Road

Hermit Falls

The hike starts down a gated, paved road on your right as you pull into the parking area. As you descend into Santa Anita Canyon, you'll pass through oak and pine. After 0.2 mile, as the road is about to turn to the left, you reach a crucial intersection. There's a bench, trash can, and a sign indicating you should turn right to get on singletrack trail and off the paved road.

Descend toward the water on switchbacks. At 0.5 mile, reach a T intersection near cabins. A sign indicates to descend to the right, not left toward a human-made check dam "falls."

Rock-hop the creek at 0.7 mile at a sign calling this place "First Water." It's a key junction and easy to miss depending on where you cross. Turn right (downhill and downstream). You climb an embankment along the left (east) portion of the creek to get around a check dam, passing a cabin. As the canyon narrows, it's shady here in the afternoon.

After 0.9 mile the creek branches into two parts. Cross the leftmost (east) branch of the creek (sometimes dry) and walk to an island between the two branches. Here, there's a No Campfire sign and unfortunate graffiti. Next, cross the right (west) branch of the creek. In winter and spring it can be intimidatingly deep.

Climb up good trail high above the creek through oaks and ferns. At 0.2 mile from the crossing, a graffitied trail reinforcement with a lock blocks a path to another cabin. Continue on the narrowing and exposed-feeling trail for another 0.3 mile— farther than you may think necessary. The creek below starts to look like it's falling through a thin, rocky chute. You may think, "Was that cascade *the* falls?"

The top of Hermit Falls is in an area with a graffiti-covered pipe looking like a factory's smokestack. The rest of the area around the falls is cliffy and impressive. The rocky slab is polished and slippery. You can't get a full view of the falls from where the official trail ends, but people have found a rope and ways to get closer via use trails. The parking lot gate is locked at 8 p.m., so be back to your car before then.

Miles and Directions

0.0 Chantry Flat trailhead starts at the gated, paved road.

0.2 Leave the pavement following signs and a narrow, dirt trail toward Hermit Falls.

0.5 Turn right at signed intersection downhill toward the creek.

0.7 Cross the creek toward a sign on the other side indicating "First Water Crossing." Turn right, downstream.

0.9 Cross both branches of the creek with an island between.

1.1 Ignore side trail near trail reinforcement.

1.4 Top of Hermit Falls. Return the way you came.

2.8 Arrive back at the trailhead.

6 Sturtevant Falls

This must-see waterfall follows a well-defined, shaded old road past historic cabins to a 50- to 80-foot year-round waterfall.

See map on page 20.
Height: About 50–80 feet
Beauty rating: ★★★★★
Distance: 3.5 miles out and back
Elevation gain: 500 feet
Difficulty: Easy
Best season: Fall, winter, spring, summer
County: Los Angeles
Trailhead amenities: 100+ parking spots on a terraced lot, Adams' Pack Station sells Adventure Passes, maps, and other goods including sometimes hot dogs and burgers (usually weekends), trash/recycle bins, picnic area, barbecues, outhouses. This is a very busy trailhead. Overflow parking along road.

Land status: Angeles National Forest
Maps: Tom Harrison Mt. Wilson; USGS Mount Wilson; Tom Harrison Angeles Front Country (but not in the best detail)
Trail contact: Angeles National Forest/San Gabriel Mountains National Monument, San Gabriel River Ranger District; 110 N. Wabash Ave., Glendora 91741; (626) 335-1251; www .fs.usda.gov/main/angeles/home
Fees and permits: Display Adventure Pass. Nearby Adams' Pack Station has overflow parking for an extra fee (not covered by your Adventure Pass). Adventure Pass required everywhere else. Gates locked from 8 PM to 6 AM.

Finding the trailhead: Google Maps: Chantry Flat Picnic Area. From I-210, take exit 32 in Arcadia. Head north on Santa Anita Avenue, which turns into Chantry Flat Road—a two-lane mountain road that ends 4.9 miles later. The road is subject to landslides; call to make sure it's open. The parking lot is notoriously crowded on weekends. Gate to road locked from 8 PM to 6 AM. **GPS:** N34 11.463' / W118 01.217'

The Hike

Although this is the longer of the two waterfall hikes from Chantry Flat, it's the more straightforward and kid- and dog-friendly. The falls themselves are one of the most impressive in the area with an 80-foot drop that runs year-round.

Sturtevant Falls were named for William Sturtevant, a burro-packer from Colorado who built many of the San Gabriel trails, opening Sturtevant Camp (found farther up Santa Anita Canyon) in 1898.

The hike starts as for Hermit Falls, down a gated, paved road on your right as you pull into the parking area. This is the Gabrielino Trail. Keep following the paved road as it descends Santa Anita Canyon. You travel through oak and pine as the trail curls down switchbacks.

After 0.6 mile and hundreds of feet of elevation loss, the pavement ends. On your left there's a "falls"—a human-made cascade created by a check dam on Winter

Sturtevant Falls is a rewarding finish point on a popular, well-marked trail.

THE GABRIELINO TRAIL

As you hike in Angeles National Forest, you're likely to use or cross the Gabrielino Trail (including on several of the hikes in this book). It's a 28.5-mile-long National Recreation Trail, open to bikes, horses, and hikers, named for the Spanish American name for the Tongva people, the Native American tribe whose ancestral land this trail passes. Parts of the trail, like those near Switzer Falls, were closed for almost a decade following the Station Fire in 2009. The trail fully reopened in spring 2018 with the help of volunteers.

Creek. It was built in the early 1960s as part of the LA County Flood Control District. Cross Roberts Bridge over Winter Creek.

This flat area at the confluence of Winter and Big Santa Anita Creeks is called Roberts Camp after a resort founded here in 1912. During LA's Great Hiking Era (1895–1938), the spot had a store, restaurant, and even a post office and branch of the LA Public Library. Now there's a rough outhouse.

This spot is a four-way intersection with the Winter Creek Trail. Don't take the Winter Creek Trail to the left or right. Instead, follow signs heading straight/right on a wide, dirt road up the Gabrielino Trail, following signs for the waterfall along the left (west) side of the creek. The trail here is shaded with oaks and alders. You'll pass eighty or so cutesy, turn-of-the-twentieth-century cabins. They were historically serviced by burro train from Chantry Flats (where you parked) by an early horse-packer named Charlie Chantry.

In about 0.8 mile you reach an important signed junction called Fern Lodge. The Gabrielino Trail continues uphill to the left, but you stay straight, following the creek upstream. One hundred yards later, the trail turns right, crossing Big Santa Anita Creek at Fiddler's Crossing. It's usually a rock-hop or crossable on debris and won't yield wet feet. But 0.2 mile later you cross again, and this sometimes can be a foot-wetter.

You can see the falls, but a final crossing leads to the base. When the water is going, the mist and wind created from the falls can be cooling and impressive.

Miles and Directions

0.0 Start on the Gabrielino Trail on a paved road headed downhill on switchbacks.

0.6 Roberts Bridge/Camp; junction with Winter Creek Trail.

1.4 Stay straight at junction with Gabrielino Trail.

1.45 Fiddler's Crossing to right side of creek.

1.6 Cross creek to left side toward brown privy.

1.65 Final creek crossing to the right.

1.75 Base of falls. Return the way you came.

3.5 Arrive back at the trailhead.

7 Eaton Canyon Falls

One of the most popular and crowded hikes in this book, this year-round waterfall is close to the city but has a wild feel. As described by John Muir in 1877, Eaton Canyon Falls ends in a shady grotto in a narrow canyon, and the trailhead boasts one of the best free nature centers in the Southland.

Height: 30–40 feet
Beauty rating: ★★★★
Distance: 3.7 miles out and back
Elevation gain: 600 feet
Difficulty: Easy to moderate
Best season: Winter, spring
County: Los Angeles
Trailhead amenities: Free nature center, parking lot with 100+ spots, trash/recycle bins, public pay phone, vending machine (may not be operating), drinking fountains, shaded

picnic areas; lower equestrian parking lot has 100+ spots. Leashed dogs allowed, but it can get very hot with little shade.
Land status: Angeles National Forest; Eaton Canyon Nature County Park
Maps: Tom Harrison Mt. Wilson; USGS Mount Wilson; free map available at nature center
Trail contact: Eaton Canyon Nature Center; 1750 N. Altadena Dr., Pasadena, CA 91107; (626) 398-5420; www.ecnca.org
Fees and permits: Display Adventure Pass

Finding the trailhead: From I-210, take exit 29A, Sierra Madre Road. Continue straight as it turns into Maple Street, then, 0.3 mile later, turn right on Altadena Drive. Stay on this for 1.5 miles and turn right into the signed Eaton Canyon Natural Area. If the upper lot is full, you can access the equestrian dirt parking area below. A signed horse trail takes you the 0.2 mile from the equestrian lot to the main trailhead sign. Parking is also available on Altadena Drive.
GPS: N34 10.42' / W118 05.477'

The Hike

Eaton Canyon Falls is one of Southern California's most visited waterfalls and for good reason. It's close to the population center, yet feels wild and secluded. John Muir applauded Eaton Canyon Falls for its "round mirror-pool." The canyon is home to many native species, including the recently discovered *Kovarikia oxy* scorpion, classified in 2018 by an Occidental College professor. (Don't worry: If it took this long for scientists to discover, it's highly unlikely you'll see one.)

In the 1860s, Judge Benjamin Eaton—former LA district attorney—piped water from what was then called Precipio Canyon (for its steep walls) to his grapevines. He proved skeptical neighbors wrong by making serious money from his grapes, starting a short-lived vineyard trend in the San Gabriels. In 1930 the canyon became a permanent bird and game sanctuary, and in 1963 its first nature center was built and named after local leader Robert McCurdy.

Much of Eaton Canyon burned in the 1993 Altadena fire, started by an illegal campfire. Today, much of the chaparral, coastal sage, and oak sycamore woodland vegetation has grown back, and many hikers are surprised to learn a fire happened here. The excellent free Eaton Canyon Nature Center (rebuilt in 1998) has displays of all that was left of the old nature center after the fire, including a melted Macintosh computer.

The nature center has a small collection of rescued native animals, including a particularly active rattlesnake. The center teaches environmental education to kids from local schools. While you're there, consider donating a few bucks to their Bus Fund to get kids out in nature.

The trailhead sits at the north end of the parking lot, marked with a sign and yellow gate. Because Eaton Canyon is so popular, it has stricter rules than other areas. Read the regulations before hiking.

Take the trail on the right toward the kiosk (the trail on the left passes a picnic area and drinking fountain and meets up with the main trail 0.25 mile later). After the two trails meet, follow the wide, sunny trail for 0.2 mile to a prominent T intersection marked with signs and trash cans. Turn left, following signs to Eaton Canyon and the waterfall. The Eaton Canyon Trail gently ascends a wide wash using an old toll road operated from 1890 to 1911.

After 0.4 mile stay straight, ignoring signs on the right for Coyote Canyon and, 0.2 mile later, Walnut Canyon. The sandy alluvial wash becomes open, in part due to 35 inches of rain that washed away canyon walls in the 1960s.

At 1.2 miles there is a critical intersection. Reach a small, wooden sign on the left with "Falls 0.5 mile ahead." Take the narrow trail *behind* this sign, not the wide trail heading uphill to the right—that connects to the Mt. Wilson Toll Road (and the bridge ahead).

At 1.25 miles your narrow trail goes *under* the Mt. Wilson Toll Road bridge. You can see why early Spanish settlers called this shady, steep, and narrow canyon "El Precipio." A small creek is usually flowing, and you'll ford it from side to side. Watch for remnants of removed small dams and old pipes.

At 1.7 miles into the canyon, you reemerge into the sun. In high water you may need to cross the creek on a logjam. Scramble up a small, steep hill. A sign at the top of the hill makes your destination clear, but there's not one clear path up.

Eaton Canyon Falls drops into a surprisingly secluded canyon grotto with a cold pool of water underneath.

Between 2011 and 2013 numerous people perished attempting to access the second falls above Eaton Canyon Falls. As a result all access has been closed to the area surrounding the upper falls. Do not attempt to access these falls, which were rendered dangerous due to landslides and flooding after numerous fires in the area.

◀ *Eaton Canyon Falls*

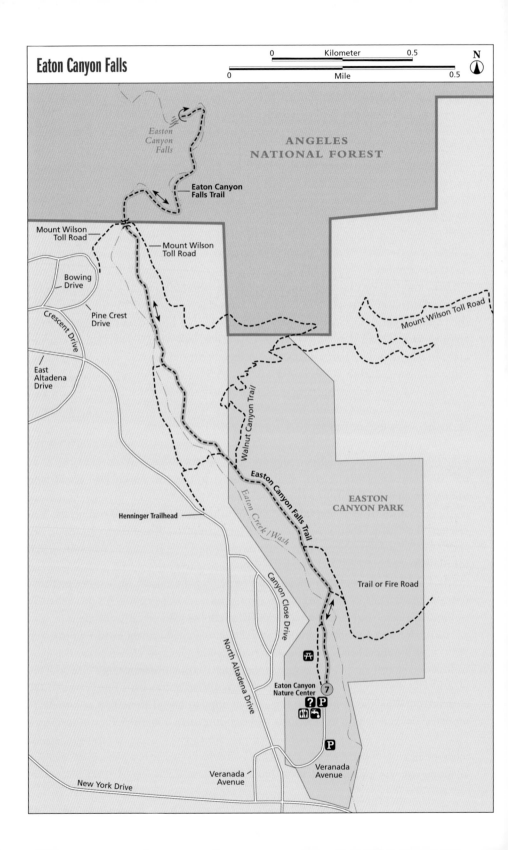

Eaton Canyon Falls

Eaton Canyon Falls

ANGELES NATIONAL FOREST

Eaton Canyon Falls Trail

Mount Wilson Toll Road

Mount Wilson Toll Road

Bowing Drive

Crescent Drive

Pine Crest Drive

East Altadena Drive

Mount Wilson Toll Road

Walnut Canyon Trail

Easton Canyon Falls Trail

Eaton Creek / Wash

Henninger Trailhead

EASTON CANYON PARK

Trail or Fire Road

Eaton Canyon Nature Center

7

Canyon Close Drive

North Altadena Drive

Veranada Avenue

Veranada Avenue

New York Drive

The year-round Eaton Canyon Falls can be a cool place to hike on an early summer morning.

Miles and Directions

0.0 Start at the parking lot.

0.2 Turn left at T intersection with trash cans.

0.4 Stay straight at intersection with Coyote Canyon.

0.6 Stay straight at intersection with Walnut Canyon.

1.2 Signed intersection for falls; take slight left onto narrower trail.

1.25 Cross under Mt. Wilson Toll Road bridge.

1.85 Base of falls. Return the way you came.

3.7 Arrive back at the trailhead.

8 Millard Falls

This year-round, kid-friendly hike leads to an impressive 80-foot falls in a grotto at the end of a narrow canyon. Best for warm spring days when you don't mind getting your feet wet, it can be more of an adventure in higher water or a trickle in the summer.

Height: About 60–80 feet
Beauty rating: ★★★★★ (when flowing)
Distance: 1.2 miles out and back
Elevation gain: 200 feet
Difficulty: Easy; moderate in highest water
Best season: Winter, spring, summer
County: Los Angeles
Trailhead amenities: 50+ parking spots, more along the side of the road into the parking area (watch for No Parking signs), campground with 5 sites, toilet. Dogs on-leash allowed.

Land status: Angeles National Forest, Los Angeles Gateway District
Maps: Tom Harrison Angeles Front Country; USGS Pasadena
Trail contact: Angeles National Forest, Los Angeles Gateway District; 12371 N. Little Tujunga Canyon Rd., Sylmar 91342; (818) 899-1900; www.fs.usda.gov/recarea/angeles/recarea/?recid=41674
Fees and permits: Display Adventure Pass

Finding the trailhead: Google Maps: Millard Trail Camp (do not Google the actual falls themselves). From I-210, take exit 23 in Altadena. Head north on Lincoln Avenue for 2 miles. Turn right onto the residential Loma Alta Drive. Turn left (north) on Chaney Trail, following signs for the recreation area. Pass the Chaney Trail gate (closed 8 p.m. to 6 a.m.) and continue up for 1.2 miles until you reach a T intersection. Turn left, following signs to the Millard Campground.
GPS: N34 12.585' / W118 08.47'

The Hike

Millard Falls is one of the most popular (and crowded) hikes in the Southland and it's clear why: A short, scenic hike up a shaded canyon leads to one of the taller falls in the region. Because it follows water on soft ground and is relatively shady, it's one of the better hikes for a leashed dog. This canyon was damaged by debris following the 2009 Station Fire (though it didn't burn much itself) and was closed until 2015. The canyon and falls are named for Henry Millard (pronounced Mill-ARD), a beekeeper who lived here with his family from 1862 to 1872.

From the day-use parking, follow the use trail from the east end of the lot toward Millard Campground. You pass a grand private cabin on your right dating to the early twentieth century, back when the US Forest Service leased land here for less than $20 per year. The path curves, generally following Millard Creek, giving you an idea of what kind of flow to expect at the waterfall.

The seasonal Millard Falls gushes in the winter and early spring. ▶

After 0.1 mile you reach a junction with the Sunset Ridge Trail, which goes uphill to the right. Instead, stay straight on the road, following a sign to "Campground and Falls."

Walk through the campground, passing a rough outhouse and trash cans on the right. Turn right, off the road and onto singletrack, following the creek upstream and signs for the falls. Do not go straight on the road to ford the cement-lined creek here—that leads to El Prieto Canyon ("dark one"). It's allegedly named after former slave Robert Owen, who lived and was a woodworker here. He saved money to free his family in Texas and bring them to LA.

The dirt singletrack trail has you scramble up a check dam where there may be a cascade. Once above the dam, ford the (dirt-lined) creek at 0.2 mile, crossing to the left side of the creek. In high water, use this ford to judge whether you should continue. If the water is high and this doesn't sound fun, consider visiting on another day. On a hot day, it could be just what your party wants. Similar creek crossings are ahead.

After crossing the creek back to the right side, the next 0.1 mile can be confusing. The creek can wash out the main trail. If unsure, head upstream.

The narrow Millard Canyon is a riparian habitat.

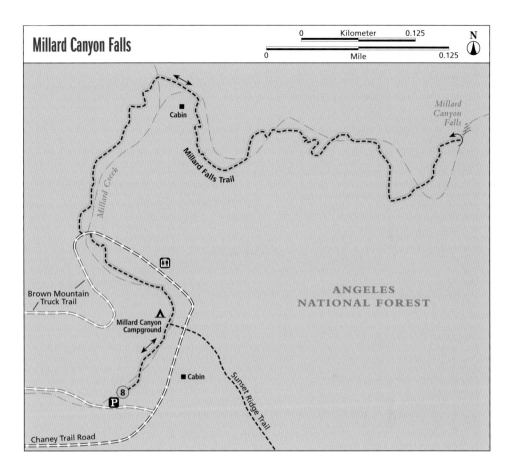

Millard Canyon Falls

As the canyon narrows and its walls become steep on one side or the other, you're crossing back and forth. Depending on water levels, you may walk in the water. During summer you likely can walk on dirt or rock-hop instead. Ferns and moss grow on the rocky canyon walls shaded with oaks and alders.

After boulder-hopping, there's Millard Canyon Falls. The trail leads to its base in a narrow grotto. The area doesn't accommodate many people. The falls tumble 80 feet with an upper tier partially in view.

Miles and Directions

0.0 Start at the day-use parking area.

0.1 Stay straight at junction with Sunset Ridge Trail on the right.

0.2 Turn right onto a singletrack trail signed for Millard Falls.

0.3 First creek crossing (trail goes to left side of creek).

0.6 Base of waterfall. Return the way you came.

1.2 Arrive back at the trailhead.

9 Switzer Falls

For almost a century, this has been one of the most popular waterfall and hiking destinations in the area. Although you can only see the bottom of the falls, this hike is pleasant, scenic, and a classic.

Height: Bottom cascade easily reached by foot: 15 feet; total falls height visible from a distance from the trail: 50–70 feet
Beauty rating: ★★★
Distance: 4 miles out and back
Elevation gain: 650 feet
Difficulty: Moderate
Best season: Fall, winter, spring
County: Los Angeles
Trailhead amenities: 50+ parking spots, more at upper parking lots and along the side of the road (watch for No Parking signs), dogs on-leash allowed though last half of hike can be hot and exposed
Land status: Angeles National Forest, Los Angeles Gateway District
Maps: Tom Harrison Angeles Front Country; USGS Condor Peak
Trail contact: Angeles National Forest, Los Angeles Gateway District; 12371 N. Little Tujunga Canyon Rd., Sylmar 91342; (818) 899-1900; www.fs.usda.gov/recarea/angeles/recarea/?recid=41674
Fees and permits: Display Adventure Pass

Finding the trailhead: Google Maps: Switzer Falls Picnic Area. From I-210 in La Cañada Flintridge, take the Angeles Crest Highway (CA 2) north for 10 miles to the signed Switzer Falls Picnic Area. Lower trailhead parking can get crowded on weekends and holidays. Upper overflow lots require you to walk past the fire road gate down the paved road for 0.3 mile (and 300 feet elevation). Occasionally, the gate to the road leading to the picnic area is closed and you have to park on the Angeles Crest Highway.
GPS: N34 15.576' / W118 08.411'

The Hike

For more than a century, this area has been among the most popular in the San Gabriel Range. It's also been one of the most deadly. A 1990 *LA Times* article speculated that in twenty years Switzer Falls claimed more than one hundred lives and was the most dangerous spot in Angeles National Forest. In the past thirty years, however, signage and easy-to-follow trails make it safe for most to travel here.

Start at Switzer Falls Picnic Area, following signs for Gabrielino Trail/Switzer Falls as you gently drop into Arroyo Seco Canyon. The shady oak, maple, willow, alder, and sycamore groves are a great place to linger and play. Cross the creek on a bridge to a wide trail heading downhill.

After a mile you reach the facility-free Commodore Switzer Trail Camp. It's hard to tell now, but in 1884 this was one of the most famous trail resorts in the range—

An old Forest Service wood burning stove at Switzer Camp.

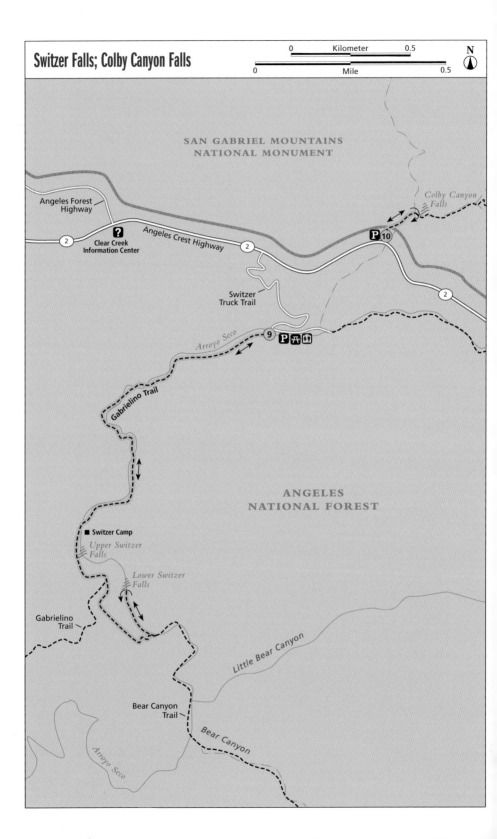

Switzer Falls; Colby Canyon Falls

0   Kilometer   0.5

0   Mile   0.5

N

SAN GABRIEL MOUNTAINS
NATIONAL MONUMENT

Colby Canyon
Falls

Angeles Forest
Highway

Angeles Crest Highway

2

2

P **10**

Clear Creek
Information Center

Switzer
Truck Trail

2

Arroyo Seco

9 **P** 🏕 🚻

Gabrielino Trail

ANGELES
NATIONAL FOREST

■ Switzer Camp

Upper Switzer
Falls

Lower Switzer
Falls

Gabrielino
Trail

Little Bear Canyon

Bear Canyon
Trail

Bear Canyon

Arroyo Seco

hundreds of people visited each weekend. Back then they came by foot, horse, or burro via an 8-mile trail from Pasadena with over sixty stream crossings. When guests reached the resort, the Austin family proprietors had a trout dinner (caught in the stream) ready for them. Visitors here included Henry Ford, Shirley Temple, Clark Gable, and Mary Pickford. There was a library, dance floor, tennis and croquet courts, and the Christ Chapel (the only building whose ruins remain today). In 1959 all but the chapel were removed (or were damaged by floods in the 1930s).

From the camp, follow the obvious trail to cross the creek. It's hard to find these days, but do not take the narrower use path through the bushes, which passes a graffitied sign warning not to continue any closer to the falls and citing the 118 deaths of those who did.

After crossing the creek, the trail climbs high on the west slope among chaparral. You're out of the shade and into the heat. The drop-off to your left is steep and exposed, although a chain-link fence separates you and the falls. Those who don't like heights should take it slowly. There are impressive views of the chapel ruins and the gorge. Among the foliage you may spot the top third of Switzer Falls and its middle pool.

About a quarter mile from the camp, reach a Y intersection with the Gabrielino Trail going uphill on the right (southwest). To reach Switzer Falls, stay straight toward Bear Canyon, breaking away from the Gabrielino Trail, which otherwise continues down the Main Branch of Arroyo Seco to Oakwilde Camp and Pasadena.

Descend steep switchbacks to the Arroyo Seco gorge, reaching the creek below the falls at 1.7 miles. Follow signs pointing left to the falls, heading upstream on a less-defined trail for 0.3 mile. The lower falls is 15 feet tall with a small pool underneath. People have been injured or killed climbing above here, but there is a use trail on the right that leads to a pool below the plunge. Continue at your own risk.

Miles and Directions

0.0 Start at Switzer Falls Picnic Area.

1.0 Switzer Trail Camp.

1.2 View of Switzer Falls.

1.3 Gabrielino Trail breaks off to the right; stay straight.

1.7 Reach Arroyo Seco Creek; head left upstream.

2.0 Base of bottom cascade. Return the way you came.

4.0 Arrive back at the trailhead.

10 Colby Canyon Falls

This close-to-the-city but unmarked falls is an easy add-on whenever you're in the area. Visible from the road but only a very short hike (if you want it to be), it's highly ephemeral, so best to visit after a storm.

See map on page 36.
Height: 30 feet
Beauty rating: ★★★
Distance: 0.2 mile out and back, more if you want to see more falls
Elevation gain: Mostly flat
Difficulty: Easy
Best season: Winter, spring
County: Los Angeles
Trailhead amenities: 6 parking spots right in front of the trailhead and 4 in an attached parking "lot"; outhouses, trash/recycle bins,

and picnicking at the nearby Switzer Falls Picnic Area
Land status: Angeles National Forest, Los Angeles Gateway District
Maps: Tom Harrison Angeles Front Country; USGS Condor Peak
Trail contact: Angeles National Forest, Los Angeles Gateway District; 12371 N. Little Tujunga Canyon Rd., Sylmar 91342; (818) 899-1900; www.fs.usda.gov/recarea/angeles/recarea/?recid=41674
Fees and permits: Display Adventure Pass

Finding the trailhead: Google Maps: Colby Canyon Trailhead. From I-210 in La Cañada Flintridge, take the Angeles Crest Highway (CA 2) north for 10 miles to the signed Switzer Falls Picnic Area. Pass the signed picnic area. Between mile markers 34.5 and 34.55, there's a pullout on the left side of the road.
GPS: N34 16.104' / W118 08.266'

The Hike

The trailhead sits at the mouth of Colby Canyon on a trail signed with carbonite (a thin, plasticky brown post). Continue on the left (west) side of the creek. You immediately have less than 10 feet of rocky area to cross. When it's dry, you may not even notice. When wet, it may be slippery.

Continue on the sandy trail to the base of the falls, which is visible from CA 2. For those wanting a longer hike, continue up Colby Canyon Trail as it climbs toward Josephine Saddle between Josephine and Strawberry Peak. You'll pass several other small, seasonal waterfalls. They mostly run only after a storm, but it's a worthy hike regardless of whether there is a falls or not.

Miles and Directions

0.0 Start at the CA 2 pullout.
0.1 Base of falls. Return the way you came.
0.2 Arrive back at the trailhead.

11 Cooper Falls

This cool, alpine hike is a gem utilizing a popular PCT alternate and the PCT the entire way. This is a rare Southern California hike where your trail follows the creek from above, past the plunge point, then down to the bottom. Starting at a shady campground and following a good, signed trail throughout the entire trip, it makes a great first wilderness hike.

Height: About 40–50 feet
Beauty rating: ★★★★★
Distance: 3.2 miles out and back
Elevation gain: 715 feet
Difficulty: Easy to moderate
Best season: Spring, summer, fall
County: Los Angeles
Trailhead amenities: About 12 parking spots, dog-friendly, more parking outside campground exit or in the campground for overnight guests
Land status: Angeles National Forest/San Gabriel Mountains National Monument, Santa Clara/Mojave Rivers Ranger District; Pleasant View Ridge Wilderness
Maps: Tom Harrison Angeles High Country; USGS Waterman Mountain
Trail contact: Angeles National Forest, Santa Clara/Mojave Rivers Ranger District Office, 33708 Crown Valley Rd., Acton 93510; (661) 269-2808; www.fs.usda.gov/recarea/angeles/recarea/?recid=41674
Fees and permits: Display Adventure Pass

Finding the trailhead: Google Maps: Burkhart Trailhead in Buckhorn Campground (closed late fall through early spring). From La Cañada Flintridge, take Highway 2 (closed during winter) for 35. 1 mile to Buckhorn Campground. There's limited parking, so if you have a campsite, it's best to leave your car where it is and walk over. If you're here for a day hike, there's limited parking at the Burkhart trailhead. When the campground is closed, you may have to park outside the exit gate and walk into the campground, adding 1.4 miles round-trip to your walk. If you're driving to the trailhead, be aware that a creek crosses the road and in high water it may be difficult for low-clearance vehicles to get across. The trailhead is near campsite 24.
GPS: N34 20.509' / W117 54.399'

The Hike

The only problem with this hike is that, like for many waterfalls, it's a reverse hike. Like the Grand Canyon, you start the hike by heading downhill, only to have the hardest climbing at the end of the day when legs are tired. Keep this in mind as you plan your hike, and allow for plenty of time to take breaks on the return.

Start at the far end of the Buckhorn Campground at the parking lot for the Burkhart Trail (10W02 High Desert National Recreation Trail). Follow signs to the Burkhart Trail/PCT, soon passing a sign indicating you have entered the Pleasant View Ridge Wilderness.

As you gently descend the canyon, pass incense cedars. A quarter mile in, the forest becomes more open and you'll lose your shade.

Just feet off the PCT, Cooper Falls is a beautiful hike in the autumn.

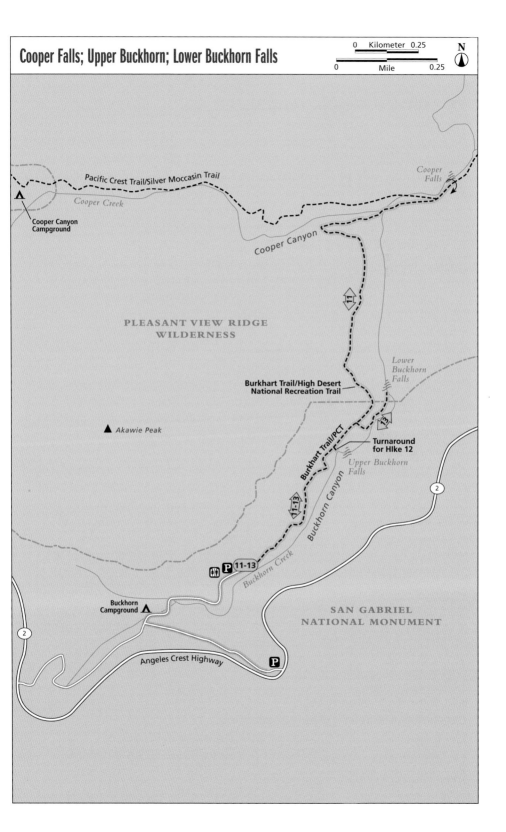

Cooper Falls; Upper Buckhorn; Lower Buckhorn Falls

0   Kilometer 0.25

0   Mile   0.25

N

Pacific Crest Trail/Silver Moccasin Trail

Cooper Creek

Cooper Falls

Cooper Canyon Campground

Cooper Canyon

11

PLEASANT VIEW RIDGE WILDERNESS

Lower Buckhorn Falls

Burkhart Trail/High Desert National Recreation Trail

▲ *Akawie Peak*

12

Turnaround for Hike 12

Burkhart Trail/PCT

Upper Buckhorn Falls

2

Buckhorn Canyon

11-13

11-13

Buckhorn Creek

Buckhorn Campground

SAN GABRIEL NATIONAL MONUMENT

2

Angeles Crest Highway

P

At 0.45 mile in, at a very large conifer, the trail widens and you reach a three-way junction with an unmarked use trail. This is the junction to Upper Buckhorn Falls, which makes a great side trip on the way to Cooper Falls or an alternative hike if you're looking for something shorter. Stay straight on the Burkhart Trail, which parallels Buckhorn Creek high above on the hillside. As you hike deeper into the canyon, you'll lose your view of the creek but gain views of the wilderness beyond.

Ignore what appears to be an intersection to your right at 0.6 mile in. The trail here has reinforcement to prevent falling into the canyon, but the use trail doesn't provide any satisfying views and gets dangerously loose and close to the edge of the cliffs. Instead, continue downhill on the good Burkhart Trail. As you descend, there's a section of trail that gets rocky with a steep drop to your right. It may feel exposed. Take your time and use your judgment.

After a little more than a mile, switchback into shaded Cooper Canyon, now following Cooper Creek downstream. This narrow, incense cedar–laden canyon is different than the wide-open Buckhorn Canyon you left moments ago.

Around 1.3 miles in, reach the confluence of Cooper Creek and Buckhorn Creek—the creek you followed on the way down into Cooper Canyon.

At 1.5 miles in, reach a three-way junction. To the left is the Silver Moccasin Trail/PCT north headed to Canada. To the right is the PCT south—although the Forest Service has closed part of it for over a decade to protect an endangered frog. Your path up to Cooper Falls is open, though, so head straight ahead on the PCT. The trail is the perfect viewpoint to watch the creek peacefully meander down the slope. Then it starts cascading at a lower angle before a full-on plunge off the edge, disappearing below.

To get to the bottom of the falls, take the PCT 500 feet past the junction. Look for a steep use trail to the left past wooden trail reinforcements. Scramble to the creek on the steep, narrow, and often muddy use trail. There may be a rope to help lower yourself, but as with any rope, assess its condition and where it's anchored before making your own decision whether it is safe enough to use.

At the plunge pool and grotto at the bottom, you are in a magical world of ferns, moss, alder trees, and incense cedar. It is serene and feels like a temperate forest, so unlike the dominant ecosystems in the rest of Southern California. You can only see three-quarters of the falls from this vantage point, but it's lined with greenery. The canyon alcove stays shaded. Across the creek are large, flat rocks for picnicking (if they aren't underwater during higher snowmelt years).

Miles and Directions

0.0 Start at the Burkhart trailhead.

1.3 Confluence of Buckhorn Creek and Cooper Creek.

1.5 Three-way junction with PCT north and south. Stay straight on PCT south.

1.6 Scramble down to base of Cooper Falls on a use trail. Return the way you came.

3.2 Arrive back at the trailhead.

12 Upper Buckhorn Falls

Starting at a shady mountain campground, this family-friendly hike gives you a taste of the beauty of the falls on Buckhorn Creek via a short, safe route.

See map on page 41.
Height: 10-15 feet
Beauty rating: ★★★★
Distance: 1 mile out and back
Elevation gain: 140 feet
Difficulty: Easy
Best season: Spring, summer, fall
County: Los Angeles
Trailhead amenities: About 5 parking spots, dog-friendly, free maps at information kiosk

Land status: Angeles National Forest/San Gabriel Mountains National Monument, Santa Clara/Mojave Rivers Ranger District
Maps: Tom Harrison Angeles High Country; USGS Waterman Mountain
Trail contact: Angeles National Forest, Santa Clara/Mojave Rivers Ranger District Office, 33708 Crown Valley Rd., Acton 93510; (661) 269-2808; www.fs.usda.gov/recarea/angeles/recarea/?recid=41674
Fees and permits: Display Adventure Pass

Finding the trailhead: Google Maps: Burkhart Trailhead in Buckhorn Campground (closed late fall through early spring). From La Cañada Flintridge, take Highway 2 (closed during winter) for 35. 1 mile to Buckhorn Campground. There's limited parking, so if you have a campsite, it's best to leave your car where it is and walk over. If you're here for a day hike, there's limited parking at the Burkhart trailhead. When the campground is closed, you may have to park outside the exit gate and walk into the campground, adding 1.4 miles round-trip to your walk. If you're driving to the trailhead, be aware that a creek crosses the road and in high water it may be difficult for low-clearance vehicles to get across. The trailhead is near campsite 24.
GPS: N34 20.509' / W117 54.399'

The Hike

Start at the far end of the Buckhorn Campground at the parking lot for the Burkhart Trail (High Desert National Recreation Trail). Follow signs to the Burkhart Trail/PCT, soon passing a sign indicating you have entered the Pleasant View Ridge Wilderness.

Just short of half a mile in, you can hear the creek below you. Reach an unsigned three-way junction with a use trail to the right. You'll notice it when the trail widens. Switchback down on the pine needle–covered trail, losing 125 feet of elevation over 250 feet of walking. When you're quite close to the water, you'll have to use your hands in a rocky area.

The falls itself is a short, moss-covered cascade with a small pool underneath. It's shady and lined with ferns. This is a nice place to relax, play by the creek, and reset in nature.

THE PACIFIC CREST TRAIL AND A RARE FROG

The Pacific Crest Trail is a 2,650-mile-long continuous hiking trail from Mexico to Canada. Many of the waterfall hikes in this book are near the PCT. Each year a few hundred experienced hikers walk from one end to the other in a season.

A section of the PCT south of here is closed to protect the rare habitat of the southern mountain yellow-legged frog (*Rana muscosa*). Considered by ecologists to be among the most endangered amphibians on the planet, the frog only lives in perennial streams in the San Gabriel, San Bernardino, and San Jacinto Mountains and the southern Sierra. Ravaged by disease, habitat loss, climate change, and invasive predators, in 2018 the Los Angeles Zoo released captive-bred tadpoles in the creeks near the Cooper Falls and Upper and Lower Buckhorn Falls hikes in this book. Many PCT hikers, including this author, walk around the endangered species closure by taking CA 2 to the Burkhart Trail.

Miles and Directions

0.0 Start at the Burkhart trailhead, passing the wilderness sign.

0.45 Turn right at an unsigned use trail when you can hear the creek.

0.5 Small pool at base of falls. Return the way you came.

1.0 Arrive back at the trailhead.

Take the short, family-friendly hike to Upper Buckhorn Falls, a three-season cascade near a campground.

13 Lower Buckhorn Falls

This adventurous route involves scrambling; loose, steep dirt; and travel on brushy, unmarked use trails. The route leads to one of the biggest hidden falls, but requires navigational skills and is not recommended for solo hikers or during high water.

See map on page 41.
Height: About 70 feet
Beauty rating: ★★★★★
Distance: 1.8 miles out and back (mostly off-trail)
Elevation gain: 450 feet descent/ 140 feet gain
Difficulty: Very difficult navigation
Best season: Fall, winter, spring
County: Los Angeles
Trailhead amenities: About 100 parking spots, dog-friendly, free maps at information kiosk

Land status: Angeles National Forest/San Gabriel Mountains National Monument, Santa Clara/Mojave Rivers Ranger District
Maps: Tom Harrison Angeles High Country; USGS Waterman Mountain
Trail contact: Angeles National Forest, Santa Clara/Mojave Rivers Ranger District Office, 33708 Crown Valley Rd., Acton 93510; (661) 269-2808; www.fs.usda.gov/recarea/angeles/recarea/?recid=41674
Fees and permits: Display Adventure Pass

Finding the trailhead: Google Maps: Burkhart Trailhead in Buckhorn Campground (closed late fall through early spring). From La Cañada Flintridge, take Highway 2 (closed during winter) for 35. 1 mile to Buckhorn Campground. There's limited parking, so if you have a campsite, it's best to leave your car where it is and walk over. If you're here for a day hike, there's limited parking at the Burkhart trailhead. When the campground is closed, you may have to park outside the exit gate and walk into the campground, adding 1.4 miles round-trip to your walk. If you're driving to the trailhead, be aware that a creek crosses the road and in high water it may be difficult for low-clearance vehicles to get across. The trailhead is near campsite 24.
GPS: N34 20.509' / W117 54.399'

The Hike

Start at the far end of the Buckhorn Campground at the parking lot for the Burkhart Trail (High Desert National Recreation Trail). Follow signs to the Burkhart Trail/PCT, soon passing a sign indicating you have entered the Pleasant View Ridge Wilderness. At 0.45 mile in, at a very large conifer, the trail widens and you reach a three-way junction with an unmarked use trail. This is the junction to Upper Buckhorn Falls. Stay straight on the Burkhart Trail, which parallels Buckhorn Creek high above on the hillside.

About 0.5 mile in, pass several cedars by a flat rock that looks like a good place to sit. Shortly after, you'll see a use trail to the right. It's inconspicuous and unsigned, sharply turning to the right, paralleling part of the main trail for a short period before switchbacking more steeply down to the creek. This area is not vegetated and is covered with pine needles.

Lower Buckhorn Falls is a rugged, steep, loose, and scrambling alternate for those with the experience and skills to visit it.

From the Burkhart Trail to the falls is only 0.4 mile and 300 feet of elevation loss on the way down (and gain on the way back). But it's a slow-going adventure that takes you to what feels like a very different place from the nicely signed PCT alternate you were on.

After switchbacking down, reach the creek. Follow the creek downstream on its left bank on a wide trail/old dirt road, passing a fire pit and campsite. Follow the trail over a large fallen tree trunk. Near a medium-sized cedar, it appears as if a rock cliff blocks off the left bank. But if you look closely, the use trail continues, going about 10 feet up the rock cliff, following close to the creek. (There are higher use trails farther away from the creek, but this is the most direct and safest route.) When we visited, the use trail was slightly obscured by two bushes on either side of the trail. It soon becomes more obvious, looking almost as if it was blasted out of the rock by a trail crew. As the trail disappears, lower yourself to the creek, which requires minor rock climbing skills. It's not technical, but be careful of slippery rocks, high water, and ice.

After crossing the creek, work your way through willows to find the use trail again. Follow it downstream until the creek slows near the top of the falls. Your trail appears to cliff-out at a rocky area, but actually curves to the right. Make a left on an animal trail down a narrow, steep gully of dirt and roots. It's loose, exposed, and steep, requiring use of both hands. Hiking poles are recommended.

You reach a secluded rock amphitheater surrounded on almost all sides and not visible from any spot above. When willows are turning yellow in autumn, these falls are one of the tallest and most magical in the San Gabriels.

Miles and Directions

0.0 Start at the Burkhart trailhead.
0.5 Take use trail to the right.
0.9 Base of falls. Return the way you came.
1.8 Arrive back at the trailhead.

Option: Follow the Burkhart Trail past the use trail at 0.6 mile to the confluence of Buckhorn and Cooper Creeks at 1.3 miles. Follow Buckhorn Creek South for 0.8 mile.

The main route is shorter and involves less trampling in the sensitive riparian area (also, less exposure to poison oak). However, it has more exposure and requires a higher level of dirt and rock climbing skills. Either route is best left to those who have the requisite skills, experience, and self-sufficiency to travel safely off-trail.

14 Trail Canyon Falls

Framed with a wilderness-like backdrop, this falls looks taller than its recorded height. Reminiscent of the Southern California classic Bridge to Nowhere hike, you cross creeks through wild terrain to view a treasure of the San Gabriels.

Height: 30-40 feet
Beauty rating: ★★★★★ (in high water)
Distance: 4.7 miles out and back
Elevation gain: 725 feet gain/60 feet descent (one-way)
Difficulty: Moderate (difficult in high water)
Best season: Winter, spring, fall, summer
County: Los Angeles
Trailhead amenities: 50+ parking spots, plus more along the side of road into parking area (watch for No Parking signs); dogs on-leash allowed, but not recommended in summer or on warm days
Land status: Angeles National Forest, Los Angeles Gateway District
Maps: Tom Harrison Angeles Front Country; USGS Sunland
Trail contact: Angeles National Forest, Los Angeles Gateway District; 12371 N. Little Tujunga Canyon Rd., Sylmar 91342; (818) 899-1900; www.fs.usda.gov/recarea/angeles/recarea/?recid=41674
Fees and permits: Display Adventure Pass

Finding the trailhead: Google Maps: Trail Canyon Trailhead. From I-210 West, exit onto Sunland Boulevard, turning right; 0.7 mile later, turn left on Oro Vista Ave. In 1 mile it turns into Big Tujunga Road. Enter the national forest in 2.9 miles, then, 1.3 miles later, turn left onto a dirt road signed for the Trail Canyon trailhead (or park along the road here). If you've reached Ottie Road, you have gone too far. The trailhead is between mile markers 2.01 and 2.05.
GPS: N34 18.192' / W118 15.191'

The Hike

Trail Canyon Falls is a year-round hike with views of the rugged Fox, McKinley, and Condor Peaks in a proposed wilderness study area that encompasses the Lower and Upper Big Tujunga watersheds in the western San Gabriels. According to wilderness advocates, there is strong evidence condors have returned. Once you get past the cabins, this hike feels remote—even though you'll likely be sharing the trail with others.

The hike to Trail Canyon Falls may remind you of the popular Bridge to Nowhere hike. They both require creek crossings to view your goal at the end. In the winter and spring, or after rains, bring hiking poles to safely ford. If visiting during warmer months, start early, bring plenty of water, a hat, and sunscreen (and don't expect much of a show from the falls).

Trail Canyon Falls has a proposed wilderness as a backdrop. Its flows vary by season. Here, it is seen after a winter storm.

▶

From the parking area along Big Tujunga Road, take FR 3N34, following signs to Trail Canyon Falls. After 0.2 mile, at a Y junction with Gold Creek Road, stay right (straight) on the road and descend toward signed private residences.

At 0.4 mile from your car, reach the official trailhead in front of the cabins (sometimes, you can drive directly here). Look for a trail kiosk, trash can, and trail register. Turn left, through a yellow gate, continuing to follow the road as it follows the creek upstream.

At 0.45 mile the road makes a sharp turn to the right across the creek. Stay on the road and cross the creek, heading toward a private residence on the other side. (Ignore a faint use trail on the left side of the creek—we saw multiple people make that mistake.) There's a trail signpost on the other side of the creek, placed out of view from those trying to decide whether to take the faint use trail or continue on the road. In low water it's much clearer that you want to stay on the road here.

Continue on the road past more residences. In another 0.3 mile you reach another Y junction in the road. Stay straight. Do not take the road crossing back over the creek (a better-placed signpost may guide you here). Staying on the right side of the creek, a carbonite (a thin, plasticky brown post) indicates "Trail Not Maintained." This is your trail. It narrows here. There's a circular, cement water storage unit on your left. On your right is a rocky cliff 80 to 100 feet tall, home to a bonus waterfall after rains. At 0.9 mile cross the creek you've been following, a tributary that joins Trail Canyon Creek below.

Climb up switchbacks to pass a large burnt oak on the left. This next section is among my favorites. Walk on a hilly promenade with views of Mount Lukens and the backside of the Angeles frontcountry. From this promenade you can still spot evidence of the 2009 Station Fire—the burnt trunks of pine trees. The chaparral plants of sage, yucca, chemise, and yerba buena grow robustly here, but will the pine forest ever return?

The trail curls to the right, following a new waterway: Trail Canyon Creek. Head downhill and upstream to meet the creek and cross it at 1.15 miles. Until now, you saw remnants of when this was a paved road and what's left of an old bridge. That's about to end at a "No Campfire/No Trash Service" sign. You are about to enter a wild area.

If you're visiting in the wet season, this is the first of seven crossings of Trail Canyon Creek and likely the easiest (it often has downed debris and logs to cross on). You'll wade through four more times in the next 0.25 mile. High water levels can come up to your knees or thighs if you are unable to find a log. Try to scout out areas where the water isn't as deep and isn't moving quickly. Use your poles and judgment. If levels are too high, come back when water is lower.

Before the last crossing you climb high enough to get views of Mount Lukens (and its towers) again. At 1.4 miles, pass a picnic table and potential campsite on the left.

At 1.6 miles, cross the river again in a wide-open riverbed. This crossing can be the most difficult one in high water but a rock-hop in low water. From here

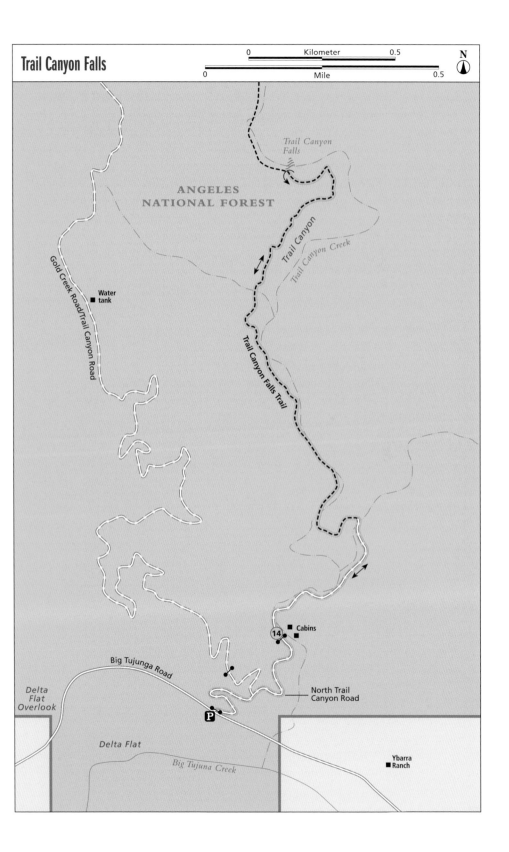

Trail Canyon Falls

N

0   Kilometer   0.5

0   Mile   0.5

ANGELES
NATIONAL FOREST

Trail Canyon Falls

Trail Canyon

Trail Canyon Creek

Gold Creek Road/Trail Canyon Road

Water
tank

Trail Canyon Falls Trail

14

Cabins

Big Tujunga Road

North Trail
Canyon Road

*Delta
Flat
Overlook*

P

Delta Flat

Big Tujuna Creek

Ybarra
Ranch

until the end, your feet will stay dry as you climb up switchbacks to contour high above on the mountainside.

It feels wild and remote with no views of roads, houses, radio or cell towers, or any other sign of humans but the trail and hikers. The creek channel is far below you. Across the canyon you may spot other falls tumbling down toward the creek.

As the trail curls around a bend, you'll get your first view of Trail Canyon Falls and its freefall drop over an almost 90-degree nickpoint. Framed against Condor Canyon and the wild mountains above, it has a grand Sierra-like look (see Rainbow Falls hike) that makes it appear taller than its stated height. In wet conditions there's a pool below.

Rough, rocky, loose use trails and sometimes a rope lead down to its base (not recommended for kids, those afraid of heights, or dogs). A better use trail continues straight for a view of the nickpoint as the creek goes tumbling down.

Miles and Directions

0.0   Start at parking on Big Tujunga Road. Take dirt Forest Service road.

0.2   Stay straight at intersection with Gold Creek Road.

0.4   "Official" trailhead. Go through yellow gate.

0.45 Stay on road, making a sharp right over the creek and toward residences.

0.75 Ignore road going back over the creek on your left. Stay straight and shortly reach a "Trail Not Maintained" sign.

0.9   Cross tributary of Trail Canyon Creek.

1.15 First Trail Canyon Creek crossing.

1.4   Picnic table.

1.6   Last Trail Canyon Creek crossing.

2.35 Trail Canyon Falls viewpoint. Return the way you came.

4.7   Arrive back at the trailhead.

15 Placerita Canyon Falls

This classic, family-friendly hike is a 10-minute drive from Santa Clarita, starts at a nature center, and ends at a waterfall. It even has an opportunity to fill up water bottles along the way. But be warned that the falls only flow after heavy rain.

Height: About 15-25 feet
Beauty rating: ★★★
Distance: 4.8 miles out and back
Elevation gain: 350 feet
Difficulty: Easy to moderate (due to distance and heat)
Best season: Winter, spring, fall (only flows right after heavy rain)
County: Los Angeles
Trailhead amenities: Nature center open 9 a.m. to 5 p.m. with water, picnic sites, restrooms. Park open sunrise to sunset; those staying later are subject to arrest (except for those with camping reservations). Leashed dogs allowed.
Land status: LA County Department of Parks and Recreation
Maps: USGS San Fernando; free map at nature center
Trail contact: Placerita Canyon Nature Center, 19152 Placerita Canyon Rd., Newhall 91321; (661) 259-7721; www.placerita.org
Fees and permits: None

Finding the trailhead: Start point: Google Maps: Placerita Canyon Nature Center. From CA 14 (Antelope Valley Freeway), exit on Placerita Canyon Road. Turn right (east) 2 miles to Placerita Canyon County Park near the nature center.
GPS: N34 22.407' / W118 28.035'

The Hike

Note: This area was damaged by the Sand Canyon Fire in 2016 and subsequent rains and debris flows in 2017. The trails described below are closed until at least fall 2019, although other trails in the park are open. Check regulations before hiking.

A rare, gentle hike on the northern slope in the western San Gabriel Mountains, this east–west canyon is a family-friendly place to learn about local ecology and history.

Unsurprisingly, given its proximity to movie studios, Placerita Canyon is often used as a movie set, including for *The Cisco Kid* (1950). The excellent Placerita Canyon Nature Center can give you a free map and has information on local history and the live animals cared for at the center.

From the nature center, take the multiuse Canyon Trail east, following the creek through a wooded, riparian ravine. The trail gradually climbs through sycamores and oaks. The area burned in 1979 and 2003. In 2005 record rainfall, flooding, and debris flow destroyed trails. Park literature says it would take fifteen years until vegetation returned to its pre-fire levels. In a cruel twist of fate, the area burned in 2016. But chaparral on the slopes above may be a hundred years old, seemingly immune to the wildfires that come through here every few decades.

Placerita Canyon Falls

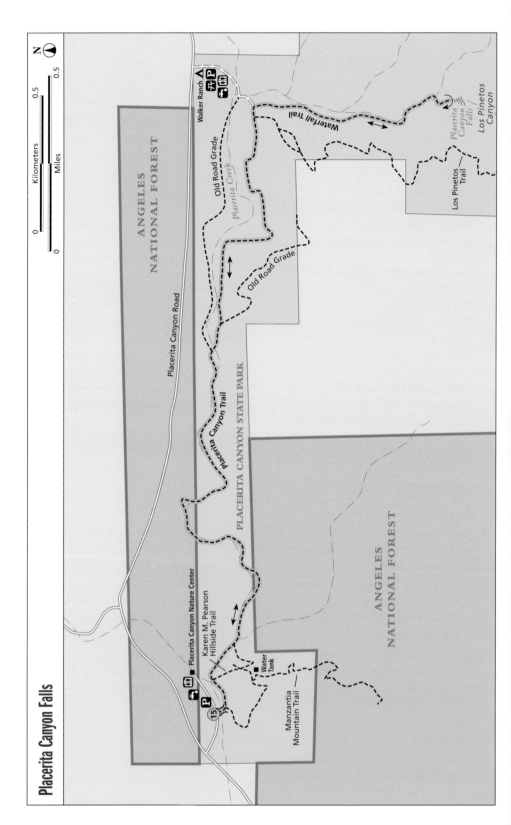

THE REAL FIRST DISCOVERY OF GOLD IN CALIFORNIA

In 1842–seven years before James Marshall's 1849 gold "discovery" at Sutter's Mill–the first California gold rush happened here in Placerita Canyon. Legend has it Mexican geologist Jose Francisco de Garcia Lopez dreamed of discovering gold while napping under an oak tree. That afternoon he discovered a nugget while digging up onions for dinner. The San Fernando Placers–which included prospectors, outlaws, and Chinese laborers–came to this canyon searching for gold–giving the canyon its name.

Pass intersections for trails on the right to Manzanita Mountain (2,063 feet).

The canyon narrows at 0.75 mile. High canyon walls ahead are evidence of the hydraulic mining used in the late 1800s to wash away the hillside in search of gold. The practice was banned in 1884 after farmers downstream complained of destroyed waterways. About 1 mile in you have the opportunity to cross the creek or stay straight on the Canyon Trail. Either way, after 1.8 miles the two trails meet near the Walker Ranch Picnic Area, which has picnic tables, a drinking fountain, and a trail kiosk. Frank Walker hand-built a house for his family of twelve kids in 1920.

You'll see signs for the Los Pinetos Trail and then for the Waterfall Trail, which climbs 300 feet in 0.6 mile. If the falls is flowing, you're likely to get wet feet crossing the creek on the Los Pinetos Trail. Take the less-used dirt singletrack Waterfall Trail south along Los Pinetos Canyon's west wall. When the canyon splits, turn right (west) up the trail along the narrower of two tributaries. When the canyon curves to the left and forks again, turn right, scrambling a short distance into a grotto with the seasonal 25-foot waterfall.

Miles and Directions

0.0 Nature center parking lot; take the Canyon Trail.
0.5 Cross creek.
0.7 Canyon narrows.
1.8 Walker Ranch Picnic Area and intersection for Waterfall Trail.
2.4 Waterfall. Return the way you came.
4.8 Arrive back at the trailhead.

Pacific Coast and Santa Monica Mountains

This region is one of the finest examples anywhere in the world of a wildland close to an urban population. Santa Monica Mountains National Recreation Area is the world's largest urban national park with over 600,000 visitors per year. Meanwhile, Topanga State Park is one of the largest parks in the world entirely within a city's boundary (Los Angeles). The open wildlands of the Pacific Coast encompass 153,000 acres from the Hollywood Hills to Malibu and extend from the San Fernando Valley to the southern part of Ventura County. These mountains are home to the Backbone Trail, a 67.8-mile long-distance hiking trail, which took more than thirty years to complete. The National Park Service says it's "the best-protected stretch of coastal Mediterranean habitat in the world."

The wildlands along the Pacific Coast were formed by geology and weather as well as the Chumash and Tongva people who called these mountains home. You can learn more from a Native American ranger or guest host at the nearby Satwiwa Native American Indian Culture Center in the Santa Monica Mountains National Recreation Area. Later, rancheros and a multi-ethnic group of homesteaders took over the area following Lincoln's Homestead Act of 1862.

Most of the hikes in this book are ocean facing, which means morning fog blocks out the sun (and keeps the area relatively moist).

This area is home to several other falls including Solstice Canyon Falls, Laurel Canyon Falls, and Sycamore Canyon Falls. Sycamore Canyon Falls can be accessed via the Big Sycamore entrance to the Santa Monica Mountains National Recreation Area and near the Satwiwa Culture Center. The trip is a good alternative to the nearby La Jolla Canyon Falls (especially while it remains closed), though not quite as scenic. Solstice Canyon Falls is accessed via a paved road and runs rather infrequently, but if you catch it in the right season, is a painless stroll. Laurel Canyon Falls near Laguna Beach is quite seasonal and the trail visits from the top, so there's not a great vantage point to see the falls. Malibu Creek State Park has three tall human-made falls: Rindge Dam, Century Lake, and Malibu Lake Dam.

The Woolsey Canyon Fire of 2018 burned 88 percent of Santa Monica Mountains National Recreation Area. By March 2019 most of it had reopened. Ecologists suspect that prior to human habitation, the chaparral plant ecosystem burned every five to fifteen years, and Native American communities used fire to actively manage brush. The plants here have evolved to live with wildfire, although decades of fire suppression management have made recent fires burn more intensely than those of the past. For your own safety and to aid with plant regeneration, stay on the trail through burned areas and follow trail closures and restrictions.

16 Paradise Falls (Wildwood Falls)

This family-friendly loop highlights this area's diverse ecosystem, geologic formations, and archaeological history and leads to an impressive year-round waterfall with a duck pond pool underneath.

Height: 40 feet
Beauty rating: ★★★★★
Distance: 3.0-mile loop
Elevation gain: 675 feet
Difficulty: Easy to moderate (for length)
Best season: Winter, spring, fall (flows year-round)
County: Ventura
Trailhead amenities: About 100 parking spots, free maps at information kiosk, leashed dogs allowed but there is not much shade or water; open to hikers, horses, and mountain bikers;

toilets and water available along the hike but not at Main Trailhead
Land status: Wildwood Regional Park, Conejo Recreation & Park District, Conejo Open Space Conservation Agency
Maps: USGS Newbury Park; free park map available at trailhead or at https://cosf.org/trails/wildwood/
Trail contact: Conejo Recreation & Park District, 403 W. Hillcrest Dr., Thousand Oaks 91360; (805) 495-6471; www.crpd.org/parkfac/parks/wildwood.asp
Fees and permits: None

Finding the trailhead: Google Maps: Paradise Falls Trailhead. Main Entrance along Big Sky Drive and West Avenida de los Arboles. From Ventura Freeway (US 101) North, exit on Lynn Drive. Drive 2.5 miles to Avenida de Los Arboles. Turn left and drive to the dirt parking lot. Neighbors frown on parking in the neighborhood. Additional parking is at Wildwood Neighborhood Park, 650 W. Avenida de los Arboles; or Wildwood Elementary School, 620 Velarde Dr.
GPS: N34 13.121' / W118 54.087'

The Hike

This loop through Wildwood Park in Ventura County leads to the impressive year-round Paradise Falls. The 1,765-acre Wildwood Park has numerous trails that can be connected into a longer hike. You can access the falls on wide and easy-to-follow fire roads in as short as 2.4 miles round-trip. The description below creates a longer near-loop that takes you to shady, quieter areas. Wildwood is a great park and well worth exploring by developing your own route. Free trail maps are available at the trailhead or can be downloaded to your phone via a QR code.

Although the trailhead is located in a neighborhood, from inside the park, it's easy to forget civilization is anywhere nearby.

Though many trails lead to the falls, the most obvious route is well-signed at the western edge of the parking lot near an information kiosk. Grab a free map of the park, which shows the major route described here.

Paradise Falls is tucked into a grotto and runs year round because part of its flow comes from the surrounding neighborhoods.

WILDWOOD PARK

The Conejo Open Space Foundation (www.cosf.org) reports more than 250 unique plant species in Wildwood Park. It's a connecting point of seven different distinct ecosystems: southern oak woodland, chaparral, coast sage scrub, desert scrub, California grassland, and freshwater marsh. It also is home to sixty species of birds, thirty-seven mammal species, and twenty-two species of reptiles and amphibians.

For 8,000 years the area was home to the Chumash Native Americans. After disease and forced conscription into the Mission System ravished Chumash populations, nineteenth-century Spanish colonizers grazed cattle and sheep in what they called Rancho El Conejo. There is still evidence of the grazing days in the park. Because it's an easily accessible wildland area, it was a Hollywood film site from the 1930s to 1960s, including for *Spartacus*.

The Conejo Recreation & Park District first acquired open space for this park in 1966 with a goal of creating a ring of open space around Conejo Valley. The City of Thousand Oaks' General Plan calls for 41 percent of its planning area to be open space, including the nearby Conejo Canyons, Los Robles Trail, and Dos Vientos and Lang Ranch/Woodridge Open Space Trails. Because of the city's more than 150 miles of trail, the American Hiking Society has designated Thousand Oaks a Trail City USA.

Take the wide fire road, the Mesa Trail, straight and directly west, ignoring a spur trail to the parking lot on the left. After 0.25 mile, pass a vehicle barrier. There's a panoramic view of rock cliffs over grassland. Continue on the Mesa Trail as it climbs and descends a small hill, ignoring the signed Santa Rosa Trail. After 0.4 mile turn left, following signs for the Teepee. Stay on the wide North Teepee Trail, heading south. About 0.1 mile later, pass a sign on the left for the Stagecoach Bluff Trail, which connects back up 0.2 mile south of here.

Continue on the North Teepee Trail. Note the sign for the Moonridge Trail on your left. You'll be taking this narrow but beautiful trail back to the parking lot. For now, though, descend the hill toward the Teepee. This rest area has shade, sitting areas, and a drinking fountain. Fill up your bottles and then turn downhill and right on the Teepee Trail to the Wildwood Canyon area, following signs to Paradise Falls.

Option: After another 0.2 mile the fastest way to the falls is via Paradise Falls Spur Trail. It's a signed, narrow trail to the left off the fire road.

If you have more time and energy, stay straight on the fire road, curving through the canyon to the left. About 0.1 mile later you have an unmatched view of the whole falls from a spot directly across the canyon from the falls.

After 0.15 mile you reach the Wildwood Canyon Picnic Area and its shady oaks, toilets, and water. Reach a T intersection 0.2 mile later. There are more than ten picnic

Paradise Falls (Wildwood Falls)

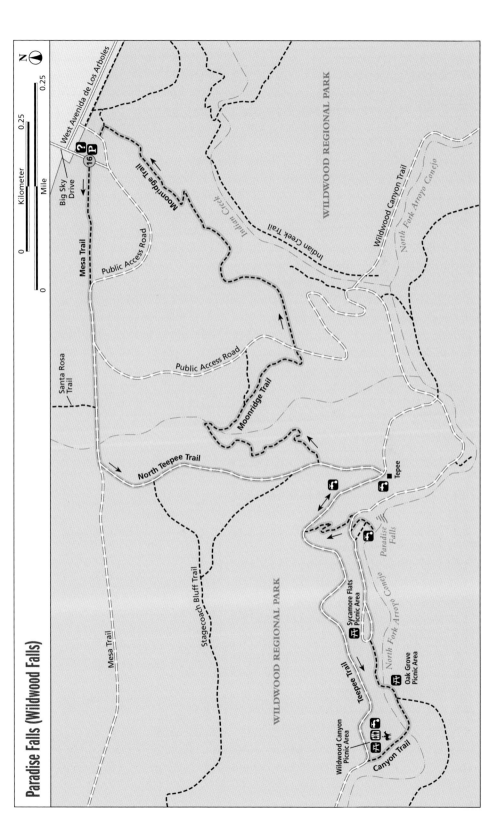

tables, shade, trash, restrooms, and more drinking fountains. Turn left, following signs to Wildwood Canyon Trail, which is still a wide fire road.

Shortly after the picnic area, cross a creek on a board plank. Enjoy the reeds and oaks. Continue on the wide path, following the creek upstream, passing the Oak Grove Picnic Area. Cross the creek again and continue past the Sycamore Flats Picnic Area on narrower trail.

Take a steep trail to the left to an intersection with the Paradise Falls Spur Trail. There is a trash can and drinking fountain nearby. Follow the trail toward the falls, taking wooden stairs down to the base. The falls tumble down a cliff into a picturesque duck pond pool below.

To return, take the wooden steps back up to the trail. Continue straight up another flight of wooden stairs to connect with the Paradise Falls Spur Trail. Follow switchbacks back up to the fire road and turn right, back toward the Teepee.

From the Teepee, turn left on the North Teepee Trail. After 0.1 mile turn right on the signed Moonridge Trail. The narrow trail contours a canyon high above the ridge with open views of the Teepee and surrounding hillsides. It twists and winds and feels remote like the background of a Wild West movie. Just 0.2 mile later the trail dips down to a canyon on wooden stairs and then climbs back up. A quarter mile later the Moonridge Trail crosses a wide fire road, the public access road.

Cross the fire road, staying on the signed Moonridge Trail. The ecosystem now has more oaks. Half a mile later you emerge at the southeast corner of the parking lot.

Miles and Directions

0.0 Start at the western part of the parking lot at the kiosk, heading west on the Mesa Trail (fire road).

0.4 Turn left on the wide, signed North Teepee Trail.

0.75 Teepee Picnic Area with drinking fountain. Turn right on Teepee Trail.

0.9 *Option:* Take the Paradise Falls Spur Trail to the left (0.2 mile to the falls). Otherwise, stay straight on the fire road.

1.25 T intersection at Wildwood Canyon Picnic Area; turn left.

1.35 Pass Oak Grove Picnic Area.

1.45 Pass Sycamore Flats Picnic Area.

1.55 Meet back up with the Paradise Falls Spur Trail.

1.7 Base of Paradise Falls.

1.8 Return to Teepee Trail. Turn right toward Teepee Picnic Area.

2.0 Return to Teepee Picnic Area. Turn left on North Teepee Trail.

2.1 Turn right on Moonridge Trail.

2.5 Stay on Moonridge Trail, crossing the public access road.

3.0 Return to southeast corner of parking lot.

17 La Jolla Canyon Falls

This ocean-view hike is a Southern California classic through what is considered to be the finest coastal park in the region. Enjoy this trip through canyons and up ridges as a quick trip to the waterfall, a day hike loop, or an overnight backpacking trip.

Height: 10–20 feet
Beauty rating: ★★ for falls, ★★★★★ for the hike
Distance: 1.6 miles out and back to waterfall; 7.6-mile loop
Elevation gain: 250 feet to falls; 1,200 feet on loop
Difficulty: Moderate
Best season: Late winter, spring
County: Los Angeles

Trailhead amenities: Free street parking, no dogs on trails
Land status: Topanga State Park
Maps: Tom Harrison Point Mugu; USGS Point Mugu
Trail contact: Topanga State Park, 20828 Entrada Rd., Topanga 90290; (310) 455-2465 ext. 106; www.parks.ca.gov/?page_id=629
Fees and permits: Parking fee ($12 as of 2019), ranges depending on time spent

Finding the trailhead: Google Maps: Ray Miller Trailhead in Point Mugu State Park. From Santa Monica, take the Pacific Coast Highway (CA 1) for 32 miles north (west) toward the La Jolla Valley entrance of the park (not the Sycamore Canyon entrance that you pass first). It's west of Thornhill Broome State Beach Campground. You can park on the PCH (check for No Parking signs) or inside the park for a fee ($12 as of 2019).
GPS: N34 05.104' / W119 02.127'

The Hike

Note: The western portion of the hike (the La Jolla Canyon Trail including the direct route to the waterfall) burned in the 2013 Springs Fire, and loose soil and storms damaged the trail further. The area around the waterfall was washed away and the park closed the trail in mid-2017 for safety concerns. As it's a classic hike considered among the finest in the region, it's included with a route description based on the trail prior to closure. Call rangers before your trip to determine the most recent conditions.

The seasonal and small waterfall here isn't the highlight of this trip. Instead, this hike through what is considered the finest coastal park in the region is notable for springtime flowers and ocean views to the Channel Islands, and as a cluster-point for the monarch butterfly migration.

From the trailhead, you have a choice. Turn left for the quickest route to see the waterfall, up the mouth of the canyon on the wide La Jolla Canyon Trail. For either direction, cover up, use sunscreen, check for ticks, and watch for poison oak.

For the loop—which can be enjoyed as a day hike or a backpacking trip (see ranger for permit)—turn right on the Ray Miller Trail (aka the Backbone Trail).

THE BACKBONE TRAIL

The Ray Miller trailhead where you start this hike is the western terminus for the 67.8-mile-long Backbone Trail, whose eastern terminus is Will Rogers State Historic Park. Created by the National Park Service and California Department of Parks and Recreation, construction of the Backbone started in the 1980s and was completed in 2016. One reason it took so long is the trail weaves through a patchwork of public and extremely expensive private land. To complete the trail required purchasing and receiving land acquisitions and rights-of-way from private owners such as former California governor Arnold Schwarzenegger, fitness celebrity Betty Weider, and movie director James Cameron.

Climb on a well-graded, gradually ascending trail with springtime wildflower displays and sweeping ocean views. Turn left in 2.4 miles on the Overlook Trail Fire Road high on the ridge, with views of Sycamore Canyon and Boney Ridge to the east.

At 4.5 miles in you reach the most confusing part: a five-way intersection. Take the left (west) La Jolla Valley Loop Trail to La Jolla Valley Nature Preserve. It's one of the only places where you can see fields of wild California bunchgrass (although it's becoming a popular landscaping plant). Disease, grazing, and opportunistic non-natives have reduced grasslands to less than 1 percent of their historic range, making the native tall prairie grass ecosystem one of the most endangered in the country.

For those of you backpacking in, call it a day at one of the La Jolla Valley Walk-In Camps, which have restrooms, picnic areas, and potable water. Otherwise, top off your water bottle and keep hiking. Ambitious hikers may want to take the Loop Trail west to visit Mugu Peak (1,266 feet). Here we describe a shorter route, which takes you toward the seasonal reedy pond near the campground. From there you'll walk south on the La Jolla Canyon Trail for 2.4 miles back to your car.

In about a mile on the La Jolla Canyon Trail, on your right, reach a junction with the trail connecting to Mugu Peak. The canyon is narrow and rockier here. The Chumash who lived here used these caves for shade. Plant enthusiasts find this downhill section intriguing because of springtime blooms of the up to 10-foot-tall, yellow, sunflower-looking, "Dr. Seuss" giant coreopsis. Common in the Channel Islands, it's much rarer on the mainland.

At 6.8 miles from the trailhead, reach the small, seasonal, two-tiered La Jolla Canyon Falls. It's best after a rain. In the past a use trail brought you toward the upper falls. After the fire and storm damage, hikers who visited before the closure said rocks in the area have washed away the falls and to pass through requires a rappel, climbing equipment, and the skills and experience to navigate safely. Check with rangers before attempting a visit to these falls.

Continue on the trail at the bottom of the canyon between tall ridges. Join a dirt road before arriving back at the trailhead.

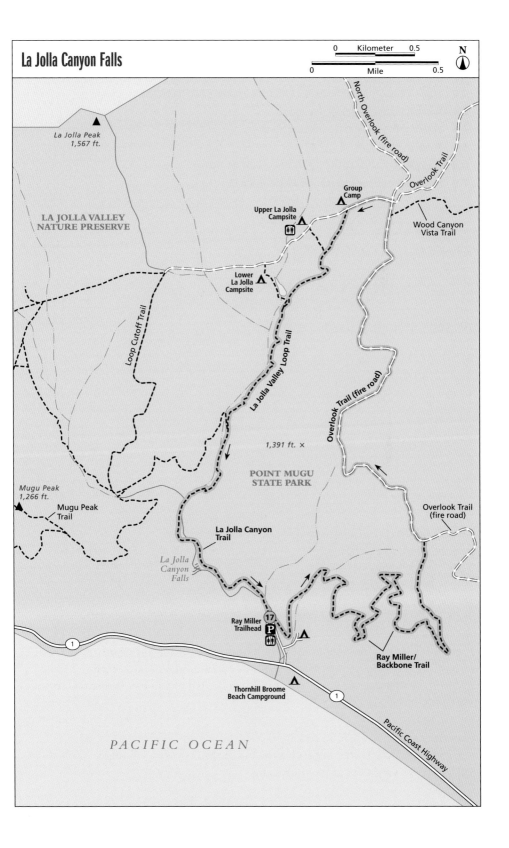

La Jolla Canyon Falls

0   Kilometer   0.5

0   Mile   0.5

N

▲ La Jolla Peak
1,567 ft.

North Overlook (fire road)

Overlook Trail

Group
Camp ▲

Upper La Jolla
Campsite ▲

LA JOLLA VALLEY
NATURE PRESERVE

Wood Canyon
Vista Trail

Lower
La Jolla ▲
Campsite

Loop Cutoff Trail

La Jolla Valley Loop Trail

Overlook Trail (fire road)

1,391 ft. ×

POINT MUGU
STATE PARK

Mugu Peak
1,266 ft. ▲

Mugu Peak
Trail

Overlook Trail
(fire road)

La Jolla Canyon
Trail

La Jolla
Canyon
Falls

Ray Miller
Trailhead

17
P

▲

Ray Miller/
Backbone Trail

Thornhill Broome
Beach Campground ▲

1

1

Pacific Coast Highway

PACIFIC OCEAN

Miles and Directions

0.0 Start at the Ray Miller trailhead; turn right on Ray Miller/Backbone Trail.

2.4 Turn left on Overlook Trail (fire road).

4.5 Five-way intersection; turn left toward campsites.

5.2 Pond.

6.8 Waterfall.

7.6 Finish the loop back at the Ray Miller trailhead.

18 Escondido Falls

Arguably the finest falls in this region when it has a strong flow, these surprising falls are among the tallest in the area with options for hikers of various skillsets.

Height: Lower tier: 50 feet; upper tiers: at least 150 feet
Beauty rating: ★★★★
Distance: 3 miles out and back
Elevation gain: 200 feet
Difficulty: Easy to lower tier; difficult to upper tiers
Best season: Winter, spring
County: Los Angeles
Trailhead amenities: About 10 parking spots, dogs allowed on-leash

Land status: Escondido Canyon Park managed by the Mountains Recreation Conservation Authority
Maps: USGS Point Dume
Trail contact: Mountains Recreation Conservation Authority and Santa Monica Mountains Conservancy; (310) 589-3200 or (323) 221-8900; http://smmc.ca.gov
Fees and permits: None

Finding the trailhead: Google Maps: Visitor Parking for Escondido Falls. Take the Pacific Coast Highway (CA 1) for 17.7 miles north of Santa Monica. Turn right on Winding Way and park in a small dirt lot on the west side. You can also park along the PCH, but watch for numerous No Parking signs.
GPS: N34 01.337' / W118 46.478'

The Hike

The official trailhead is nestled in a fancy neighborhood and locals don't want hiker traffic on the road. You'll have to park at a dirt lot below and walk 0.8 mile up the paved Winding Way "Trail."

On the left is a large sign for "Edward Albert Escondido Canyon Trails and Waterfalls" as part of the Santa Monica Mountains Conservancy. Edward Albert was an award-winning actor and dedicated environmentalist known for his part opposite Goldie Hawn in *Butterflies are Free* (1973). The son of Eddie Albert of *Green Acres* fame, Edward Albert served on the California Coastal Commission and Native American Heritage Commission; he died in 2006, when the SMMC named the trailhead after him.

Take the trail down to Escondido Canyon Park. The trail is surprisingly shaded by canyon live oaks and sycamores. In spring you'll see mustard flowers, bluebonnet, and fennel. You cross the creek at least five times, but it's usually a rock-hop (and is often dry). Climb out of the shaded oaks to sunny chaparral before dropping to the base of the lowest tier of the falls at 1.5 miles. The base is shady and makes a great picnic area (but those with sulfur odor sensitivities may complain). Those with the skills and experience to climb and scramble above can visit the

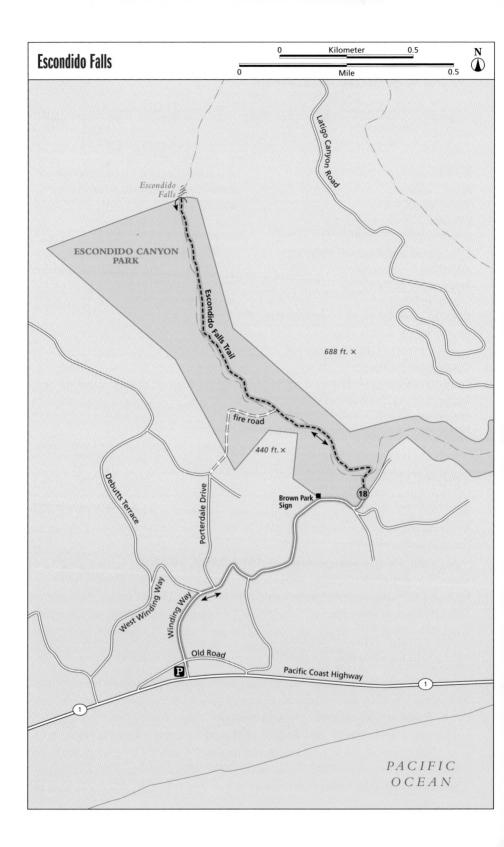

Escondido Falls

Kilometer
0   0.5

Mile
0   0.5

N

Escondido
Falls

Latigo Canyon Road

ESCONDIDO CANYON
PARK

Escondido Falls Trail

688 ft. ×

fire road

440 ft. ×

Debutts Terrace

Porterdale Drive

Brown Park
Sign

18

West Winding Way

Winding Way

Old Road

P

Pacific Coast Highway

1

1

PACIFIC
OCEAN

Upper Escondido Falls requires climbing skills to access. It can be quite slippery. Visit at your own risk.

middle falls and upper falls, which tumble down a limestone cliff. But it's not recommended for most hikers, especially young children. Attempt at your own risk.

Miles and Directions

0.0 Start at the Winding Way parking area and walk up paved Winding Way.

0.8 Turn left at the sign for Escondido Falls at the Santa Monica Mountains Conservancy entrance.

1.5 Base of lower falls. Return the way you came.

3.0 Arrive back at the trailhead.

19 Newton and Zuma Falls

A short downhill hike on the famous Backbone Trail in the Santa Monica Mountains National Recreation Area takes you to a rugged use trail down to a close but hidden waterfall. Scrambling and a longer trip can give you views of more falls including nearby Zuma Falls.

Height: About 30 feet for Upper Newton Falls
Beauty rating: ★★★
Distance: 1 mile out and back for Upper Newton Falls
Elevation gain: 600 feet
Difficulty: Easy to moderate to Upper Newton; moderate to strenuous and difficult for the other falls
Best season: Winter, spring
County: Los Angeles
Trailhead amenities: Parking lot with about 20 spots, street-side parking, privy, shaded bench, lots of signage at Backbone Trail kiosk, trash/recycle bins
Land status: Santa Monica Mountains National Recreation Area
Maps: Tom Harrison Zuma and Trancas Canyons; USGS Point Dume
Trail contact: Santa Monica Mountains National Recreation Area, 26876 Mulholland Hwy., Calabasas 91302; (805) 370-2301; www.nps.gov/samo/index.htm
Fees and permits: None

Finding the trailhead: Google Maps: Newton Canyon Parking Lot. Park at the Kanan Road trailhead, after the T-1 tunnel. Nearby is a blue street sign for private Newton Canyon Road and a gate on the left. The parking lot is on the right and holds about 20 cars.
GPS: N34 04.333' / W118 48.552'

The Hike

Note: This area burned in the 2018 Woolsey Fire. As of 2019 Zuma/Trancas Canyons were among the last sections of the Santa Monica Mountains National Recreation Area to still be closed. Check local regulations before you go.

This is a short hike in a scenic spot in Santa Monica Mountains National Recreation Area. Follow signs to the Zuma Ridge Motorway, shown as 2.5 miles away, passing the privy on your left. Start downhill on a wide, sometimes rocky trail. Moss and ferns line this oak ecosystem, which is green with grass in the spring. Zuma is derived from the Chumash word for "abundance."

The trail makes a switchback to the right. Follow along high above the bank of a creek, which is visible below. Take note of this creek, as it's fed by Upper Newton Falls. After 0.3 mile cross a creek bed, which is almost always dry. The trail turns left.

A short 0.05 mile later, you encounter a sign on the left indicating the Backbone Trail continues right and uphill. Instead, turn left on the use trail heading gently downhill paralleling the creek.

Upper Newton Falls is just off the Backbone Trail, but easy to miss if you don't know where to look.

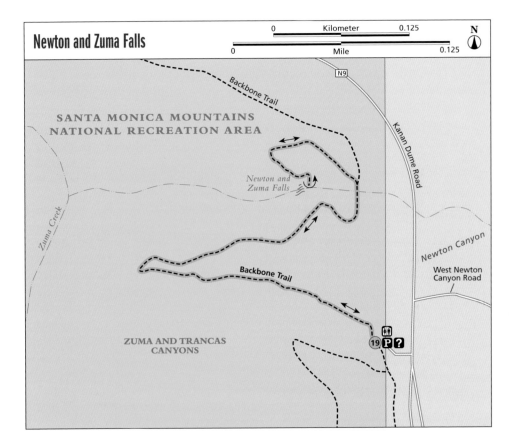

SANTA MONICA MOUNTAINS
NATIONAL RECREATION AREA

Backbone Trail

Newton and
Zuma Falls

Zuma Creek

Backbone Trail

Kanan Dune Road

N9

Newton Canyon

West Newton
Canyon Road

ZUMA AND TRANCAS
CANYONS

19 P

Shortly after, you encounter a grand oak tree on your left. A well-trodden path from the oak tree visits the top of the waterfall, which can be dangerous and is less scenic than the view from the bottom. Instead, stay high (the use trail to the right) to connect to the path leading down to the creek bed. The use trail has several branches and can at times be hard to follow.

At the end the use trail turns to head upstream. The last 50 feet to the base of the waterfall can be a slight scramble on rock and over a tree branch. This rough trail deposits you at the base of the falls.

For those with route-finding skills and physical stamina, continue downstream. There's not much trail so you'll need to scramble and/or get your feet wet. It's slow going and can be brushy. Watch for poison oak, which is seemingly everywhere.

Depending on water flow, it can be moderate or strenuous and difficult to reach Lower Newton Falls. Southern California guidebook author, the late Jerry Schad, startled snakes in here. Take care not to go off a cliff when you reach Lower Newton Falls. For the even more adventurous, a third waterfall, Zuma Falls, is nearby.

Miles and Directions

0.0 Start at the parking lot trailhead.

0.2 Switchback downhill to the right.

0.3 Cross a dry creek bed.

0.35 Turn left onto use trail at sign for Backbone Trail.

0.5 Base of Upper Newton Falls. Return the way you came.

1.0 Arrive back at the trailhead.

The author near the base of Upper Newton Falls during a spring with little rain. After storms, this fall looks even more impressive.

20 Santa Ynez Falls

A short hike takes you into a sandstone cliff–lined "slot" canyon that ends in a shady grotto. Here a short waterfall tumbles down among maidenhair ferns.

Height: 15–20 feet
Beauty rating: ★★★★★
Distance: 2.6 miles out and back
Elevation gain: 120 feet gain/30 feet descent
Difficulty: Easy to moderate (for scrambling at end)
Best season: Winter, spring
County: Los Angeles

Trailhead amenities: Free street parking, no dogs in Topanga State Park
Land status: Topanga State Park
Maps: Tom Harrison Topanga State Park; USGS Topanga
Trail contact: Topanga State Park, 20828 Entrada Rd., Topanga 90290; (310) 455-2465 ext. 106; www.parks.ca.gov/?page_id=629
Fees and permits: None

Finding the trailhead: Google Maps: Santa Ynez Canyon Trailhead. Park at the intersection of 17300 West Vereda de La Montura and the private road, Camino de Yatasto.
GPS: N34 04.414' / W118 34.028'

The Hike

This short hike starts in a neighborhood but requires an adventurous spirit to complete. Topanga State Park is all within the LA city limits and is considered the world's largest wildland within a major city. Watch for poison oak. Dogs are not allowed in the state park.

The trail starts at a gated walkway on Vereda de La Montura Road. Follow a short set of wooden stairs down to a sign marking Topanga State Park and the Santa Ynez Trail/Trippet Ranch. Stay straight on the paved trail, ignoring a branched trail on the left.

The pavement quickly ends and you ford a cement-bottomed "creek" on cement stepping-stones. Directly across the creek is a dirt trail. Continue on this dirt trail (do not walk up the cement "creek"). Follow this dirt trail up through several creek crossings (usually dry).

About 0.25 mile in there's a large sandstone formation to your right. A side trail leads to a "cave" inside. After a short visit, stay on the main route.

At about 0.5 mile in, head left at a brown post marked "trail." The trail goes under a sideways trunk of a grand oak tree. Cross another dry bed before reaching a T intersection. A signed post indicates to head right, toward the waterfall. Immediately cross another likely dry creek bed. Follow signs pointing to the left toward the waterfall, warning you "this is not a through trail."

Head upstream through a shady area. Even in drought years, this creek has water in the spring. After 0.9 mile from the trailhead, drop to the creek, following a sign indicating the trail is to the right. After about 50 feet of what may be wading up the creek, go back up to the right bank. The trail crisscrosses the creek. After about 0.1 mile, notice that the gorge has gotten deeper. Above, you'll notice a tributary that reaches the left bank of the creek, cutting into the mountainside. Keep following the main creek upstream, though, staying in the shaded canyon.

After 1.2 miles there's a sign for the waterfall. Stay in the stream here (do not follow the trail behind the sign). At this point you walk in the stream bed. In high water you may need to scramble up to the right above the bank. This part of the canyon is very narrow with vertical cliffs to the left and right.

After 1.25 miles you reach a pool. A small waterfall trickles down from an area with a boulder and rock jam. A small, easy scramble can get you above the boulder. Less than 500 feet later, the actual waterfall tumbles down from a grotto. You'll know it's the actual falls if you see a rope hanging to the left on a boulder with carved footholds. Maidenhair ferns line the canyon walls.

BRIAN DAVIDSON

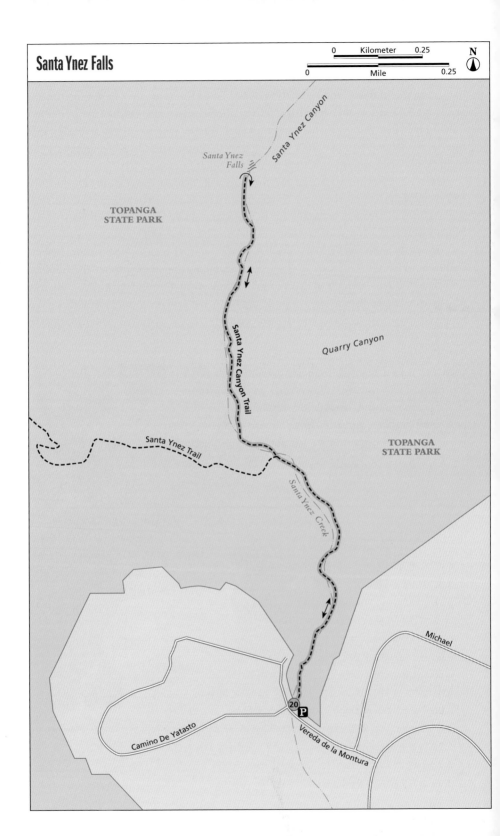

Santa Ynez Falls

0 ___ Kilometer ___ 0.25

0 ___ Mile ___ 0.25

N

Santa Ynez Canyon

Santa Ynez Falls

TOPANGA STATE PARK

Santa Ynez Canyon Trail

Quarry Canyon

Santa Ynez Trail

TOPANGA STATE PARK

Santa Ynez Creek

Michael

20 P

Camino De Yatasto

Vereda de la Montura

BRIAN DAVIDSON

Miles and Directions

0.0 Start at the gate following signs for the Santa Ynez Canyon Trail.

0.6 Ford a creek on cement stacks.

0.8 Cross a creek again.

0.26 Pass a large sandstone cave.

0.28 Three dry crossings.

0.5 Pass parts of a metal fence.

0.52 Trail heads left at a brown post marked "trail."

0.6 T intersection; follow sign right, toward waterfall.

0.9 Drop to creek; head into the creek following brown signs for trail pointing right.

1.05 Cross creek and walk upstream on left bank.

1.2 Sign for waterfall. Head upstream into the narrow canyon (not to area behind the sign).

1.25 Pool and narrow rock jam.

1.3 Base of falls. Return the way you came.

2.6 Arrive back at the trailhead.

21 Temescal Canyon Falls

This popular hike to a seasonal falls in the heart of civilization comes with views of the city, ocean, mountains, and shady oak groves. The trail is routed to keep out views of hillside mansions, so it feels more remote than it actually is.

Height: About 10–15 feet
Beauty rating: ★★
Distance: 2.6 miles out and back or 5+ miles as a loop with Temescal Ridge Trail
Elevation gain: 425 feet one-way
Difficulty: Easy to moderate (due to climbing)
Best season: Winter, spring, fall, summer (it's shaded)
County: Los Angeles
Trailhead amenities: 100+ parking spots
Land status: Temescal Gateway State Park, LA Department of Parks and Recreation,

Mountains Recreation and Conservation Authority, Topanga State Park
Maps: Tom Harrison Topanga State Park; USGS Topanga
Trail contact: Mountains Recreation and Conservation Authority; (310) 454-1395; https://mrca.ca.gov and Topanga State Park, 20828 Entrada Rd., Topanga 90290; (310) 455-2465 ext. 106; www.parks.ca.gov/?page_id=629
Fees and permits: Parking fee (machine takes credit cards), annual parking pass available

Finding the trailhead: Google Maps: Temescal Gateway Park, 15601 Sunset Boulevard, Pacific Palisades, CA 90272. From I-10, take the Pacific Coast Highway (CA 1) north for 3.2 miles. Turn right onto Temescal Canyon Road for 1 mile to Temescal Gateway Park (at the intersection with Sunset Boulevard). Free parking on Sunset Boulevard or Temescal Canyon Road. Reportedly there is a stop-sign camera (with associated ticketing) inside the park. **GPS:** N34 03.137' / W118 31.343'

The Hike

Temescal Canyon has a series of trails for easy-to-access nature and a workout.

In the 1920s to 1930s, this was the western headquarters of the Chautauqua movement. From the 1940s to mid-1990s, the Presbyterian Church used it as a retreat. When the Santa Monica Mountains Conservancy took over, they built trails and still use the cabin and retreat facilities for kids' summer camps.

From the Temescal Canyon Road, walk the paved road (or the dirt trail paralleling it on the right) toward the restroom and information area. After topping off a water bottle, continue up the paved road for 0.25 mile as it corves to the right. Turn left onto a wide, flat dirt road that's chained off.

Continue through shady oak, maple, and sycamore forest. In 0.2 mile you pass an old building, picnic table, and trash cans.

Start a steady climb on a well-defined trail. Cross into Topanga State Park, which doesn't allow dogs. Ascend out of the shade and into sunny, exposed chaparral. There are sweeping views of the canyons below and the ocean—if it isn't obscured by the morning marine layer.

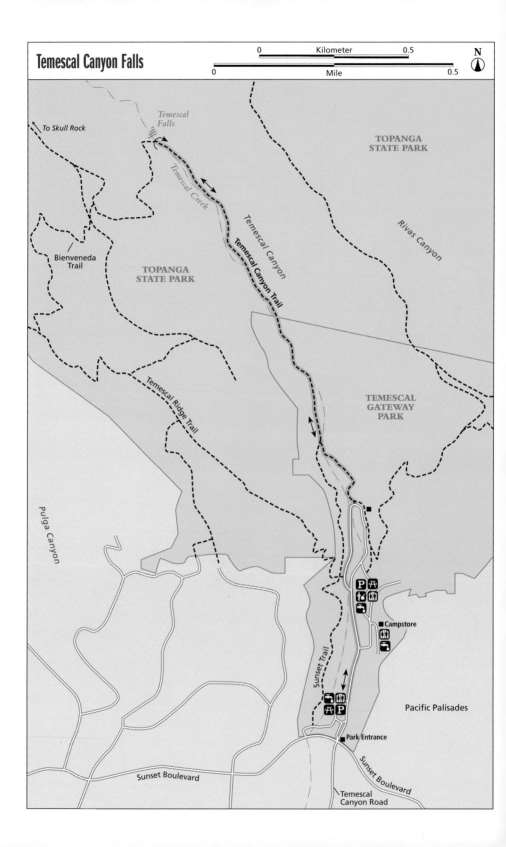

Temescal Canyon Falls

0   Kilometer   0.5

0   Mile   0.5

N

To Skull Rock

Temescal Falls

TOPANGA STATE PARK

Temescal Creek

Rivas Canyon

Temescal Canyon

Temescal Canyon Trail

Bienveneda Trail

TOPANGA STATE PARK

TEMESCAL GATEWAY PARK

Temescal Ridge Trail

Pulga Canyon

Campstore

Sunset Trail

Pacific Palisades

Park Entrance

Sunset Boulevard

Sunset Boulevard

Temescal Canyon Road

Continue ascending for another 0.8 mile until you reach the bridge over Temescal Creek. From the white, wooden bridge, you can see the short 10-foot falls tumbling over boulders upstream of the trail. It's seasonal and best visited after a good rain. Below the bridge are more falls visible with a short off-trail scramble. In summer or a dry year, you may see nothing but ferns.

Return the way you came or continue uphill to make a loop with the Temescal Ridge Trail, which meets up with your route near the restrooms. This is a classic hike, though it can be hot and exposed and involves more climbing. From the top of the ridge, there are views west to Catalina Island, south as far as Palos Verdes, and even the downtown skyline to the east.

Miles and Directions

0.0 Start at restrooms and info area.

0.25 Turn left on chained-off dirt road.

0.45 Pass old buildings.

1.3 Bridge and waterfall. Return the way you came.

2.6 Arrive back at the trailhead.

Orange County

California's most densely populated county has plenty of wilderness—and most of it is lightly visited. While it can get toasty here in the summer, these hikes are prime wildflower viewing areas in winter and spring. I've read reports claiming Orange County is the second most biologically diverse county in California.

The Santa Ana Mountains extend the eastern boundary of the county and are known for their winds.

The hikes here should give you a taste of on-trail Orange County waterfalls. For adventurers willing to put in off-trail travel, Black Star Falls and the rougher Harding Falls are well worth a visit. They are both quite ephemeral and rated difficult for the average hiker for both route-finding and physical exertion. Coal Canyon "Falls" in Chino State Park is ephemeral and requires walking 1 mile next to the interstate. Additionally, there are several intriguing human-made falls in Orange County.

Much of the wild area of Orange County burned in the Wildomar Fire of October 2017 and the Holy Fire of August and September 2018. Call the ranger station and check regulations to determine whether hiking areas and roads are open before going.

You are required to display an Adventure Pass on your dashboard at most Cleveland National Forest trailheads described in this book. See How to Use This Guide for more about this fee.

22 Holy Jim Falls

Despite being one of the most popular hikes in the Santa Ana Mountains, the rough unpaved road to get here makes Holy Jim feel like a big adventure. This lush, riparian hike surrounded by chaparral and dry hillsides is an Orange County classic that has made at least one other guidebook's front cover.

Height: About 20 feet
Beauty rating: ★★★★
Distance: 3.2 miles out and back
Elevation gain: 200 feet
Difficulty: Easy
Best season: Winter, spring
County: Orange
Trailhead amenities: Parking lot with about 25 spots, picnic table, port-o-potties, trash cans; nearby parking lot down the road at the fire station holds more cars. Dogs highly not recommended
Land status: Cleveland National Forest
Maps: USGS Santiago Peak
Trail contact: Cleveland National Forest, Trabuco Ranger District, 1147 E. Sixth St., Corona 92879; (951) 736-1811; www.fs.usda.gov/main/cleveland/home
Fees and permits: Display Adventure Pass

Finding the trailhead: Google Maps: Holy Jim Trailhead. This description has tolls but there are ways around them. From CA 241 South (a toll road), take exit 19 for Santa Margarita Parkway. Drive 1.5 miles east and turn left on Plano Trabuco Road. In 0.6 mile, as you descend to a canyon, the road name changes to Trabuco Canyon Road. Turn right on an unpaved road, also called Trabuco Canyon Road, and travel 4.7 miles. If you find yourself crossing a long bridge over a mostly dry wash, you've gone too far. The unpaved Trabuco Canyon Road is rough with potholes and a creek crossing. In dry conditions it's accessible to most two-wheel-drive cars, though folks may be happier with a high-clearance vehicle.
GPS: N33 40.368' / W117 31.023'

The Hike

Note: This area burned in the Holy Fire of August and September 2018, and parts of Trabuco Canyon Road were damaged in a landslide and debris flow in January 2019. Call the ranger station and check regulations to determine whether it's open before going.

Partially named after beekeeper "Cussin' Jim," aka James T. Smith, a foul-mouthed early Santa Ana Mountains settler, it was renamed when turn-of-the-century mapmakers thought "Holy Jim" sounded more proper. Legend has it Jim's honey farm attracted the last grizzly bear in the Santa Ana Mountains, which was shot near the mouth of the canyon in 1907.

Leave the parking lot heading north and follow posted signs for the Holy Jim Trail. You start on a wide, high-clearance road heading to the left. Soon you pass what cute, rustic cabins survived the Holy Fire. Many were built in the 1930s, when the

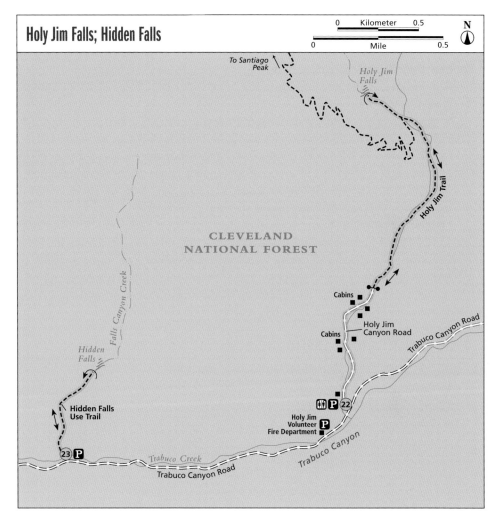

Holy Jim Falls; Hidden Falls

To Santiago Peak

Holy Jim Falls

Holy Jim Trail

CLEVELAND NATIONAL FOREST

Falls Canyon Creek

Hidden Falls

Cabins

Holy Jim Canyon Road

Cabins

Trabuco Canyon Road

Hidden Falls Use Trail

Holy Jim Volunteer Fire Department

22

Trabuco Creek

Trabuco Canyon Road

Trabuco Canyon

23

Forest Service began leasing properties to encourage city folks to experience nature, though the Holy Jim community history goes back to Civil War–era founders.

Continue heading upstream on the road, crossing back and forth over the creek.

After 0.6 mile the road ends and you reach the signed and gated Holy Jim pedestrian trailhead. During peak seasons the local volunteer fire department leaves out bottled water and collects donations for its firefighting and search and rescue efforts. Consider leaving some dollars for the fine folks who do so much for this area. It can get quite hot on this trail; do not hesitate to take water from the stash if you are unsure whether you have enough.

The trail ascends following the creek through an oak canyon, crossing back and forth over the creek. During high water these fords can be knee high or more, but often are nothing but a rock-hop. At 0.7 mile in you cross a tributary. After 0.8 mile the climb becomes more gradual. Cross under a tunnel of trees 0.9 mile into the hike.

After 1.15 miles ignore a use trail to the right that goes up a different canyon. Instead, stay on the main trail, crossing the creek shortly after.

After 1.2 miles there's a large rock on the left side of the trail that makes an excellent spot for a break. The trailside is often grassy or bushy, so this is a rare opportunity to sit. In the creek there are check dams that were built by California Fish and Game to create fishing pools.

In areas free of vegetation, you may spot Santiago Peak (5,692 feet), the highest in Orange County and the southernmost peak of the Saddleback Range. To the ancestral Juaneño Indians who lived here, the peak was called Kalawpa ("a wooded place" in Tongva language) and was home to the deity Chiningchinish. Its creek was renamed in 1769 after James the Apostle (*Sanctus Jacobus* in Latin). After locals gave it numerous other labels, the peak was officially named after the creek in 1894.

The trail to Holy Jim Falls continues to climb and cross back and forth over the creek. At 1.45 miles in, stay straight at a signed junction for the falls. The trail to the left climbs to the main divide road toward Santiago Peak and doesn't go to the waterfall.

After about 0.2 mile of rock-hopping and creek crossings, you're in a rocky grotto and at the base of Holy Jim Falls. There are shady, rocky areas where you can eat a snack and enjoy the beauty of these fern-covered, peaceful falls.

Miles and Directions

0.0 Start at the parking lot and take Holy Jim Road past cabins.

0.6 Holy Jim trailhead.

1.15 Ignore a side trail to the right.

1.2 Large lunch rock on left.

1.4 Shady lunch area on left.

1.45 Signed junction; stay straight (right).

1.6 Base of falls. Return the way you came.

3.2 Arrive back at the parking lot.

23 Hidden Falls (Trabuco Canyon Falls/ Falls Canyon Falls)

While Holy Jim Falls gets all the glory, a short but brushy hike takes you to this remote-feeling waterfall that's taller, wilder, and more remote-feeling.

See map on page 85.
Height: About 80 feet
Beauty rating: ★★★★★
Distance: 1.2 miles out and back
Elevation gain: 150 feet
Difficulty: Moderate physically; moderate to difficult navigation
Best season: Winter, spring
County: Orange

Trailhead amenities: 3 parking spots along a dirt road
Land status: Cleveland National Forest
Maps: USGS Santiago Peak
Trail contact: Cleveland National Forest, Trabuco Ranger District, 1147 E. Sixth St., Corona 92879; (951) 736-1811; www.fs.usda.gov/main/cleveland/home
Fees and permits: Display Adventure Pass

Finding the trailhead: Google Maps: Falls Canyon Falls Trailhead. From CA 241 South (a toll road), take exit 19 for Santa Margarita Parkway. Drive 1.5 miles east and turn left on Plano Trabuco Road. In 0.6 mile, as you descend to a canyon, the road name changes to Trabuco Canyon Road. Turn right on an unpaved road, also called Trabuco Canyon Road, and travel 3.4 miles. The unpaved Trabuco Canyon Road is rough with potholes and a creek crossing. In dry conditions it's accessible to most two-wheel-drive cars, though folks may be happier with a high-clearance vehicle. Park along the right side of the dirt road in an area where the road is slightly wider. It's unsigned.
GPS: N33 40.450' / W117 32.174'

The Hike

In this canyon, Holy Jim gets all the glory. But the unsigned, hard-to-find Hidden Falls is a real gem—if you're willing to search for it.

Park at a small pullout on the right side of the road (as you are driving up the canyon). It only has room for three cars. From there, walk on the road downhill for 0.1 mile until you see a steep use trail descending from the road embankment toward the creek. Google Maps shows a road where the trail is, but good luck finding it. Instead, take this rough use trail down to the creek. Cross it, watching for poison oak, which is abundant.

Look at the mountains. You are standing at the confluence of two creeks: Trabuco Creek (which you crossed) parallels the road. Falls Canyon Creek feeds into it and runs almost perpendicular. Even in spring, Falls Canyon Creek is often dry at the confluence. But if you follow it up along the use trail, it leads to Hidden Falls.

After about 0.1 mile of heading up Falls Canyon Creek on the use trail, there's a mine shaft/cave on the left (west) canyon wall. The trail crosses back and forth over

the often-dry creek. At times you may scramble over fallen logs. Depending on the season and year, this is around when you'll start seeing water in the creek.

At 0.6 mile you reach what appears to be the mouth of the canyon with the stunning Hidden Falls. A small pond lies at its base, where you may find playful orange amphibians active in aggressive spring mating practices. Take a lunch break under the shady tree. But do not take the trail on the right (east) side (as you face the waterfall), which follows a series of ropes (that is, unless you have canyoneering equipment and the skills to continue).

Miles and Directions

0.0 Start at parking alongside the road; head downhill.

0.1 Descend a steep use trail off the road to the left. Ford a wide creek.

0.15 Follow a smaller, possibly dry creek bed upcanyon. Pass a mineshaft/cave on the left.

0.2 Log crossing.

0.6 Base of falls. Retrace your steps.

1.2 Arrive back at the trailhead.

24 San Juan Falls

The short hike to this dramatic seasonal waterfall is a favorite for families and locals. The trail is what the US Forest Service describes as looking straight out of an "old West" movie, with exposed boulders, open meadows, and shaded oak areas.

Height: 15–20 feet
Beauty rating: ★★★★★
Distance: 0.6 mile out and back or as part of a 2.1-mile loop
Elevation gain: 350 feet for loop
Difficulty: Easy
Best season: Winter, early spring
County: Riverside
Trailhead amenities: 50+ parking spots, pit toilets, kiosk, shaded bench, water spigot,

Forest Adventure Passes for sale (across the street)
Land status: Cleveland National Forest
Maps: USGS Sitton Peak
Trail contact: Cleveland National Forest, Trabuco Ranger District, 1147 E. Sixth St., Corona 92879; (951) 736-1811; www.fs.usda.gov/main/cleveland/home
Fees and permits: Display Adventure Pass (available for sale at the Ortega Oaks Candy Store across the street)

Finding the trailhead: To get to the San Juan Loop trailhead, from CA 15 in Lake Elsinore, take the Ortega Highway (CA 74) for 13.4 miles. The trailhead is a large parking lot on the right (northwest) side of the road. It's across the street from the Candy Store, which also sells Forest Adventure Passes.
GPS: N33 36.459' / W117 25.359'

The Hike

From the kiosk at the San Juan Loop trailhead, descend on the well-marked San Juan Loop Trail. The loop starts above CA 74 with views of the Bear Canyon area and San Mateo Wilderness to the south. After 0.2 mile you pass the sign for the San Juan Loop Trail. Shortly after, you turn a bend around a narrow gorge and no longer see the highway. The traffic sounds disappear, and it feels like a different world.

At 0.25 mile in you pass another sign on your right for the San Juan Loop Trail and get your first views of San Juan Creek. 300 feet later, you reach a viewing platform for San Juan Falls and a wooden bench. In drier conditions the truly adventurous can find a use trail that follows the creek upstream for 100 feet to the creek area above the falls. Be aware it can get very slippery even when there isn't much water and is not suitable for most dogs. The smooth, polished granite is beautiful, but very slick.

Retrace your steps and return the way you came, or continue on the San Juan Loop Trail.

For the loop: Switchback down to the shady, oak-filled canyon along San Juan Creek. At 1 mile you reach the San Juan Creek bed for the first time. You'll see a

San Juan Falls; Chiquito Falls; Ortega Falls

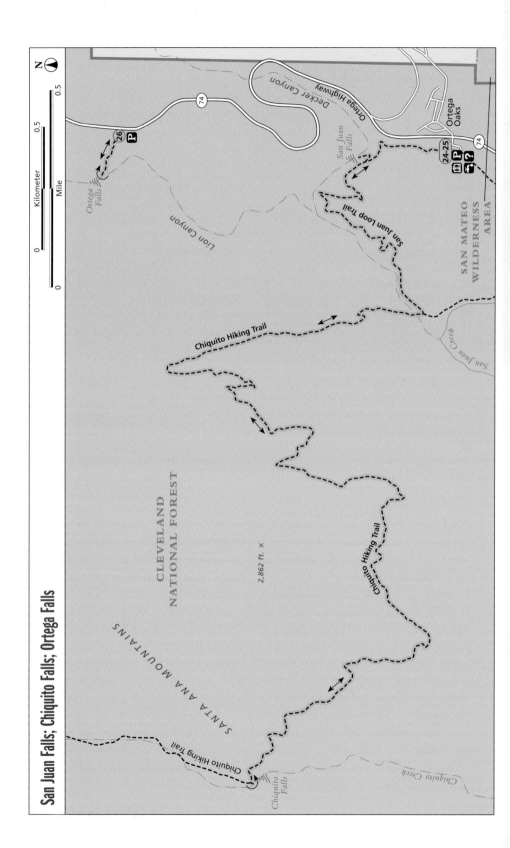

N

Kilometer
0   0.5   0.5

Mile
0   0.5   0.5

Ortega Falls

74

26   P

Lion Canyon

Decker Canyon

Ortega Highway

San Juan Falls

San Juan Loop Trail

24-25   P   i

74

Ortega Oaks

SAN MATEO WILDERNESS AREA

Chiquito Hiking Trail

CLEVELAND NATIONAL FOREST

2,862 ft. ×

SANTA ANA MOUNTAINS

Chiquito Hiking Trail

San Juan Creek

Chiquito Hiking Trail

Chiquito Falls

Chiquito Creek

carbonite marker on the right, but don't ford the creek. Instead, stay on the well-defined trail along the creek's left bank until you reach a three-way intersection, a wooden bench, and a sign. Turn left at this marked junction (right takes you to Chiquito Falls). Pass through a grove of coast live oaks alleged to be over one hundred years old. The understory here includes ferns . . . and poison oak.

Turn left to the northern edge of the Upper San Juan Loop Campground. Then, head sharply left up an open slope for 0.5 mile. The unshaded last section of trail parallels CA 74 to finish a counterclockwise loop back to your car at the Ortega Oaks parking area.

Miles and Directions

0.0 Start at the trailhead kiosk.

0.18 San Juan Loop sign.

0.26 Second San Juan Loop sign.

0.3 Viewing platform for San Juan Falls. (**Option:** Retrace steps back to the trailhead)

1.0 Trail is near San Juan Creek.

1.15 Three-way junction and bench; turn left.

2.1 Loop back to the trailhead.

25 Chiquito Falls

This long and strenuous hike visits two waterfalls: the popular San Juan Falls and the remote Chiquito Falls. In one hike you get to experience the classic views and ecosystems of the Cleveland National Forest. The climb to Chiquito Falls has elevation gain, but because you descend and climb, descend and climb, your legs and knees get breaks.

See map on page 90.
Height: About 15 feet
Beauty rating: ★★
Distance: 9.1 miles out and back
Elevation gain: 1,000 feet gain, 500 feet loss (one-way)
Difficulty: Difficult physically; moderate navigation
Best season: Fall, winter, early spring
County: Trailhead in Riverside; waterfall in Orange
Trailhead amenities: 50+ parking spots, pit toilets, kiosk, shaded bench, water spigot,
Forest Adventure Passes for sale (across the street)
Land status: Cleveland National Forest
Maps: USGS Sitton Peak
Trail contact: Cleveland National Forest, Trabuco Ranger District, 1147 E. Sixth St., Corona 92879; (951) 736-1811; www.fs.usda.gov/main/cleveland/home
Fees and permits: Display Adventure Pass (available for sale at the Ortega Oaks Candy Store across the street)

Finding the trailhead: To get to the San Juan Loop trailhead, from CA 15 in Lake Elsinore, take the Ortega Highway (CA 74) for 13.4 miles. The trailhead is a large parking lot on the right (northwest) side of the road. It's across the street from the Candy Store, which also sells Forest Adventure Passes.
GPS: N33 36.459' / W117 25.359'

The Hike

From the kiosk at the San Juan Loop trailhead, descend on the well-marked San Juan Loop Trail. Follow instructions for San Juan Falls, passing its viewing platform with a wooden bench.

Switchback down to the shady, oak-filled canyon along San Juan Creek. At 1 mile you reach the San Juan Creek bed for the first time. You'll see a carbonite marker on the right, but don't ford the creek. Instead, stay on the well-defined trail along the creek's left bank until you reach a three-way intersection, a wooden bench, and a sign. Turn right at this marked junction, leaving behind the San Juan Loop Trail—and the crowds.

Follow the wooden trail signs for Chiquito Falls. Immediately ford San Juan Creek (sometimes dry creek bed) and start following the canyon of a tributary uphill. Head

The wide Chiquito Falls.

through more oaks, climbing toward Morrell Canyon, gently ascending along a tributary on its eastern bank about 1.5 miles in. It's shady with oaks and quite pleasant.

At 1.9 miles, ford the tributary (often a dry creek bed). This is where the climbing becomes more serious and shade becomes rare.

Switchback up, heading northeast. After 2.7 miles the trail makes a sharp turn and you'll get shade as you walk on a part of the mountainside that gets more moisture. You may spot ferns or moss. There is a shaded sitting rock to take a break before more climbing.

The trail continues upward out of the trees, allowing for impressive panoramic views of the iconic peaks of the Santa Ana Mountains to the southeast: Sitton (3,273 feet)and Saddleback (5,689 feet). This is part of the San Mateo Wilderness, designated in 1984 to protect 39,413 acres of chaparral and sagebrush, home to 139 bird species, 7 fish species, 37 mammal species, and 46 species of reptiles and amphibians.

At 3.8 miles into the hike, reach the high point of the trip at (about 2,700 feet). There are good viewpoints in the next 0.5 mile of trail, including your first view of Chiquito Falls in the distance.

After curving a bend, gently descend toward Chiquito Falls and its waterway. At 4.5 miles into the hike, reach a three-way intersection right before Chiquito Creek. Turn left and, a few hundred feet later, you're at the top of Chiquito Falls.

In drier conditions you can follow a use trail near the left bank to scramble down smooth rocks to the base of the falls.

Miles and Directions

0.0 Start at the kiosk at the trailhead.

0.3 Viewing platform for San Juan Falls.

1.15 Three-way intersection and bench; turn right and ford San Juan Creek.

1.9 Ford tributary.

2.7 Shaded area.

3.8 High point of trip.

4.5 Three-way intersection; turn left on spur trail toward waterfall.

4.55 Top of Chiquito Falls. Return the way you came.

9.1 Arrive back at the trailhead.

26 Ortega Falls

This is a short hike to a stunning seasonal waterfall and swimming hole surrounded by a tall, granite amphitheater. When the waterfall isn't running, this area is a favorite place of rock climbers.

See map on page 90.

Height: Upper falls: about 35 feet; lower falls: 30 feet

Beauty rating: ★★★★★ (when flowing)

Distance: 0.3 mile out and back

Elevation gain: 200 feet gain

Difficulty: Easy

Best season: Fall, winter, spring

County: Riverside (near Orange County border)

Trailhead amenities: 5 parking spots in a dirt pullout

Land status: Cleveland National Forest

Maps: USGS Alberhill

Trail contact: Cleveland National Forest, Trabuco Ranger District, 1147 E. Sixth St., Corona 92879; (951) 736-1811; www.fs.usda.gov/main/cleveland/home

Fees and permits: Display Adventure Pass

Finding the trailhead: From CA 15 in Lake Elsinore, take the Ortega Highway (CA 74) about 11.9 miles to an unmarked dirt pullout to the right (west). It's 2 miles south of the El Cariso Visitor Center and about 1.4 miles north of the Ortega Oaks Candy Store and San Juan Loop trailhead near mile marker 4.5. The pullout can be tricky to find, so we recommend entering the GPS coordinates into your navigation system or using Google Maps for "Ortega Falls waterfall parking/viewpoint."
GPS: N33 37.332' / W117 25.345'

The Hike

This seasonal waterfall is a short hike from the car, but navigating through the brush to get to it is not as straightforward as you may expect due to the number of use trails.

From the dirt parking lot, you can see the splendid seasonal waterfall to the northwest against the brushy mountain. This short hike takes you around the lip of the canyon, where you can access the swimming hole and the base of the falls.

From the parking lot, take the established trail in the center-left. When the trail forks, in general stay high and to the right on the wider trail. For better or worse, there are rocks spray-painted with arrows indicating to continue right. Stay on the wider trail, avoiding numerous use trails that steeply go left down into the canyon. The correct path climbs on good trail through a rocky area. Once again, the established trail stays to the right and is indicated by a purple-painted arrow.

Stay high and to the right at another intersection with a very large boulder. Below to the left, there is another purple arrow with the word "road" pointing to where you came from.

You can take a very steep rock scramble down to the rock amphitheater and seasonal swimming hole. Orange flagging (may not always be there) indicates a higher path directly above the purple arrow leading to the main waterfall and rock climbing area. In low water years and off-seasons, the upper waterfall may have a trickle. The lower waterfall amphitheater can be a difficult scramble but is surprisingly beautiful, and reminiscent of a Roman bath, even when the water isn't flowing. However, graffiti and other evidence of people who don't care for the area detract somewhat from its beauty.

The lower "Roman bath" portion of Ortega Falls. When water is flowing, the pool below the author fills and becomes a great soaking area.

The upper Ortega Falls. During lower flow springs (as shown) or after it is dried up in the summer, the area just left of this photo is popular with rock climbers.

Miles and Directions

0.0   Start at the dirt pullout.

150 feet Follow yellow arrow to the right.

400 feet Follow purple arrow to stay right.

0.15   Intersection between trail to base of upper waterfall and rock scramble down to rock amphitheater and lower waterfall. Return the way you came.

0.3   Arrive back at the trailhead.

27 Tenaja Falls

This seasonal falls is among the tallest in the Southland and an unlikely find in one of the driest parts of the semisarid Cleveland National Forest. It's a short hike but quite remote, as it requires a 5-mile drive into the national forest via a one-lane, paved road. Tenaja Falls has at least four cascades and three pools, though finding an angle where all are visible can be tricky.

Height: 150 feet over 5 tiers
Beauty rating: ★★★★★ (if flowing)
Distance: 1.6 miles out and back
Elevation gain: 350 feet
Difficulty: Easy to moderate
Best season: Spring
County: Orange (near Riverside County border)
Trailhead amenities: 50+ parking spots, pit toilets, kiosk, shaded bench, water spigot, Forest Adventure Passes for sale (across the street)
Land status: Cleveland National Forest, San Mateo Canyon Wilderness
Maps: USGS Sitton Peak
Trail contact: Cleveland National Forest, Trabuco Ranger District, 1147 E. Sixth St., Corona 92879; (951) 736-1811; www.fs.usda.gov/main/cleveland/home
Fees and permits: Display Adventure Pass

Finding the trailhead: Google Maps: Tenaja Falls Trailhead. From I-15 in Murrieta, take Clinton Keith Road for 6 miles west until it turns into Tenaja Road. Take this for another 1.7 miles. Turn right to stay on Tenaja Road and follow for 4.2 miles. Turn right on Cleveland Forest Road (also called Tenaja Truck Trail or FR 7S02). Cross into Cleveland National Forest in 0.9 mile. Travel another 5.1 miles on a paved, single-lane road (passing the similarly named Tenaja trailhead on your left shortly after you enter the forest). You have to drive slowly and use pullouts if other cars come by, but the road doesn't require high-clearance or four-wheel drive. Park at the Tenaja Falls trailhead kiosk on the left side of the road lined with metal posts. The "No Alcohol" signs may be more prominent. The lot fits fifteen cars and remarkably has trash service.

A former route accessed the falls via Killen Trail (South Main Divide Road) from the Ortega Highway (CA 74), but it was damaged in the Wildomar Fire and as of 2019 is closed to the public.
GPS: N33 32.566' / W117 23.396'

The Hike

From the lot, find the trailhead by the wooden kiosk sign. Travel down a well–defined trail. There's a trail register and sign stating all visitors must sign into San Mateo Canyon Wilderness. Designated in 1984, it preserves 39,413 acres of chaparral and coastal sage habitat in one of the most populated counties in the country.

After 0.1 mile, reach a three-way junction at a sign. Left goes to Fisherman's Camp. During the 1930s through 1950s, anglers visited its pools looking for steelhead and trout. Nowadays, lower water tables and droughts have made it difficult to support substantial fish populations.

People standing at the upper-most tier of Tenaja Falls during a dry winter. The other tiers are equal in size, which should give you an idea of just how tall these falls are. It's almost impossible to get it all in one photo.

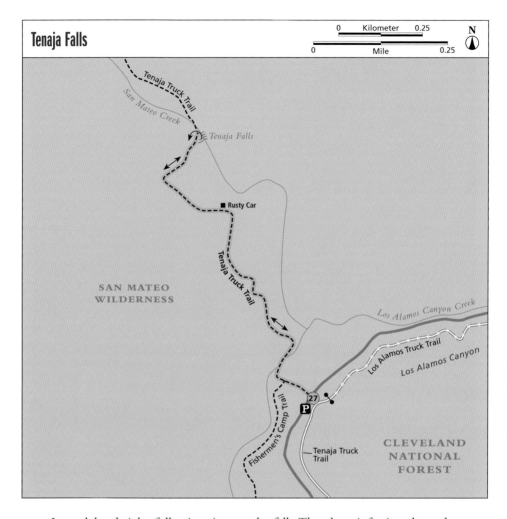

Instead, head right, following signs to the falls. There's an info sign about threatened steelhead fish that once lived here. Shortly you come to an "Unimproved Crossing" sign. The trail forks here. Turn left. The area behind the crossing sign immediately fords the creek on a rock-hop near cattails. Do not follow the creek upstream to scramble over car-sized boulders. While this route eventually leads to the falls, it has led to obvious riparian damage and has confused even experienced hikers.

After crossing the creek at 0.2 mile, pass a wooden post that says "falls." Ascend out of the creek bed on a wide, shady trail through oaks, laurels, and even ferns. Side trails to the right lead to a large, shady campsite (0.3 mile) with big oaks and flat spots. A permit is required to camp here, but it's a great spot.

Keep ascending on the trail, popping out of the trees as the vegetation changes to lower-lying chaparral. This makes for easy views of the surrounding peaks—without a building or tower in sight.

Half a mile in, turn left (southwest) up the canyon. A side trail near the turn goes to the right. Within steps there's a rusted, crashed abandoned car. Another hiker identified it as a 1970s Ford Galaxy. What do you think it is?

Back on the main trail, you get your first view of the falls on the right, up the canyon. Continue ascending gently, contouring along the left edge of the canyon. Because the trail ends at the top of the falls, the best views of the entire height of the falls are from viewpoints along the trail. Usually, you can see only two—maybe three—of its four or five tiers.

After curling around the edge of the Los Alamos Canyon, the trail makes a final turn toward the top of the falls. A shady tree with a flat spot on the left makes a good picnic spot. A cement platform helps you cross the stream that feeds the falls. Watch for cattails, willows, and riparian vegetation. In dry times you may find a well-worn metal USGS marker on the slab rock.

The rock on top of the falls is smooth and slick, so take care when approaching the water. There are use trails people have created to approach the falls, but they only slightly mar the beauty. There's a little graffiti. The granitic rock is polished and smooth, and exploration requires rock climbing skills, experience, and caution. A fall here could be deadly. It's so remote, search and rescue could take a long time.

Miles and Directions

0.0 Start at the trailhead by the kiosk.

0.1 T junction; turn right.

0.2 Cross creek.

0.3 Campsite.

0.5 Short side trail to rusty car and first view of falls.

0.8 Top of falls. Return the way you came.

1.6 Arrive back at the trailhead.

San Diego County

Although San Diego County has among the least rainfall in Southern California, almost a quarter of San Diego County is public land open to everyone for recreation. The waterfall hikes in the San Diego area are generally in the wetter, higher-altitude areas of the Cuyamaca Mountains and the drier Laguna Mountains to the south. The land is managed by Cleveland National Forest, among the first established in the country. El Prado Ranger Station in the Laguna Mountains was one of the first built in the state, in 1911.

This is the ancestral land of the Kumeyaay people, who have lived in these mountains during the summer for at least the last 7,000 years. The Kumeyaay called the Cuyamacas the Ah-ha-Kwe-ah-ma, or "place where it rains" or "rain yonder." In this dry climate the more than 30 inches of mountain rainfall (versus an average of 10 to 15 inches annually in the city of San Diego) is notable. Bedrock millstones called *moteros* ("deep holes") used for acorns can be found along trails here. Please respect any cultural artifacts you find and leave them in place.

Waterfalls in San Diego County include those that feed into the Upper San Diego River drainage, which falls from Julian to the western slopes of the Cuyamaca Range into El Capitan Reservoir. These falls, most notably Cedar Creek, Three Sisters, and Mildred (not part of this book) fall over igneous and metamorphic rock. When smaller rocks are caught below the falls, the churning water and rock mixture carves out a punchbowl, making great swimming holes.

The 2003 Cedar Fire burned much of Cuyamaca Rancho State Park and impacted about half the hikes described in this book, including those outside the park. Started by a hunter who got lost and hoped the fire would alert rescuers (keep the impact of this fire in mind if you ever become lost), the fire escaped and grew to become the largest fire in California history at the time (exceeded by the Thomas Fire in 2017). It killed fifteen people and destroyed more than 2,000 homes.

Enough time has passed that vegetation has returned. Although the fire burned so hot it destroyed seedbanks in the soil, various groups have reintroduced native conifers to create islands of forest in what would otherwise become chaparral.

Other waterfall hikes in the San Diego region take you to the foothills. While these falls are seasonal, we included them for their easy access and family-friendliness. Furthermore, they are spectacular examples of how proactive cities and the county can set aside open space for recreation and watershed protection.

For those seeking further San Diego falls, Barker Valley and Oriflamme are among the most noted in the area, although they both require four-wheel drive and/or high-clearance vehicles to access.

You are required to display an Adventure Pass in Cleveland National Forest.

28 Cedar Creek Falls

This famous 80- to 100-foot waterfall requires a permit for day hiking, but is well worth the extra hassle. It has a large punchbowl that is a notable swimming hole.

Height: 80–100 feet
Beauty rating: ★★★★★
Distance: 5.5 miles
Elevation gain: 950 feet descent/125 feet ascent (900 feet of climbing on the way back)
Difficulty: Moderate to difficult (physically due to heat); easy navigation
Best season: Winter, spring
County: San Diego
Trailhead amenities: 2 shaded accessible picnic tables, trash/recycle bins, water bottle filling faucets, cool-off shower faucet, dog bowl and faucet, outhouses, kiosk with rangers who check permits, 30 day-use-only parking spots and neighborhood parking. Don't block fire road gates when parking. Dogs not recommended.
Land status: Cleveland National Forest
Maps: USGS Tule Springs
Trail contact: Cleveland National Forest, Palomar Ranger District, 1634 Black Canyon Rd., Ramona 92065; (760) 788-0250; www.fs.usda.gov/main/cleveland/home
Fees and permits: In addition to the Adventure Pass, a permit ($6 fee) is required. Get information at www.fs.usda.gov/recarea/cleveland/recarea/?recid=80293 and reserve a permit in advance at www.recreation.gov. Up to 75 groups per day may be issued permits, and each group can have up to 5 people.

Finding the trailhead: Google Maps: Cedar Creek Falls Trailhead. From the intersection of Main Street and San Vicente Road in Ramona, take San Vincente for 6.5 miles. It turns into Ramona Oaks, which you'll then take for 2.8 miles. Turn right onto Thornbush Road into the residential neighborhood of the same name and drive to road's end 0.2 mile later. The Google Maps description is accurate, and most carriers have service all the way to the trailhead.
GPS: N32 59.427' / W116 45.227'

The Hike

You can't miss the trailhead for Cedar Creek: right where the rangers are checking permits. Everyone in your party needs a photo ID, at least a gallon of water, and to sign in before they let you go. While it's bureaucratic for a day hike, it's the Forest Service's attempt to improve safety by educating hikers and to reduce the almost daily helicopter rescues in this canyon.

Part of the reason this hike causes hikers so much grief is it's a "reverse hike": Like the Grand Canyon you start on the easy part going downhill. When you're tired during the heat of the day, you must climb back. It's also why it's recommended to leave dogs at home. Rangers regularly remove the bodies of overheated dogs. While it's legally ok to bring a dog, heed the numerous warning posters at the trailhead.

Even when the water isn't flowing, the grotto, pool, and cave under Cedar Creek Falls are a worthy destination.

If you're up for the challenge (and get a permit), descend northeast on a wide, sandy trail. For most of the hike, the trail is almost impossible to lose. At times the trail is fenced in on one if not both sides like bumper-lanes at a bowling alley for kids.

You'll get expansive views of the wilderness to the southeast as you leave behind the suburban views to the west.

The first third has benches every quarter mile. Each bench is labeled with a number. If you or someone in your party has an emergency, report the bench number to help search and rescue find you. There are clear signs every quarter mile for the entire length of the trip that mark how far it is to the falls and how far back to the trailhead. Pay close attention to these signs and use them to help judge if and when to turn back.

Pass through chaparral, descending as the trail curls southeast to prominent views of Eagle Peak. After 0.5 mile there are no more views of houses and your trail is visible winding down the hillside below. About halfway down you have expansive views of the San Diego River valley. In autumn (December and January around these parts), the whole valley turns golden with the changing leaves of the cottonwood trees.

From here you can see the headwaters of the San Diego River, including Mildred Falls. The largest falls in San Diego County, we omitted it from the book because it only runs every few years after near record-breaking rain (and even then, allegedly it relies on a rancher upstream releasing water). Nonetheless, as you descend you can see its impressive rock cliff and a prominent trail descending from Eagle Peak. That trail starts at Saddleback/Eagle Peak Road and is an original route to Eagle Creek Falls. Between the two routes, the one you're on is more fun and scenic.

From here you may also see the mouth of the small, vegetated canyon winding behind the arm of Eagle Peak. That's Cedar Creek!

The most confusing use trails on this hike have been signed off or fenced off. At 1.75 miles in, pass under a large, obelisk-Pacman-shaped boulder on your left. As you climb back on the return, it can be a good marker for how far you've come.

You'll meet the steepest part of the entire trail after the "waterfall 1 mile" sign. It's short and heads straight southeast toward the San Diego River. When you get close to the river, the trail becomes flat and shaded with oaks and sycamores. The air smells of riparian plants. The trail feels less open and far different from where you started.

At a large, signed three-way junction in the oaks, the trail heading right and downhill is the San Diego River Canyon Trail. The trail to your left uphill is the "alternate" to the falls that you could see for most of the hike. The path you want is straight ahead, through wooden fences, with numerous loud signs saying you can only enter with a permit.

Continue through a tunnel of oaks. The canyon walls get taller as you head deeper into the canyon, which turns left toward the falls. Cross a creek bed 2.5 miles in, then cross back over again. The last 0.25 mile is filled with shoe- and shoebox-sized rocks. Watch your ankles. The trail feels boxed in now.

Cedar Creek Falls

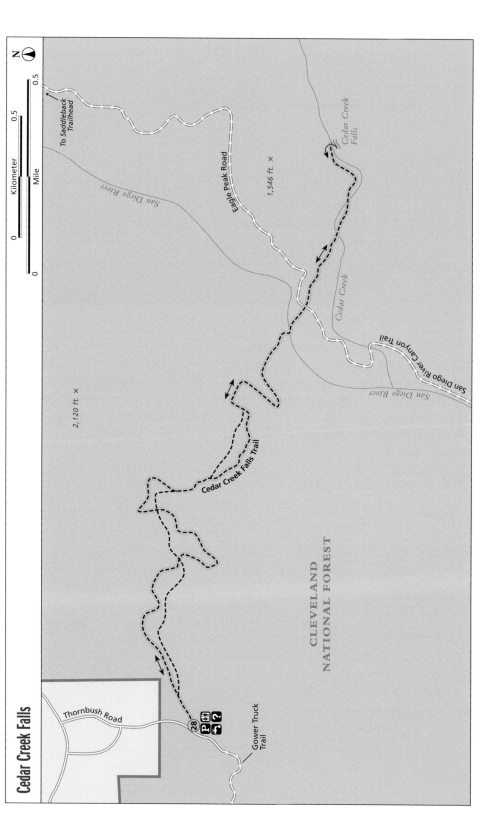

N

Kilometer
0   0.5   0.5

Mile
0   0.5

To Saddleback Trailhead

San Diego River

Eagle Peak Road

1,546 ft. ×

Cedar Creek Falls

Cedar Creek

2,120 ft. ×

Cedar Creek Falls Trail

San Diego River Canyon Trail

San Diego River

CLEVELAND
NATIONAL FOREST

Thornbush Road

28

Gower Truck Trail

You walk down into this valley with views of Eagle Peak and the small canyon that is home to Cedar Creek.

The falls is 100 feet tall and has a punchbowl-like pool that is at least 6 feet deep. It sits in a rocky amphitheater surrounded by cottonwoods. A cave-like mini grotto is on the far right and covered in ferns. Swimming is allowed, but at your own discretion. As multiple signs note (and your permit states), alcohol, rock climbing, and jumping from cliffs are prohibited. This is a popular swimming hold but do so at your own risk.

Miles and Directions

0.0 Start at the trailhead kiosk.

2.0 Cross the San Diego River.

2.25 Four-way junction; stay straight.

2.75 Cedar Creek Falls. Return the way you came.

5.5 Arrive back at the trailhead.

29 Three Sisters Falls Trail

In spring 2018 the US Forest Service built a new, safer trail to one of San Diego County's most popular—and up until now most deadly—waterfalls. This three-tiered falls wedged in a narrow valley used to require minor rock climbing and canyoneering skills, but can now be reached via a nice trail. The Middle Sister is the largest falls, dropping 50 feet into a 10-foot-deep pool in best conditions. During wildflower season the hillside is covered in poppies and wild mustard.

Height: 3 distinct tiers—the lowest about 30 feet, middle about 50 feet, and upper about 25 feet
Beauty rating: ★★★★★ (at full flow)
Distance: 4.0 miles out and back
Elevation gain: 1,035 feet gain on the return
Difficulty: Moderate to strenuous (physically); easy to moderate navigation
Best season: Winter, spring
County: San Diego

Trailhead amenities: 2 port-o-potties, trash/recycle bins. The parking lot holds at least 100 cars, but the dirt road outside the gated lot has numerous No Parking signs.
Land status: Cleveland National Forest
Maps: USGS Santa Ysabel
Trail contact: Cleveland National Forest, Palomar Ranger District, 1634 Black Canyon Rd., Ramona 92065; (760) 788-0250; www.fs .usda.gov/main/cleveland/home
Fees and permits: Display Adventure Pass

Finding the trailhead: Google Maps: Three Sisters Falls Trailhead. From Julian, head west on CA 79. Turn left on Pine Hills, which has signs for YMCA and Girl Scout Camps. After 1.6 miles, turn right on Eagle Peak Road. Then turn left on Boulder Creek Road and continue on it for 13 miles. The last 5.8 miles are on a dirt road and are passable with a two-wheel-drive car when conditions are dry (aka it hasn't rained recently). The road passes through the Inaja Indian Reservation. You are allowed to drive on the road through here, and the No Trespassing signs are there to ask you to stay on the road only. At a sharp bend to the left in the road, reach a gate and sign for the trailhead.

You can also reach the trailhead from the town of Descanos. Follow Boulder Creek Road for 12.6 miles (there are mile markers along the narrow road). Five miles out of town, the road becomes dirt. About 10 miles from town, you pass near Rancho Margarita where there may be a water crossing (manageable by two-wheel drive most of the time).
GPS: N32 59.046' / W116 40.375'

The Hike

Note: This trail may be closed in the summer during extreme heat advisories over 95°F (check with the Palomar Ranger District at 760-788-0250).

The Forest Service recommends you bring 3 to 4 liters of water per person (we suggest bringing electrolytes and plenty of salty snacks, too). Emergency air rescues

For much of the hike, you'll see all three tiers of the waterfall. The trail takes you right to the middle pool of the three-tiered Three Sisters.

happen almost daily here during the summer. During the warmer months, so much of the trail is exposed to the sun that there is high potential for dehydration, heatstroke, or exhaustion. For this reason it is not recommended for dogs, kids, or people with known health conditions. Like Cedar Creek Falls, it's an inverted hike. So while going down at the beginning is easy, the return is uphill during the heat of the day when you are most tired. For all hikers we recommend starting early and hiking during the coolest parts of the day.

Take the wide, flat dirt trail at the gate at the *far* end of the trailhead, not the closed road headed downhill to the right as you enter the parking lot (that goes to Eagle Peak).

The first 0.5 mile goes west on an old ranch road, staying high on a flat ridgetop. Sunshine Mountain (3,154 feet) is to the north, and there are views of Cuyamaca Mountain (the highest peak in San Diego at 6,152 feet). Mineral Hill (with towers) is to the southeast. About a quarter mile in, there are oak trees to the left where folks picnic. This is the last shade for a while.

At 0.3 mile the dirt road takes a rocky descent, still on the spine of the ridge passing through chaparral. This hike burned in the 2003 Cedar Fire, but is mostly recovered.

Reach a wooden post after 0.55 mile. Make a sharp turn left and downhill on a narrower trail (avoid going straight on a fainter narrow trail, which goes to Eagle Peak). Your trail descends, curling around the mountain toward the Boulder Creek Gorge. From this vantage point you may spot the top of Three Sisters Falls, nested in a distinctive V-shaped notch across the valley.

After 0.9 mile, pay attention at a confusing unmarked intersection. (When we visited in 2019, however, the other trail that goes straight to Sheep Canyon was blocked off by stones.) Your trail wraps a hairpin turn to the right to cross a tributary of Boulder Creek (likely dry). Then the trail heads downhill, following the creek on its left bank downhill. There are oaks and even ferns in this shady area (watch out for poison oak).

You pop into the sun, contouring the hillside to the south, with unblocked views of the canyon ahead and the surroundings peaks. You also have views of the falls here—from 1,000 feet above it.

After 1.35 miles you reach the new section of trail contouring high above the creek. This well-defined trail gently descends, curling west toward the falls. Look back on the trail you came down and scan the old route, which left an ugly scar on the hillside and was responsible for injuries and rescues. In contrast, the new route is graded and only has one spot where you have to climb over a small boulder on a stone step.

As you approach the creek, descend on two tight minor switchbacks. Follow the creek upstream. 2 miles from your car, you are deposited at an angled stone slab on the left (east) side of the falls. This is smooth and slick granite and feels exposed with a drop down to the creek below. This is where one of us was toppled by an off-leash

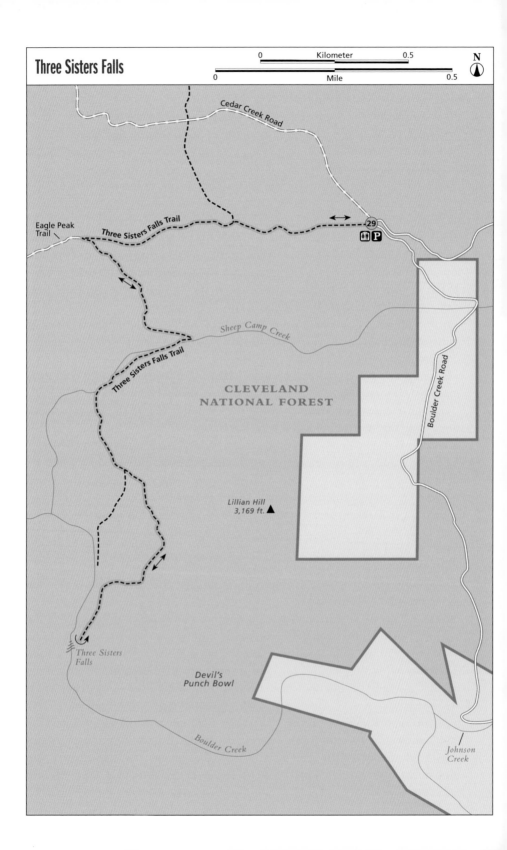

Another view of the waterfall.

dog that an unscrupulous owner brought on this hike. We don't recommend bringing dogs here, and if you do, they should be on-leash.

The trail ends at the base of the 50-foot Middle Sister in a circular grotto. You'll also get a good view of the smaller lower falls.

Miles and Directions

0.0 Start at trailhead near campsite 74.

0.55 Turn left at junction at wooden post.

0.9 Turn right at unmarked junction with Sheep Creek, heading downstream.

2.0 Stone slab between the lower and middle falls. Return the way you came.

4.0 Arrive back at the trailhead.

30 Jack Creek Falls

This is about as kid-friendly a hike as you can get. These ephemeral falls are easy to access from the city. Even when the falls aren't flowing (which is most of the time), this is a pleasant hike that can be extended to visit a cave and venture around a small lake with abundant picnic areas and even a playground and barbecue area for lunching.

Height: About 10–20 feet
Beauty rating: ★★
Distance: 0.8 mile out and back or 2.4 miles as a loop
Elevation gain: 100 feet loss there/100 feet gain on the way back
Difficulty: Easy
Best season: Winter, early spring
County: San Diego
Trailhead amenities: Numerous sheltered picnic areas. The upper picnic area, Hilltop, has a playground, barbecue pit, restrooms with running water and flush toilets, drinking fountains, and trash/recycle bins. There is abundant parking inside and outside the park.
Land status: Dixon Lake Recreation Area, City of Escondido
Maps: Park map may be available at entrance.
Trail contact: Dixon Lake Ranger Station, 1700 La Honda Dr., Escondido 92027; (760) 839-4045; www.escondido.org/dixon-lake.aspx
Fees and permits: Parking fee on weekends, holidays, and special events; cash only ($5 as of 2019). Gates open 6 a.m. to 6 p.m.

Finding the trailhead: Google Maps: Dixon Lake, Escondido. Park in the Hilltop picnic area (turn right after the entrance fee station). More than 200 spots are available in a dirt parking lot outside the park entrance (shared parking with the Daley Ranch Open Space next to the park). **GPS:** N33 09.553' / W117 03.050'

The Hike

Jack Creek Falls is a short, ephemeral boulder cascade surrounded by palms and eucalyptus. It has views of the natural-looking reservoir Dixon Lake nestled among the rocky hills. Willows fill the creek and turn golden in fall. While these waterfalls only run right after a good rain in a city that only gets 15.2 inches of rain per year, this hike and the surrounding amenities of Dixon Lake Recreation Area are enjoyable throughout much of the year.

Right beyond the car fee entry station, the road Ts. Here, to the right of the "Park Directory" sign, is a trailhead kiosk for the 2.4-mile Grand Loop Trail. From the kiosk, head 250 feet straight and then right downhill. Keep going straight on the dirt path when you intersect a gravel road best suited for a golf cart. Your narrower dirt trail stays high, contouring the hillside through the trees and shade between the upper picnic area (Hilltop) and lower picnic area.

Pass several formal and less formal-looking paths leading between the upper and lower picnic areas, but stay straight until you see a bridge. Take the path with wooden stairs going down to Jack Creek and the bridge.

Jack Creek Falls only runs right after a rain storm (and even then, can be dry), but Dixon Lake Park and the hike to the reservoir are a fun, scenic family-friendly destination close to civilization.

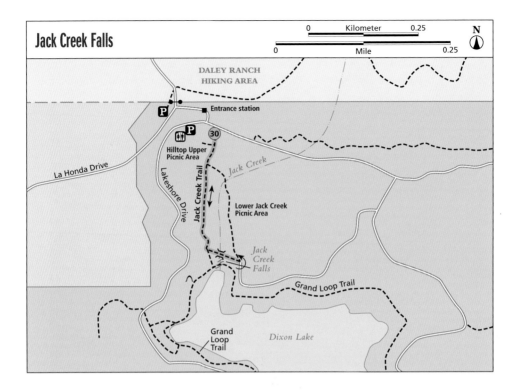

While this park can seem like a maze of picnic areas, you need not worry about getting lost. If you find yourself not on the "right" trail, head for the lower picnic area. Your path and the bridge are behind the picnic shelter named Sage.

When you stand atop the bridge, you are looking down from the top of Jack Creek. If you have very little ones with you, this is the safest viewpoint. If you feel confident of the abilities of those with you, there are three ways to get better views of the falls.

First option: Continue across the bridge and walk about 40 feet up. There's a use trail on the right descending 25 feet to the top of the falls.

Second option: Continue across the bridge and stay on the main trail (passing the use trail described in the first option). Pop out to views of Dixon Lake before descending. If you want to do the whole Grand Loop Trail, stay straight. Otherwise, when you're about 250 feet from the bridge, take a trail to the right. After 150 feet on this side trail, you reach Jack Creek. From there it's a bushwhack and tricky scramble for about 200 feet upstream to the base of the falls. It may be impassable, especially when wet, as the rocks are quite smooth and slippery. Of the three options, this is the one most suited for adults or advanced adventurers.

Third option: From the bridge, backtrack on the trail to the three-way junction behind the Sage picnic shelter. Turn left on a trail at the junction (not uphill on the wooden stairs back toward the upper picnic area). This is the end point of the 2.4-mile Grand Loop Trail (for those who started at the bridge heading clockwise). You contour the hillside above Jack Creek for about 300 feet. Stay on the trail until you reach a small cave. This is the best viewpoint of Jack Creek Falls and the lake.

For those who have time and the wherewithal, the 2.4-mile Grand Loop Trail circles Dixon Lake back to the third viewing option by the cave and can be a fun way to extend your hike.

Miles and Directions

0.0   Start at the trailhead kiosk.

0.2   Cross path between lower and upper picnic areas.

0.4   Top of falls at bridge. Return the way you came.

0.8   Arrive back at the trailhead.

31 Los Peñasquitos Falls

Surrounded by suburbia, the Los Peñasquitos Canyon Trail and Falls is a respite from the city in one of the largest urban parks in the world. This short tumble of water over boulders isn't one of the great falls of Southern California, but it's remarkable for its unlikeliness given the terrain and its proximity to civilization. It is located along the flat, shady, multiuse Los Peñasquitos Canyon Trail, which can be enjoyed by foot, bike, or horse.

Height: About 10–15 feet
Beauty rating: ★★
Distance: 6.2 miles out and back
Elevation gain: 200 feet loss there/200 feet gain back
Difficulty: Easy (aside from distance)
Best season: Winter, spring
County: San Diego
Trailhead amenities: 50+ parking spots, drinking fountain, outhouse; dogs on-leash allowed

Land status: Los Peñasquitos Canyon Preserve, City of San Diego
Maps: USGS Del Mar
Trail contact: San Diego Parks and Recreation Department, Open Space Division, Los Peñasquitos Canyon Preserve; (858) 538-8066; www.sdparks.org
Fees and permits: None

Finding the trailhead: Google Maps: Peñasquitos Canyon Trailhead on Black Mountain Road.
GPS: N32 56.177' / W117 07.463'

The Hike

What makes this hike so good is not the destination itself, but the pleasant walking through the Los Peñasquitos Canyon Preserve to get to these boulder falls (Peñosquitos means "little cliffs" in Spanish). While there are shorter routes to the falls, this is the most scenic and pleasant, avoiding most of the sun and views of electrical towers found on some of the shorter variations. It's on a wide, shady trail that is suited for side-by-side walking conversations with friends. It's also one of few waterfall trails accessible by bike.

Start at the eastern Los Peñasquitos Canyon trailhead on Black Mountain Road. From the parking lot, go through the wooden gate next to the trail information sign, taking the wide, unpaved road west. Soon you reach a junction with another trail. This connects to another part of the parking lot and the eastern section of the much longer Los Peñasquitos Canyon Trail. The whole trail is part of the 140-mile-long Trans San Diego County Trail. The TSDCT starts at the Salton Sea, crosses Anza-Borrego Desert State Park through the Cuyamaca Mountains, and ends at Torrey Pines Beach.

Keep heading left (west) on the main Los Peñasquitos Canyon Trail. Along the main trail you'll find signed intersections with narrower trails (usually with "No Bikes" signs).

Los Peñasquitos is one of the flattest, shadiest waterfall hikes in Southern California.

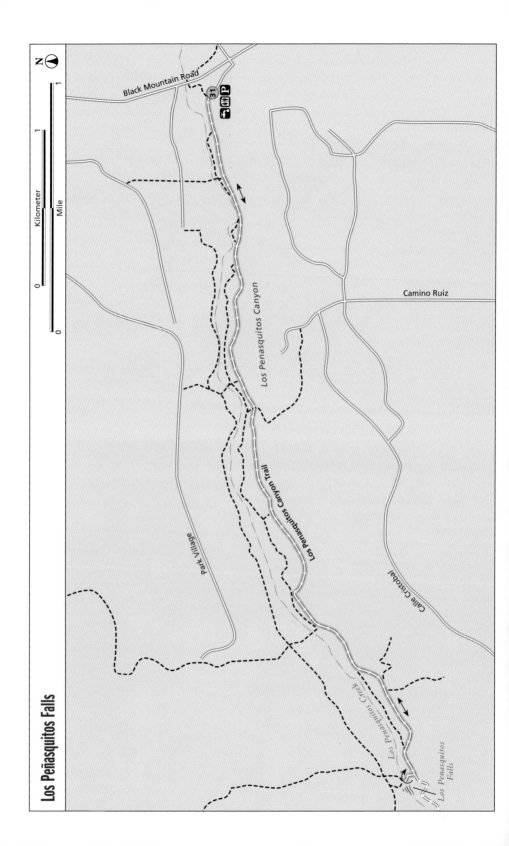

Los Peñasquitos Falls

N

Kilometer
0   1

Mile
0   1

Black Mountain Road

Park Village

Los Penasquitos Canyon

Los Penasquitos Canyon Trail

Los Penasquitos Creek

Los Peñasquitos Falls

Calle Cristobal

Camino Ruiz

The notable thing about Los Peñasquitos Canyon is how surrounded it is by suburbia. Above on the hilltops, you can see houses, parks, and neighborhoods. It is one of the first Mexican land grants in California titled to Francisco de Maria Ruíz in 1823. Totaling 4,000 acres over 7 miles, Los Peñasquitos Canyon is one of the largest urban parks in the world and home to over 500 plant species. Travel through an oak woodland ecosystem, which provides shade for most of the hike throughout the year. The oak habitat is important to many species. Birds of prey perch in branches. Rodents feast on the acorns.

About 2 miles into your hike (with an elevation loss of about 50 feet), the vegetation opens up. At 2.25 miles a prominent trail joins from the right.

About 3 miles from the trailhead (near a mile marker letting you know as much), look for a signed intersection for the falls to your right. It looks like a dirt turnaround pullout for cars.

Take this trail and hike 0.1 mile down some stairs. There's a wooden railing that people use to lock up bikes before the rockier section down to the creek. The trail takes you to the top of the boulder falls and even continues across the creek. Depending on the season, you may get your feet wet.

Linger here and enjoy the unlikely flow of water in a dry, flat area so close to civilization. It's difficult to get a good vantage point to see the entire height of this falls, but after a good rain, you can hear it roar below.

Miles and Directions

0.0 Start at the Black Mountain Road Los Peñasquitos Canyon trailhead.

2.25 Stay straight on Los Peñasquitos Canyon Trail when a trail joins from the right.

3.0 Leave main Los Peñasquitos Canyon Trail at a junction on the right to the falls.

3.1 Top of Los Peñasquitos Falls. Return the way you came.

6.2 Arrive back at the trailhead.

32 Sweetwater Falls

Featuring the only human-made pool in the book, this small, seasonal falls utilizes a fire road for most of the hike, with views of the wild Cuyamaca State Park. It can be enjoyed as a short hike or used to connect the Green Valley Falls hike into a longer route along the Sweetwater River.

Height: About 10 feet
Beauty rating: ★★
Distance: 1.8 miles out and back
Elevation gain: Easy to moderate
Difficulty: Easy
Best season: Winter, spring
County: San Diego

Trailhead amenities: 40+ parking spots, ranger house nearby, drinking fountain, cell service at parking lot
Land status: Cuyamaca Rancho State Park
Maps: USGS Descanso
Trail contact: Cuyamaca Rancho State Park; (760) 765-3023; www.parks.ca.gov/?page _id=667
Fees and permits: Day-use fee

Finding the trailhead: Google Maps: Merigan Fire Road, Descanso, CA or 24910/24912 Vieja Road. **Note:** Neighbors have signed "no trailhead parking." From I-8, take the exit for CA 79 for 2.9 miles. Turn left on Viejas Boulevard toward the town of Descanso, following it for 0.9 mile. The Merigan trailhead is on your right. If you reach the T in the road by the elementary school, you've got too far.
GPS: N32 51.547' / W116 36.667'

The Hike

This hidden falls would be a local's secret, except it's inside Cuyamaca State Park. We found it while perusing maps looking for waterfalls off the beaten path. On a hunch, we explored and were pleasantly surprised by what we found. Though it's human-made (at least the pool is created by a silt diversion dam), it's a neat little alcove not far from the busier Green Valley Falls. If you do visit the falls, please take extra care to pack out your trash; refrain from carving, painting, or marking any of the rocks or boulders; and be respectful of the area and the neighbors.

The falls flows seasonally but features a year-round reflective pool. To approach the falls, you must walk in the waterway of Sweetwater Creek. This isn't a big deal for most of the year, but on Valentine's Day 2019, the area received close to 10 inches of rain in 24 hours. As with almost all the waterfalls in this book, do not visit during high rains and flash flood warnings.

From the trailhead, take the fire road past the gate following signs to Dead Horse (listed as 0.7 mile away). The "trail" here is a wide, gravel road. Pass two ranger residences on the right. This is a multiuse trail open to bikes and horses and follows under

Sweetwater Falls tumbles down a small rockface.

a telephone line. On the left is an open field with houses in the distance. Pass the skeletons of oaks and the boulder-strewn hillsides so iconic of this part of Southern California.

After 0.25 mile the gravel road turns to a dirt fire road. It's still wide and easy to follow, climbing through oaks and manzanitas. The climb starts gently, then becomes steeper. You can still see houses to the right. The vegetation becomes less open with lots of chemise and manzanita, and no shade. The trail levels out past 0.5 mile before climbing through yucca and chaparral.

At the top of a hill, reach a signed and posted intersection 0.7 mile from your car. Turn left, following signs down to the Dead Horse Trail/California Riding and Hiking Trail. The sign notes it's 0.1 mile to the Sweetwater River—the source of this falls.

As you break off from the fire road, the trail becomes narrow and switchbacks steeply down to the river. You drop 125 feet in just over 0.1 mile. Watch for poison oak. The view of houses and the sounds of other users disappear. You could be hundreds of miles away in the wilderness.

After 0.1 mile—right before you get to the river—keep your eye out for a small, signed arrow on your right. It points to the left, but this is a marker for the main trail. To get to the falls, take a use trail to the right. If you find yourself crossing the water on the main trail, you've gone too far.

Follow the use trail upstream along Sweetwater Creek for 0.1 mile. It can be overgrown. You pass an old copper pipe and may need to wade in the creek bed (use your

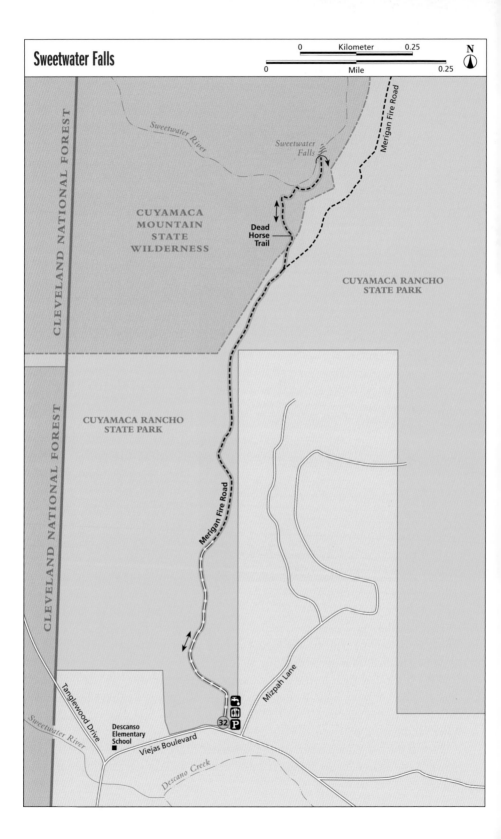

Sweetwater Falls

CLEVELAND NATIONAL FOREST

Sweetwater River

Sweetwater Falls

Merigan Fire Road

CUYAMACA
MOUNTAIN
STATE
WILDERNESS

Dead
Horse
Trail

CUYAMACA RANCHO
STATE PARK

CLEVELAND NATIONAL FOREST

CUYAMACA RANCHO
STATE PARK

Merigan Fire Road

Mizpah Lane

Tanglewood Drive

Sweetwater River

Descanso
Elementary
School

32

Viejas Boulevard

Descano Creek

0   Kilometer   0.25

0   Mile   0.25

N

The dammed up pool below Sweetwater Falls holds water yearround.

judgment as to whether it looks safe). When the canyon narrows, reach a small cascade (possibly dry). If it looks safe for you, scramble on rocks to follow the creek above.

Reach a magnificent pool bolstered by what Southern California guidebook author, the late Jerry Schad, describes as a "silted-in diversion dam." Even in dry times the water looked to be 2 feet deep. Nestled in a grotto, this enchanted water hole in the desert is free from trash and graffiti. We beg you to do all you can to keep it that way by picking up litter.

A 10-foot falls drops into the pool. An upper pool is above it, but it's difficult to see from the narrow grotto.

Miles and Directions

0.0 Start at the Merigan parking and trailhead.

0.25 Gravel road turns to dirt.

0.7 Turn left at signed intersection for Dead Horse Trail.

0.8 Turn right at arrow up a use trail.

0.9 Pool at base of falls. Return the way you came.

1.8 Arrive back at the trailhead.

Option: For those wanting a longer adventure, from Sweetwater Falls, return to Merigan Fire Road and turn left, uphill and north. Follow above the path of the Sweetwater River for 1.25 miles with 250 feet gain until you reach a junction with the California Riding and Hiking Trail and the Sweetwater Trail. In another 0.5 mile on the Sweetwater Trail, reach another falls in a gorge-like area. In another 0.5 mile, turn left on the South Boundary Fire Road to the Falls Fire Road leading to Green Valley Falls, 1 mile later. Those wishing to experience the hike while walking mostly downhill can start at Green Valley Falls and end at the Merigan trailhead. Both one-way routes require setting up a car shuttle.

33 Green Valley Falls Trail

This family-friendly trail starts in a shady campground and picnic area. Despite the hike's short distance and the falls' short height, these are beautiful year-round falls.

Height: Upper falls: about 20 feet for 2 cascades; lower falls: 15 feet for 2 tiers
Beauty rating: ★★★★★
Distance: 0.8 mile out and back
Elevation gain: 80 feet loss/80 feet gain on the return
Difficulty: Easy
Best season: Winter, spring (falls run year-round)
County: San Diego

Trailhead amenities: 100+ parking spots, flush toilets (when campground is open), faucets with drinking water (when campground is open), camping, helpful staff at the ranger station
Land status: Cuyamaca Rancho State Park
Maps: Available at entrance or at www.parks .ca.gov, USGS Cuyamaca Peak
Trail contact: Cuyamaca Rancho State Park; (760) 765-3020; www.parks.ca.gov
Fees and permits: Day-use parking fee

Finding the trailhead: Google Maps: Green Valley Area Campground. From downtown San Diego, take I-8 east toward El Centro for 23 miles. Take exit 40 for CA 79 North/Japatul Valley Road toward Julian.
For picnic area: From exit 40, turn left onto CA 79 North/Japatul Valley Road and take it for 7.4 miles to Green Valley Campground. Turn left into the park and pay the $10 entrance fee. Park in the Green Valley Falls Picnic Area (lower area), which can be found by driving on the road past campsite 76 (but not in the campsite's designated parking spot as described in route descriptions). While the upper picnic area has signed posts that lead to the falls, it's less scenic (but a good option if the parking in the bigger lower area is full).
GPS: N32 54.188' / W116 35.043'
Optional Mesa trailhead: Google Maps: West Mesa Trailhead. From exit 40, turn left onto CA 79 North/Japatul Valley Road and take it for 6 miles. The trailhead is a dirt pullout on the right side of the road. Parking at this trailhead adds about 2 miles to hike. **GPS:** N32 56.419' / W116 33.952'

The Hike

On the drive to this campsite from I-8, you'll cross a bridge marked "Sweetwater Creek." This hike takes you to a tributary of Sweetwater Creek upstream of the bridge crossing.

Cuyamaca Rancho State Park is home to 6,512-foot-high Cuyamaca Peak. Over half of its 24,700 acres of oak and conifer forests and meadows are state wilderness. It was home to the ancestors of today's Kumeyaay Indians. As the native population dwindled, miners arrived and searched here for gold before capitalist Ralph M. Dyar bought the rancho. He'd hoped to develop it but only built his own Dyar House before the Great Depression led him to sell the property to the new California State

The Lower Green Valley Falls are surrounded by flat slabs for picnicing and sitting by the water.

Park System. The Civilian Conservation Corps improved the park throughout the 1930s. In 2003 the Cedar Fire burned most of the park including the former park headquarters at the old Dyar House. With time and active reforestation projects, much of the vegetation has grown back.

Despite what Google or the California State Parks website may say, the campground to access these falls isn't always open in the fall, winter, and spring—the months when most people are searching for waterfalls. Call ahead. Otherwise, the falls are accessible by adding 2 miles of easy, flat hiking from the La Mesa trailhead along CA 79 (which is an option year-round if you're looking to avoid paying the car entrance fee).

Maps and directions at the La Mesa trailhead kiosk spell out how to access the falls almost as if the park preferred waterfall chasers started here rather than in the campground. It's 0.5 mile along a mostly flat trail to the campground. Carefully cross the road to enter the campground. From the entrance station, looking straight across a field, you can see the picnic trailhead area. But here's the annoying part: You have to walk a circuitous paved road around the campground to access the trailhead at the picnic area. The attendant may point you toward a more direct route across the creek.

Whether you hike in or drive in, once you're at the picnic area, signposts point you toward Green Valley Falls. Follow the obvious trail past picnic tables and faucets (be sure to top off your water bottles). You'll be traveling through oaks, pines, manzanitas, and poison oak.

Continue following signs for the falls to dirt-and-wooden steps. Pass a "No Diving Sign" and "No Dogs" sign. After 0.1 mile you descend wooden steps paralleling the creek. On the way down, two side trails go left. The first curls around (almost a U-turn) and leads to a rock outcropping above the upper falls. But as it's above the falls, the view isn't as grand as from the other angle.

The second side trail to the left leads about 20 feet to a rock outcropping lookout over the upper falls. But we think the view of the upper falls is better sticking to the main trail, which goes down stairs and then climbs more to a "high point." The upper falls is a 20-foot falls with two streams squeezing through boulders. At the bottom is (sometimes) a pool of water. In winter it even holds ice.

From the high point, descend more wooden steps. More use trails go left toward the water. These take you to the base of the falls, but should be approached with caution because of slippery rocks and abundant poison oak.

If you'd prefer to continue to the double cascade at the lower falls, continue on the main dirt trail, following the creek downstream and through woods. About 0.2 mile in, look for a house-sized boulder on your right. You have to scramble over the slab skirting its left side. Because this section of trail is on rock, it can feel like you've lost the trail. Once you descend off the slab, reach the dirt trail again. Soon, it'll head right and reach a signed post for the Green Valley Falls Fire Road.

Instead, if you're feeling confident about your scrambling and slab-walking skills, look for a use trail that descends toward the creek. A smaller waterfall runs almost year-round, and when it's really flowing, it's a two-tiered 15-footer pouring over a wide slab with a nice pool underneath.

The double Upper Falls of Green Valley Falls isn't far from the picnic area and runs year-round.

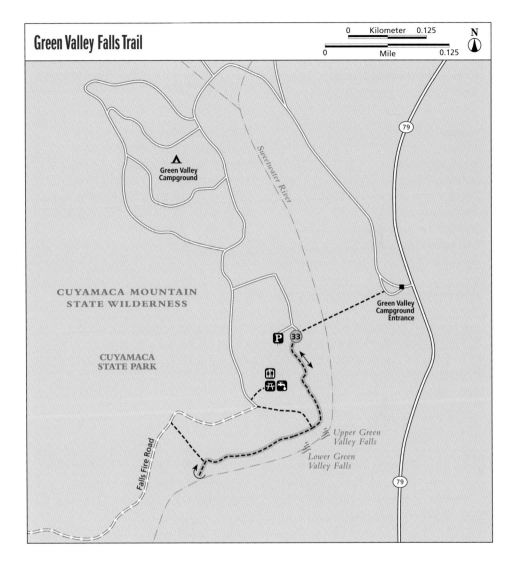

Green Valley Falls Trail

Miles and Directions

0.0 Start at the picnic area.

0.2 Upper falls.

0.4 Lower falls. Return the way you came.

0.8 Arrive back at the trailhead.

Option: Connect this with the Sweetwater Falls hike to follow the Sweetwater River down to Cuyamaca State Park's Merigan trailhead.

34 Cottonwood Creek Falls

Finding the pullout may be the most difficult part of this wild-feeling trip. The creek is lined with cactus and it feels like a waterfall in the desert.

Height: Several tiers, varying between 10-15 feet

Beauty rating: ★★★

Distance: 2 miles out and back

Elevation gain: 350 feet loss and gain (on the return trip)

Difficulty: Easy; moderate route-finding

Best season: Winter, spring

County: San Diego

Trailhead amenities: 2 port-o-potties

Land status: Cleveland National Forest

Maps: USGS Mount Laguna

Trail contact: Cleveland National Forest, Descanso Ranger District, 3348 Alpine Blvd., Alpine 91901; (619) 445-6235; www.fs.usda .gov/main/cleveland/home

Fees and permits: Display Adventure Pass

Finding the trailhead: Google Maps: Cottonwood Falls, 7432 County Rte S1, Pine Valley 91962. From I-8, take exit 47 to the Sunrise Highway. After climbing 1.8 miles up the mountain, park at a giant unsigned parking lot on the left (northwest) located between mile markers 15 and 15.5. It has great views of I-8 and Pine Valley below. A red boulder is toward the far end of the lot, and there's a lone picnic table for watching sunsets. A large parking lot is on the right (east) almost across the street from it.
GPS: N32 49.368' / W116 29.453'

The Hike

From the parking lot, look back on the great views of Pine Valley and I-8 where you drove. This is a grand start to this short but wild hike to Cottonwood Creek.

From the northwest parking lot (left side), carefully cross the Sunrise Highway to an unsigned footpath. Look for it north of where the guardrail ends on the opposite side of the highway from where you parked. Follow this footpath under an electrical pole, following below the Sunrise Highway. You may see evidence of old cable wire. The trail may get faint and brushier until you intersect with another use trail coming from the other (east) parking lot 0.25 mile in. That use trail also parallels the Sunrise Highway but is steeper.

Now there is but one trail. It follows the electrical lines all the way down. But first you must take a leap of faith by following the trail into a tunnel of chaparral. The trail here isn't overgrown (you won't feel like you need a machete), but it does feel like the trail has been blasted through the vegetation like a tunnel is blasted through rock. Look at the Google Maps satellite view before you go.

Cottonwood Creek has a diversity of plants growing next to it and is one of few falls with cacti growing right next to the water.

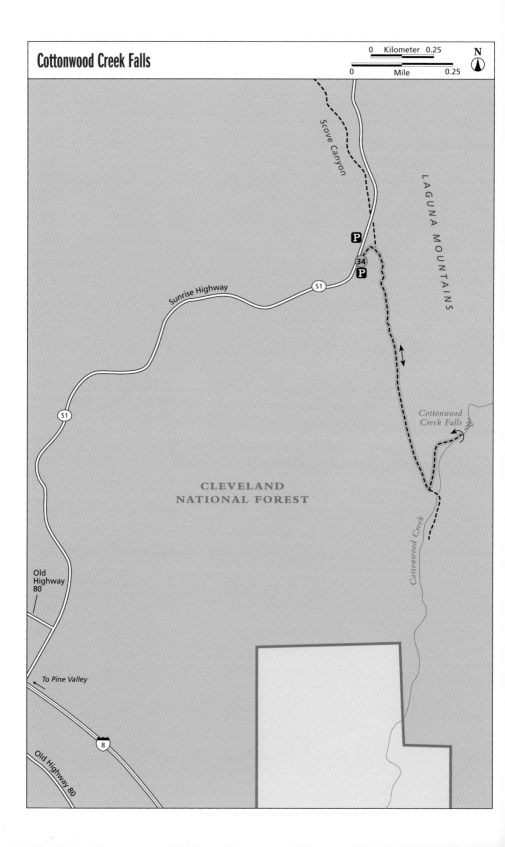

Cottonwood Creek Falls

0   Kilometer   0.25

0   Mile   0.25

N

Scove Canyon

LAGUNA MOUNTAINS

P

34

P

Sunrise Highway

S1

S1

Cottonwood
Creek Falls

CLEVELAND
NATIONAL FOREST

Cottonwood Creek

Old
Highway
80

To Pine Valley

8

Old Highway 80

The path twists around blind curves in the vegetation, which made me question whether we were on the right path or on an animal trail through a thicket. The first blind turn into the brushy tunnel felt the narrowest, but the trail corridor gets wider and more open after. On the return trip we ran into several folks headed downhill toward the falls who asked me, "Is this the trail?" They were thrilled when we told them they were right.

Continue through the brushy tunnel. At 0.4 mile the trail gets wider and rockier and follows below power lines on what looks like an old road, with views of the valley below. In 0.7 mile your path reaches an old jeep road that parallels the creek near a big tree. There's a little evidence of a January 2014 fire through here. Turn left on the jeep road, heading upstream.

As you approach the creek, you may see birds. San Diego has one of the highest numbers of different bird species in the United States, and this canyon is home to dozens of species. Continue toward the valley until you reach a T intersection. Turn left, following the trail and the creek uphill and upstream.

Continue upstream and pass several 15-foot cascades. Depending on water level it may be difficult to get to the higher cascades. The upper falls have a pool underneath, home to Pacific chorus frogs. Use caution around slippery rocks and slabs, and watch out for cacti!

Miles and Directions

0.0 Start at the parking lot.

0.7 Reach Cottonwood creek and turn left on an old jeep road.

1.0 Pass numerous cascades. Return the way you came.

2.0 Arrive back at the trailhead.

35 Kitchen Creek Falls

Only 0.2 mile from the Pacific Crest Trail (PCT), this massive hidden falls seems out of place in the desert not far from the Mexican border. With expansive views of the Pine Valley and falls tumbling over polished granite above, when it flows in early spring, Kitchen Creek Falls is well worth the side trip.

Height: Around 150 feet
Beauty rating: ★★★★
Distance: 5.2 miles out and back
Elevation gain: 500 feet
Difficulty: Moderate
Best season: Winter, spring
County: San Diego
Trailhead amenities: 30+ parking spots, out-houses, potable water faucets, campground
Land status: Cleveland National Forest

Maps: Halfmile free PCT maps for Section A, www.pctmap.net/maps/; USGS Cameron Corner
Trail contact: Cleveland National Forest, Descanso Ranger District, 3348 Alpine Blvd., Alpine 91901; (619) 445-6235; www.fs.usda .gov/main/cleveland/home
Fees and permits: Signs at the campground indicate a day-use fee, which may be covered by an Adventure Pass. Check with the camp host or park outside the campground along the road.

Finding the trailhead: Google Maps: Boulder Oaks Campground. (*Do not* use the Google Maps directions for Kitchen Creek Falls.) From I-8 east, take exit 54. Turn right on Kitchen Creek Road for 2.6 miles. Turn right on Old Highway 80, following it to the campground. A sign shows PCT parking in the lot to the left from the entrance.
GPS: N32 43.468' / W116 28.571'

The Hike

One of the largest falls in San Diego County, Kitchen Creek Falls are 0.2 mile from the Pacific Crest Trail, but hidden from many who hike the famous trail. Because almost the entire hike to the falls is along the PCT, the quality of trail tends to be pristine—well-signed, moderate, and free of brush. But the last 0.2 mile can be confusing, especially the intersection to turn left off the PCT.

From the parking lot it's a maze of campground loop roads to get to the PCT on the other side of Old Highway 80. The PCT follows the fenceline/road on the campground side of the road. If you can't find it, follow the road east until you see giant PCT markers indicating where the trail crosses. Watch for snakes here—on one visit we saw a fat rattler hidden in the grass inches from the trail. On subsequent trips we've opted to walk the road. After 0.2 mile, cross the paved road toward the giant PCT signs.

While walking along Old Highway 80, across from the "Rural Bus" sign, there's a tree and a large rock with Native American *morteros* (grinding holes) used for seeds, pods, and nuts. Enjoy but please respect this artifact.

Kitchen Creek Falls is dry in the summer and autumn, but leaves hints of its size and impressive height.

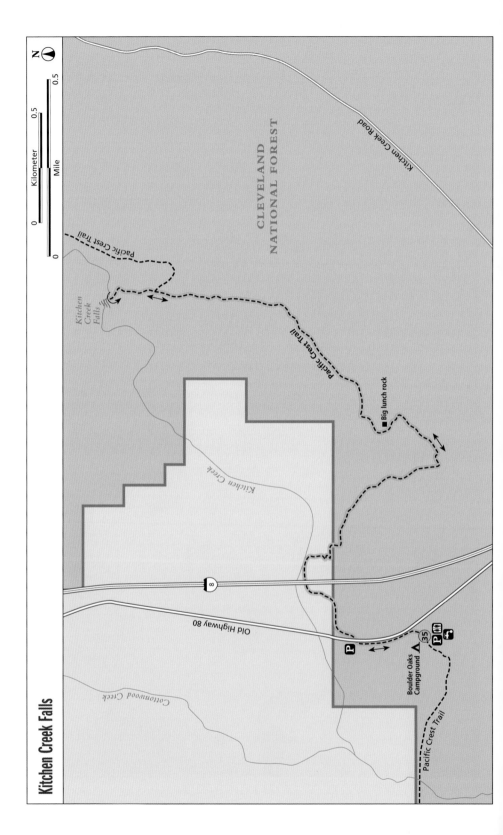

Kitchen Creek Falls

CLEVELAND NATIONAL FOREST

Kitchen Creek Road

Pacific Crest Trail

Kitchen Creek Falls

Pacific Crest Trail

Big lunch rock

Kitchen Creek

Old Highway 80

Cottonwood Creek

Boulder Oaks Campground

Pacific Crest Trail

N

Kilometer
0   0.5

Mile
0   0.5

Follow the PCT "northbound" (it heads northeast here). In another 0.2 mile, reach a sign asking you to please close the gate. In another 0.1 mile you cross under I-8, which you drove to reach the trailhead. The trail switchbacks up to another gate.

Traverse the edge of a hillside, climbing up a small canyon. Shade is limited here, unless the sun happens to be hidden behind the hillside. The PCT climbs and becomes steeper, though to accommodate horses and other users, the trail never goes above a 10 percent grade.

At 1.4 miles the trail switchbacks to the right around a large lunch rock—a giant slab on the right as you are climbing up. There are several flat camps.

At 2.4 miles from your car, notice the trail making a turn toward the right. Two carbonites (thin, plasticky looking "poles") about 15 feet apart indicate the PCT turns to the right here. This is your junction to Kitchen Creek Falls. Turn left on a faint use trail into the brush. You can see tent spots near this use trail. The trail then heads downhill.

At 0.15 mile from the PCT, the use trail has a junction to turn left, which puts you at the top of the falls. There are numerous steep, rocky, bouldery use trails to approach the falls. Use extreme caution as the rock here is quite smooth and slick when wet. I lost a pair of sunglasses when they tumbled from my head as I looked down toward the falls. The scramble down looked technical enough that I opted to let them go.

Miles and Directions

0.0 Start at trailhead at Boulder Creek Campground.
0.2 Cross paved Old Highway 80.
0.4 Gate.
0.5 Cross under I-8.
1.4 Lunch rock.
2.4 Take use trail to the left.
2.6 Reach the creek near the falls. Return the way you came.
5.2 Arrive back at the trailhead.

San Bernardino National Forest

S an Bernardino National Forest may be the most diverse in the country, encompassing San Gorgonio at 11,503 feet down to the upper stretches of the Santa Anita River. The national forest includes parts of the San Gabriel, San Bernardino, San Jacinto, and northern Santa Rosa Mountains as well as the Sand to Snow National Monument. With the help of the Wildlands Conservancy, which purchased the last private inholdings surrounded by forest, the 154,000-acre monument creates a wildlife corridor from the desert to the mountains.

These mountains were home to the Serrano and Cahuilla people. The Pervetum people lived near what is now Big Bear and the Kaiwiem near Lake Arrowhead. These were the first people to create a trail system here, which was used as a trade route. From 1851 to 1857 these mountains were logged to build the city of San Bernardino, then a Mormon outpost. Mill Creek, which you'll see on the Big Falls hike, gets its name from that history.

Geologically, faults separate the San Bernardino Range from the rest of the Transverse Ranges.

Those seeking further falls in this area will delight at the small cascades off Whitewater Creek near the Whitewater Preserve, a worthy hike regardless of the height of the falls. Additionally, Deep Creek has numerous falls best accessed by a four-wheel-drive vehicle and/or canyoneering equipment and rock climbing moves. Other falls in these mountains have been closed to protect the last remaining habitat of the arroyo toad. Please respect this endangered creature.

San Bernardino National Forest requires you to display an Adventure Pass at select trailheads. See How to Use This Guide for more details.

36 Etiwanda Falls

This easy-to-access, easy-to-follow frontcountry trail in the Inland Empire climbs through dry chaparral to a narrow, riparian canyon filled with alders.

Height: 3 tiers, ranging about 10–25 feet
Beauty rating: ★★★
Distance: 3.4 miles out and back
Elevation gain: 800 feet one-way
Difficulty: Easy
Best season: Spring, fall
County: San Bernardino
Trailhead amenities: Parking lot for 40+ cars. Do not park on the street; numerous signs say you'll be ticketed or towed. Port-o-potty. No dogs allowed.

Land status: North Etiwanda Preserve, San Bernardino National Forest; Loop Trail is on the North Etiwanda Preserve managed by San Bernardino County Special Districts
Maps: Tom Harrison Angeles High Country; USGS Cucamonga Peak
Trail contact: San Bernardino County Special Districts Department, 222 W. Hospitality Ln., 2nd floor, San Bernardino 92415; (909) 386-8800; http://web.sbcnep.org/index .aspx?page=192
Fees and permits: None

Finding the trailhead: Google Maps: Etiwanda Falls Parking Lot. From I-210 east, take exit 61, Day Creek Road, and head north into Rancho Cucamonga for 2.1 miles. Turn left onto Etiwanda Avenue for 0.4 mile. The road ends at the trailhead parking lot. Gate is open 6:30 a.m. to 6 p.m. in winter and 6:30 a.m. to 8 p.m. in summer.
GPS: N34 09.563' / W117 31.239'

The Hike

This free, easy-to-access frontcountry park in the foothills near Rancho Cucamonga is a great place for a workout or for San Gabriel foothills time. Although this area once had a reputation for graffiti and litter, the city has cleaned it up and created a destination that attracts folks from around the Southland.

It's possible to turn this hike into a much longer loop by connecting trails in the Etiwanda Preserve (of which the direct route only skirts its edge). In particular, the historical and ecological interpretive signs in the preserve gave me such an appreciation for what makes this area special. Believe it or not, there's a bog here among the dry chaparral. The trail crosses a robust metal bridge over a narrow chasm that can flash flood after a storm. It leads to the ruins of an early settler's cabin from the nineteenth century. You'll learn how the Chaffey brothers' home was among the first in the nation to be powered by hydroelectricity. You'll learn of the Tongva and Serrano native people who called the area their home prior to being unwillingly brought to Mission San Gabriel, founded in 1771.

But those exciting twists are along the loop route. Here we describe the fastest out and back to the falls. You might have cell reception for almost the whole hike

The left side canyon above Etiwanda Falls is home to another fall.

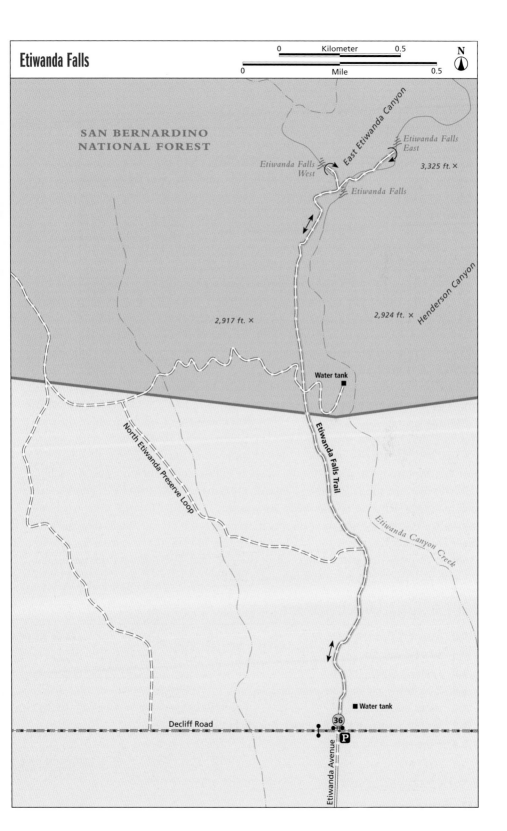

Etiwanda Falls

0   Kilometer   0.5

0   Mile   0.5

N

SAN BERNARDINO
NATIONAL FOREST

East Etiwanda Canyon

Etiwanda Falls
East

Etiwanda Falls
West

3,325 ft. ×

Etiwanda Falls

Henderson Canyon

2,917 ft. ×

2,924 ft. ×

Water tank

Etiwanda Falls Trail

North Etiwanda Preserve Loop

Etiwanda Canyon Creek

Water tank

36

Decliff Road

P

Etiwanda Avenue

and are almost always within view of the city, so we encourage you to explore the area as long as you have energy.

Like much of the San Gabriel foothills, it can get quite hot in the unshaded chaparral. Start early, bring plenty of water, and wear sun protection.

Start at the large, official dirt parking lot near the sign for the Etiwanda Preserve. There are two gates here. One path goes to the north toward the mountains and one to the west following under power lines (the end of the loop). Take the path heading north toward the mountains. You'll have great views of the San Gabriels and of the East Etiwanda Canyon, which you'll ascend into. On a clear day you can see San Gorgonio to the east.

At 0.5 mile in, reach a junction and take the right fork through a usually open gate. (The left fork loops around to meet back up with the main route and can connect to the Etiwanda Preserve, but adds more distance.)

If you stay on the main route, in another 0.5 mile you can see a trail join from the left. That's the other trail rejoining the main trail. From that junction, keep straight and heading north, deeper into the canyon as the vegetation changes. It'll start to feel like you're in the mountains instead of the floodplains. As you approach Day Creek, signs warn you that use trails are not, in fact, the trail. Stay on the main path, which is a wide, dirt fire road impossible to miss.

The last 0.5 mile can be steep as it twists up the dirt road. Pass a concrete water unit. The first 10-foot falls tumbles over a slab of rocks into a pool. Below it, another 15-foot falls drops into another pool, though it's not easy to see from where the trail spits you out. The rock slab to the viewing points can be slippery.

Stay here for a picnic. Maybe set up a hammock in the shady forest of alders. Or you can explore upstream of the two creeks whose confluence is right above the first falls. We like the falls on the creek to the left (northwest) better. There's a use trail along the left side of the creek (as you head uphill). After 0.1 mile, reach an impressive 10- to 15-foot falls that's much easier to see in its full height than the first (main) waterfall. But while the US Forest Service and volunteers have been able to clean up most of the graffiti and trash of the past from the area near the main falls, the obscure falls to the left could use some love.

Miles and Directions

0.0 Start at the parking lot.

0.5 Take the right fork.

1.0 Continue straight (north).

1.5 Pass a steel and concrete water transport unit.

1.6 Reach the first falls.

1.7 Reach the leftmost falls. Return the way you came.

3.4 Arrive back at the trailhead.

37 Bonita Falls

This is a short, kid-friendly, easy-to-access hike to the second-tallest falls in the San Bernardino National Forest. Bonita Falls shines as a natural splendor, despite the graffiti humans have left behind along the way. Consider bringing along a trash bag.

Height: Up to 400 feet over multiple tiers (not all visible)
Beauty rating: ★★ (if you can look past the graffiti)
Distance: 2 miles out and back
Elevation gain: 250 feet gain one-way
Difficulty: Easy; moderate navigation
Best season: Fall, spring, summer
County: San Bernardino
Trailhead amenities: 50+ parking spots, plus more along the side of road into parking area

(watch for No Parking signs); dogs on-leash allowed
Land status: San Bernardino National Forest
Maps: USGS Cucamonga Peak
Trail contact: San Bernardino National Forest (Lytle Creek Ranger Station); Front Country Ranger District, 1209 Lytle Creek Rd., Lytle Creek 92358; (909) 382-2851 (voice); www.fs.usda.gov/detail/sbnf/about-forest/districts/?cid=fsbdev7_007802
Fees and permits: As of early 2019, Adventure Pass not required

Finding the trailhead: Google Maps: Hiking Trail Bonita Falls. From I-15 North, take exit 119 for Sierra Avenue. Turn left and drive Lytle Creek Road for 6 miles. The trailhead is on your left, after Hidden Acres but 0.1 mile before South Fork Road.
GPS: N34 14.124' / W117 29.487'

The Hike

Start at one of two dirt parking pullouts. There are two port-o-potties to mark the area (though we wouldn't recommend going in unless you are desperate).

From the northern lot, take a use trail or scramble down the embankment toward two graffitied picnic tables. A use trail leads to a crossing over the South Fork of Lytle Creek. This can be knee-deep or more and swift in the winter and spring. Bring poles and be prepared to turn around and visit another day.

Once you've crossed, enter the wide, flat floodplain along the South Fork, headed toward the mountains to the west. It seems an unlikely place to find a falls—a narrower canyon behind the Hidden Acres private ranch nearby to the west looks more likely. Nonetheless, head toward the open floodplain following the waterway up the canyon, away from the RVs and ranches to the left (south) and right (north) side of the canyon. There are use trails through here, but those with weak ankles should know this trail is on rocky ground.

The most obvious trail hugs the left (south) side of the canyon along a graffitied rock wall. For a more scenic (but rougher route), follow the creek itself upstream close to the water. After 0.8 mile (if you've stayed on the trail along the left wall of the floodplain), reach a sign covered in graffiti. From here, the trail is well defined and climbs steeply on dirt and roots into a canyon on the left.

The canyon narrows and follows a narrow creek that feeds the South Fork. You pass a 15-foot cascade, but keep climbing. After 0.2 mile of ascending on the trail along the creek, there's a tall falls at the back of a deep, cliffy grotto.

Bonita Falls shines as one of the finest natural splendors in the area, despite the graffiti along the route. While it would be prettier without graffiti, it's still worth visiting. It's important that hikers—especially kids—see what humans can do to nature. While the impact can evoke sadness, disappointment, and even grief, it's an

Bonita Falls is the second tallest waterfall in San Bernardino National Forest. It's beautiful, despite the human impact that comes from being so close to a road.

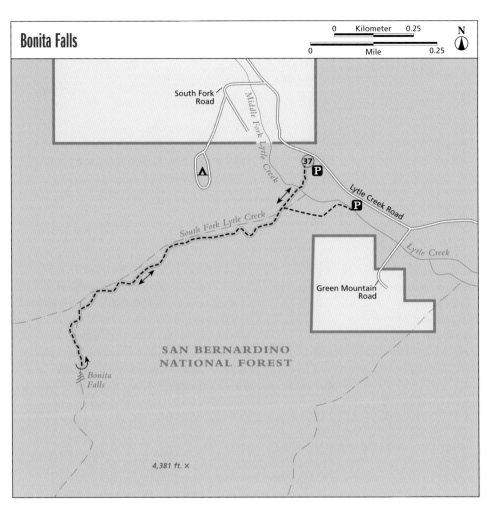

Bonita Falls

opportunity to spark discussion about how to protect and preserve natural places and support the work of agencies and nonprofits that care for public land.

Miles and Directions

0.0 Start at northern parking lot.

0.5 Enter canyon on left near a graffiti-covered sign.

1.0 Base of Bonita Falls. Return the way you came.

2.0 Arrive back at the trailhead.

38 Middle Fork of Lytle Creek Falls (Third Crossing Falls)

You'll need a wilderness permit for day hiking and a high-clearance vehicle to get here, but this rugged off-trail wilderness hike takes you to an incredible Sierra-like falls.

Height: At least 3 tiers (visible from this hike)—upper tier about 80 feet, middle tier about 80 feet, and bottom tier 100 feet

Beauty rating: ★★★★★

Distance: 5 miles out and back (more if you do not have access to a high-clearance vehicle and need to walk to the trailhead)

Elevation gain: 1,260 feet gain/65 feet loss

Difficulty: Moderate to strenuous physically; difficult navigation

Best season: Spring

County: San Bernardino

Trailhead amenities: 30 parking spots, picnic table, clean outhouse (lower lot has 50+ spots but requires a 2.2-mile hike to the official trailhead)

Land status: San Bernardino National Forest, Cucamonga Wilderness

Maps: Tom Harrison Angeles High Country; USGS Cucamonga Peak

Trail contact: San Bernardino National Forest (Lytle Creek Ranger Station); Front Country Ranger District, 1209 Lytle Creek Rd., Lytle Creek 92358; (909) 382-2851 (voice); www.fs.usda.gov/detail/sbnf/about-forest/districts/?cid=fsbdev7_007802

Fees and permits: Wilderness permit required to enter Cucamonga Wilderness, subject to quota. Call ranger station ahead for availability, or stop by on the drive there (check ranger station hours ahead of time—currently, they are closed on Tues and Wed). Display Adventure Pass when parked.

Finding the trailhead: Google Maps: Middle Fork Trail 6W01. From I-15 North, take exit 119 for Sierra Avenue. It turns into Lytle Creek Road, which you'll take for 6.1 miles into the town of Scotland. Turn left onto Middle Fork Road, which becomes unpaved shortly after. Take it for 2.8 miles up a rough dirt road. Those with low-clearance vehicles may consider parking 0.7 mile or 1 mile up the road and walking the rest of the way in.
GPS: N34 15.132' / W117 32.249'

The Hike

The stakes to get to this falls are high: a wilderness permit (even for day hiking), a high-clearance vehicle, navigation skills, and experience and physical ability to cross rugged terrain. If you feel up to it, Third Crossing Falls (aka Middle Fork of Lytle Creek Falls) is well worth the visit. Permit quotas fill up, especially for the backpacking campsites, so reserve in advance before attempting this hike.

There's good reason this area is so protected. The Middle Fork has been identified by the US Forest Service as an Area of Significance, with the watershed itself

Hidden in a north-facing canyon, the off-trail route to Third Crossing Falls can hold snow and icicles even when the rest of the canyon is warm.

identified as eligible for National Wild and Scenic protection due to (among other things) a naturally reproducing rainbow trout population. This canyon is also home to the endangered Nelson's bighorn sheep. John Robinson, the late iconic Southern California guidebook author, wrote that it's "one of few islands of subalpine wilderness left in Southern California."

The falls are on a tributary leading into the Middle Fork of Lytle Creek—not on Lytle Creek itself. The trail follows the Middle Fork for most of its length until you break away at the Third Crossing Camp, often occupied by Boy Scouts for backpacking trips. The Third Crossing refers to a historic third crossing of the Middle Fork on an old path that no longer exists. For your trip you only cross the Middle Fork once (well, twice if counting on the way back). However, you have to cross the tributary several times to reach the falls.

From the trailhead sign, head on the trail past interpretive signs. The trail switchbacks up on a wide, rocky tread. It's sunny and exposed, high on the north slope above the Middle Fork. Climb through manzanita, buckhorn, chemise, and Spanish bayonet yucca.

At 0.6 mile, reach a metal post with yellow paint at the top. Turn right up the switchback and uphill, ignoring a trail going downhill toward Stonehouse Camp. You get rare views of the Cucamonga Wilderness from the less crowded backside. If visiting in winter or early spring, there may be snow high on the shady north slope of the canyon across the creek.

At 1.1 miles the trail crosses a rocky, washed-out, wide tributary. The trail here can be rocky for about 50 feet, but there are two metal poles with yellow paint on the tips located on either side of the almost always dry tributary. If you're having trouble finding the trail, it contours the slope at the same elevation as what you were at before the washout.

At the next metal post you see, 1.35 miles in, there's a junction with a trail curling back to the Stonehouse Camp. Stay high on the right trail, continuing in the same direction you were heading. The trail is closer to the creek now. You may see an old trail going down to the water. Continue through bigcone Douglas firs as the trail becomes more shaded. At 1.45 miles enter the Cucamonga Wilderness, passing a wooden wilderness sign.

At 1.7 miles the trail again crosses a tributary before switchbacking higher. Pass a beautiful cedar grove fed by a spring above the trail. After the grove, across the creek, you may see the opening of the narrow canyon that is home to the falls.

At 1.9 miles, reach a metal post with a yellow tip right before the trail crosses the Middle Fork of Lytle Creek. Cross here (or anywhere safe) before following the Middle Fork back downstream. Remnants of use trails head off-trail and downstream. Traveling right next to the creek can be rough going. It's easier walking above the washed-out bank in the forested area. At 2.05 miles, look to your right (north) to see a narrow canyon with a creek feeding into the Middle Fork.

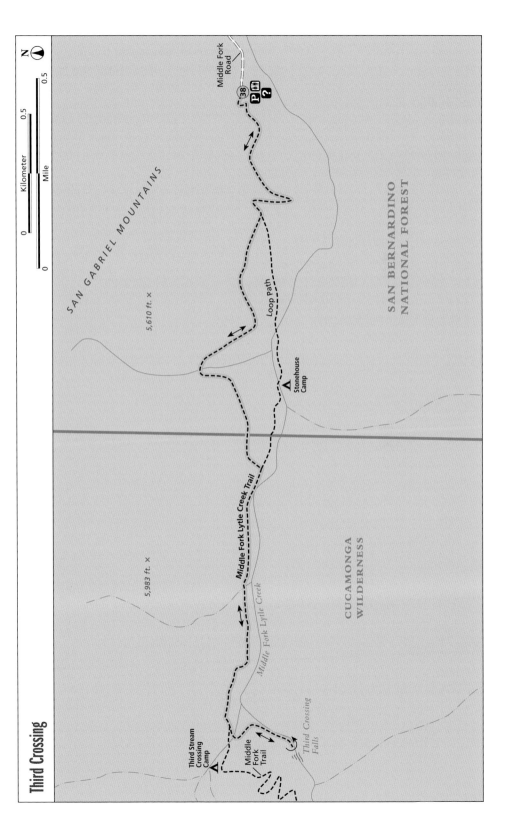

Third Crossing

N

Kilometer
0   0.5

Mile
0   0.5

SAN GABRIEL MOUNTAINS

5,610 ft. ×

5,983 ft. ×

Middle Fork Road

Loop Path

Middle Fork Lytle Creek Trail

Stonehouse Camp

SAN BERNARDINO NATIONAL FOREST

Middle Fork Lytle Creek

CUCAMONGA WILDERNESS

Third Stream Crossing Camp

Middle Fork Trail

Third Crossing Falls

38

Enter the canyon. For the next 0.2 mile, you scramble on slippery slab rock. The canyon is so narrow it's shaded, holding snow, ice, and icicles after everything else has melted. Watch for ice on slippery rock. About halfway through, the canyon narrows enough that you'll need to climb up and around a large cascade with a striking green pool below (this is a fine place to end your hike). There's nothing technical required to reach the base of the lower falls. However, it's much easier in low water. Depending on conditions, you may need to cross back and forth over the creek, though even in spring it may be possible to rock-hop across.

End at a narrow grotto below a three-tiered falls with a deep, green pool below. This canyon and falls are pristine. Please do everything you can to keep it this way.

Miles and Directions

0.0 Start at the trailhead and parking lot.

0.6 Reach yellow post at junction to Stonehouse Camp; switchback right uphill.

1.35 Stonehouse Trail joins from switchback on left.

1.45 Enter Cucamonga Wilderness.

1.9 Third stream crossing.

2.05 Enter canyon.

2.25 Base of falls. Return the way you came.

4.5 Arrive back at the trailhead.

39 Heart Rock Falls

Leading to a unique geologic "heart-shaped" rock feature, Heart Falls is one of the most unique falls in the Southland. This pleasant, family-friendly hike through a shaded forest is well worth multiple visits.

Height: 25–30 feet
Beauty rating: ★★★★★
Distance: 1 mile out and back
Elevation gain: 200 feet on the return
Difficulty: Easy
Best season: Fall, winter, spring, summer (may not flow, but is a nice hike anyway)
County: San Bernardino
Trailhead amenities: 10 parking spots, plus more along the side of road into parking area

(watch for No Parking signs); dogs on-leash allowed
Land status: San Bernardino National Forest
Maps: USGS Silverwood Lake
Trail contact: San Bernardino National Forest, Big Bear Discovery Center, 40971 North Shore Dr., CA 38, Fawnskin 92333; (909) 382-2790 (voice); www.fs.usda.gov/detail/sbnf/about-forest/districts/?cid=fsbdev7_007796
Fees and permits: Display Adventure Pass

Finding the trailhead: Google Maps: Camp Seely. From I-10, take exit 73B, Waterman Avenue. Or, from CA 210 east, take exit 76B to Waterman Avenue. Both turn into Rim of the World Scenic Byway (CA 18). Climb through the mountains for 11.5 miles and turn onto CA 138 north for 1.2 miles to a stop sign in Crestline. Go straight for 1.5 miles to turn left at the Camp Seely Road (4WO7) near mile marker 138 SBD 35.00. Follow signs for the trail, and be respectful of Camp Seely and private property along the way.

There are about 10 parking spots at the trailhead, so you may need to park along CA 138 and walk the 0.3 mile on the narrow, paved road to the trailhead. This adds 0.6 mile round-trip to your hike. There's no cell reception at the trailhead, so pay attention to driving directions on your way in. **GPS:** N34 15.196' / W117 18.204'

The Hike

Photos don't do this hike justice. In images, the rock heart looks tiny, like it's only 1 foot long, but in real life it's more than 5 feet across.

Starting at the small parking lot, follow trail signs (not the gates road) to the back of Camp Seely on a wide, shady trail. Camp Seely and the creek you're following are named after David and Wellington Seeley (different than how it's spelled on some maps), who owned a sawmill in the 1850s to help build the Mormon outpost town of San Bernardino.

Travel above the left bank of the creek as you follow it downstream. As you leave the view of the camp and a pipe near there, you can feel the denseness of this forest. The trail is soft on your feet.

About 0.5 mile from the parking lot, reach an unmarked junction to a small side trail to the right. Reach a viewpoint for the falls. Stone "stairs" descend toward the

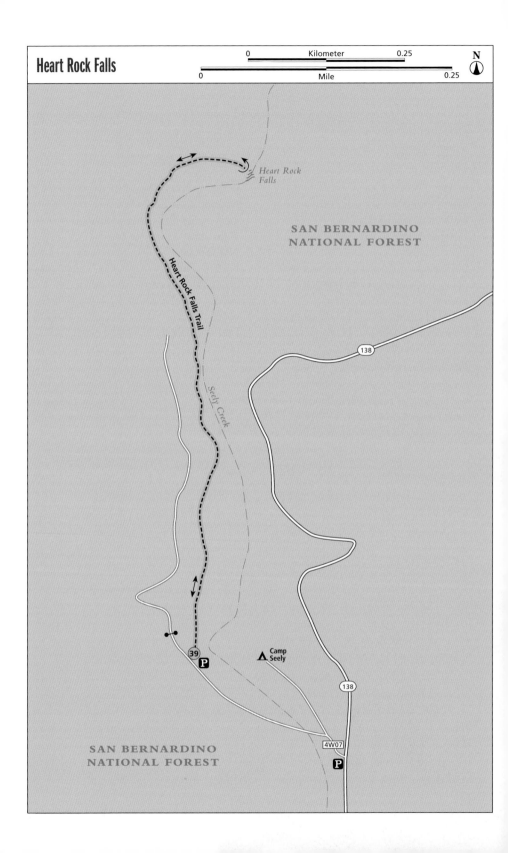

0   Kilometer   0.25

0   Mile   0.25

N

SAN BERNARDINO
NATIONAL FOREST

Heart Rock
Falls

Heart Rock Falls Trail

Seely Creek

138

39

P

Camp
Seely

138

4W07

P

SAN BERNARDINO
NATIONAL FOREST

water, though they aren't as obvious as you would think. This trail tends to attract people, so if you have trouble finding the falls, ask around.

From the viewpoint you can see a 20-foot-tall cascade tumbling down over a granite face. A large, prominent heart—often filled with water or even spitting out water itself—is poised to its left.

If you find yourself headed steeply downhill on dirt trail (losing about 60 feet of elevation over 150 feet), you missed the viewpoint junction and are headed to a lower cascade. This gets you close to the water to play on granite slabs, but isn't the main falls.

Miles and Directions

0.0 Start at the trailhead.

0.5 Three-way unmarked junction. Take a side trail to the right to an overview rock of the falls. Return the way you came.

1.0 Arrive back the trailhead.

This shaded, family-friendly site is a good place to take a loved one.

40 Aztec Falls

This popular (and often crowded) waterfall and swimming hole was the subject of a National Geographic Adventure article. It runs uphill for several miles along the Pacific Crest Trail (PCT) from the famous Deep Creek Hot Springs.

Height: 10–20 feet tall
Beauty rating: ★★★
Distance: 1.2 miles out and back
Elevation gain: 325 feet descent/200 feet ascent (one-way)
Difficulty: Easy to moderate (steep moderate scrambling at very end)
Best season: Spring, fall
County: San Bernardino
Trailhead amenities: Parking lot with about 30 spots, privy, shaded picnic area, trash/recycle bins

Land status: San Bernardino National Forest
Maps: USGS Lake Arrowhead, Butler Peak, Halfmile free PCT maps for Section C, www .pctmap.net/maps/
Trail contact: San Bernardino National Forest, Big Bear Discovery Center, 40971 North Shore Dr., CA 38, Fawnskin 92333; (909) 382-2790 (voice); www.fs.usda.gov/detail/sbnf/about-forest/districts/?cid=fsbdev7_007796
Fees and permits: Display Adventure Pass

Finding the trailhead: Google Maps: Splinters Cabin Day Use Area. The US Forest Service closes the gated road when there is snow. It's often closed throughout the winter and too hot in the summer. From Lake Arrowhead Village, drive east on Hook Creek Road through the village of Cedar Glen for 2.3 miles to a gate on FR 2N26Y. The road turns into a one-lane road. Continue on this road until you reach a signed U-shaped intersection with FR 3N34. Head left for 0.2 mile, crossing a creek before turning right at FR 3N34C, following signs for Splinters Cabin. Continue for 0.4 mile on a narrow but two-wheel-drive-manageable road (you may need to cross the creek). This trailhead is known for vandalism, so remove valuables from your car.
GPS: N34 16.210' / W117 07.448'

The Hike

The Forest Service takes great efforts to maintain this popular swimming hole and waterfall by removing graffiti and trash to keep it a pristine and fun place to visit. As a guidebook reader, chances are you are far more responsible than many Aztec Falls weekend visitors. As such, we ask when you visit, please consider bringing along an extra trash bag (and maybe a set of gloves) to make this place better for the next visitor. The parking lot has been known for vandalism.

Start at the Splinters Cabin parking lot on a well-defined trail—with the knowledge it won't always be nice trail. A set of hiking poles comes in handy at the end. Although we're headed to a waterfall, it can get very hot during the summer, which is why we advise doing this hike in the spring or fall. Don't worry: Even in December we found it to be plenty hot for swimming.

Follow signs for the PCT. About 500 feet in, you ford a small creek. Here there are two well-defined trails up to the PCT, depending on water levels. After 0.25 mile you reach the expansive Deep Creek high bridge. There are numerous signs and markers here for the PCT.

Do not cross the bridge. Instead, continue to follow the PCT north on the same slope you've been walking, contouring the mountainside high above Deep Creek. Like most of the PCT, it is well graded and well defined. However, watch your step, as the drop-off on the right side can at times feel exposed. Farther up the trail, at least one noted PCT hiker has fallen off and perished.

Follow the PCT for 0.5 mile from the trailhead. Keep your eyes peeled for a white spray-painted arrow on a boulder on the left side of the trail. It appears as the trail makes a minor turn toward the left. When we scouted here in December 2018, there was webbing tied to a tree on the right side of the trail. Avoid the use trail you see here: The wide, steep, and rooty social trail goes down toward Deep Creek way above the falls. We learned the hard way this path goes too far upstream to get a great view of the waterfall or to safely access the swimming hole.

Instead, stay on the PCT for about 50 more feet. Here you find a less obvious use trail contouring below the PCT for about 50 feet before switching back. Like many of the use trails to waterfalls, this "trail" is quite steep and loose and isn't recommended for small children, dogs, or those uncomfortable on uneven ground.

After descending about 200 vertical feet in almost as many horizontal feet, you're at the base of the waterfall and its swimming pool–sized plunge pool. The falls itself is 30 feet tall and nestled between rock walls.

Aztec Falls has multiple deep swimming holes and can attract a party crowd on warm days.

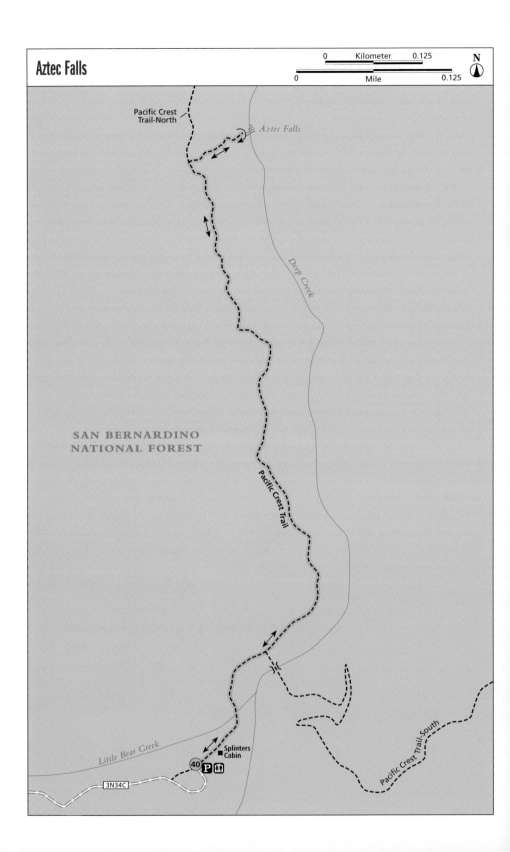

Aztec Falls

0   Kilometer   0.125

0   Mile   0.125

N

Pacific Crest
Trail-North

Aztec Falls

Deep Creek

SAN BERNARDINO
NATIONAL FOREST

Pacific Crest Trail

Little Bear Creek

Splinters
Cabin

Pacific Crest Trail-South

40 P

3N34C

There's cascades several miles upstream on Deep Creek, but the effort to get there is much tougher on vehicles and hikers than to reach Aztec Falls. LIZ THOMAS

Miles and Directions

0.0 Start at the parking lot.

0.1 Cross a creek.

0.25 Reach the PCT at one end of footbridge.

0.5 Descend off the PCT on a use trail.

0.6 Base of falls. Return the way you came.

1.2 Arrive back at the trailhead.

41 Cold Creek Falls

This easily accessible, family-friendly falls isn't a showstopper, but is a pleasant walk on an impossible-to-get-lost-on, well-graded, closed or low-traffic dirt road. It's nice to visit in the snow during the winter when the road is closed. Kids can throw snowballs on the way down and experience their first winter mountain hike in a safe environment.

Height: About 25-30 feet
Beauty rating: ★★★
Distance: 1 mile out and back
Elevation gain: 125 feet
Difficulty: Easy
Best season: Fall, winter, spring, summer
County: San Bernardino
Trailhead amenities: About 100 parking spots, dog-friendly (if there's no traffic)

Land status: San Bernardino National Forest
Maps: Shows up on Google Maps as a road
Trail contact: San Bernardino National Forest, Mill Creek Visitor Center, 34701 Mill Creek Rd., Mentone 92359; (909) 382-2882 (voice); www.fs.usda.gov/main/sbnf/home
Fees and permits: As of early 2019, Adventure Pass not required

Finding the trailhead: Google Maps: Between Angelus Oaks Lodge and Cold Creek Falls. About 0.1 mile up the road from the Angelus Oaks Lodge, park at a closed road on the right or in a big paved pullout on the left. During the winter these areas are used for putting chains onto cars before they head farther up the mountain pass.
GPS: N34 09.024' / W116 58.317'

The Hike

This hike is suitable for people who want a short, easy, well-graded trail to a waterfall where you can't get lost. This hike in cool mountain air outside the boundary of Sand to Snow National Monument is a good place to stretch your legs while on a mountain drive.

From the end of the paved parking lot about 100 yards east on CA 38 from the Angelus Oaks Lodge, look for a dirt road on your left. It's closed in the winter and receives little traffic during the summer, though it goes down to the town of Pine-zanita. A street sign marks the intersection as State Highway 38 and Middle Control Road. However, Google and other mapping services refer to the road as Mill Creek Road (carriers get service here, so you can use an app to verify you're in the right spot). Head downhill on the wide road. The drop-off to your left is steep, but the road is wide, so you have nothing to worry about.

Continue down the road for 0.5 mile past incense cedar and oaks. You have views of the valley below and the mountains across. The farther downhill you go, the taller

Cold Creek Falls is a short, easy hike to a small fall that's pretty in winter and spring.

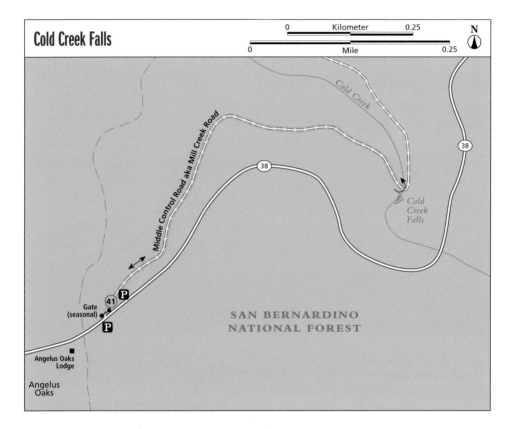

Cold Creek

38

38

Cold Creek Falls

41

Gate (seasonal)

Angelus Oaks Lodge

Angelus Oaks

SAN BERNARDINO NATIONAL FOREST

the hillside on your right appears. Near the waterfall they become tall granite walls soaring on the right.

When the road makes a hairpin turn—almost a U, you hear the water from the falls, which is to your right, dropping about 25 feet down a rock face. Your view may be blocked by a rock until you are right at the U. There's a reflective street marker with the number "2" on it right at this bend. The water from the creek goes under the road through a pipe, so you may not immediately see the water, but you can hear it. Look for a slight pullout at the U where you can get a better view of the falls.

Miles and Directions

0.0 Start at the intersection with CA 38 and Middle Control Road.

0.5 Base of the falls. Return the way you came.

1.0 Arrive back at the trailhead.

42 Big Falls

With Sierra-like views and fewer crowds, this three-tiered waterfall is the tallest in San Bernardino County—and likely in all of non-Sierra Southern California. It runs year-round (though it's harder to access in winter). It makes for a cooler-temperature hike during the summer.

Height: Main tier 150–200 feet; up to 500 feet total with all tiers
Beauty rating: ★★★★★
Distance: 0.8 mile out and back with option to add a scramble
Elevation gain: 160 feet gain/100 feet loss (more if you take the use trail)
Difficulty: Easy to viewpoint; more difficult scrambling after
Best season: Late spring, summer
County: San Bernardino

Trailhead amenities: Parking lot with about 50 spots, ranger at kiosk to enter parking lot during summer weekends, privy, shaded picnic area, trash/recycle bins
Land status: San Bernardino National Forest
Maps: Tom Harrison San Gorgonio Wilderness; USGS Forest Falls
Trail contact: San Bernardino National Forest, Mill Creek Visitor Center, 34701 Mill Creek Rd., Mentone 92359; (909) 382-2882 (voice); www.fs.usda.gov/main/sbnf/home
Fees and permits: Display Adventure Pass

Finding the trailhead: Google Maps: Big Falls Trailhead 1E13. From Redlands, take CA 38. From downtown Falls Creek, continue straight for 0.1 mile and make a slight right to stay on Valley of the Falls Road (do not go straight toward Hemlock Avenue). After 0.9 mile, reach a ranger kiosk/fee station run by the San Gorgonio Wilderness Association at the end of the road. **GPS:** N34 04.552' / W116 53.368'

The Hike

Note: At various times, the US Forest Service has opened or closed the 0.3-mile path to the Big Falls Overlook. Check with rangers to determine current conditions.

The well-signed trailhead starts at the north end of the parking lot. Follow signs for the waterfall downstream along Mill Creek. Mill Creek's headwaters are on the slopes of San Gorgonio (11,503 feet), and it travels to meet the Santa Ana River, eventually reaching San Bernardino, Riverside, and Orange Counties, then reaching the ocean near Huntington Beach.

The trail follows the western bank of Mill Creek, which is sandy and rock-lined. You pass a house on the left. About 0.2 mile in, ford Mill Creek. It's usually a rock-hop, but flash floods and landslides are common in Mill Creek, so only attempt this hike during good weather well after a storm.

After the ford the trail splits. A use trail goes straight toward a small cascade. This makes a good destination for those with children or who want a shorter hike.

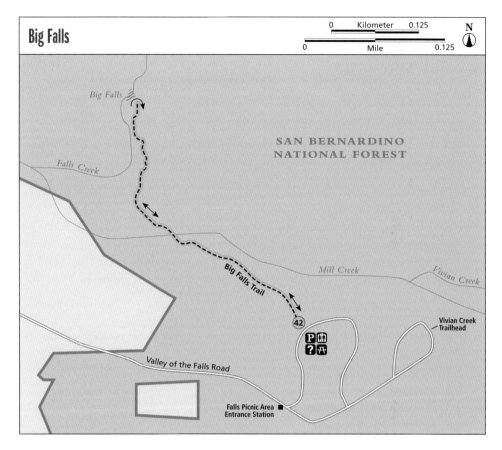

Otherwise, turn right at the sign, climbing through shady oaks and cedars, and follow Falls Creek into a shady canyon with nice sitting spots near the water. At 0.3 mile the trail becomes steep and you reach a gated viewing platform. The end of the gate has fallen off, so use caution. This is a good place to see the waterfall.

For the more adventurous it's possible to scramble to the second falls. The area is occasionally closed if there is flooding or a landslide, so check with rangers first. There is a "Closed" sign when the area is off-limits. To reach the second waterfall, follow a use trail toward the creek right *before* the gated platform. The use trail is steep, loose, and requires scrambling and climbing through rocks. It should only be attempted by competent scramblers during good weather long after a storm.

The Valley of the Falls Search and Rescue Team was founded in 1958 after a 13-year-old boy had a tragic accident at Big Falls. In 2018 an injured 15-year-old boy was rescued from the falls. Big Falls is in a narrow canyon, so helicopter rescue isn't always possible. Volunteer SAR crews instead conduct Big Falls rescues with mountain ropes skills. Proceed around Big Falls with caution.

When you count all the tiers, Big Falls is the largest fall in San Bernardino NF.
BRIAN DAVIDSON

Once at the base of the second falls, do not attempt to climb farther. A boulder at the base of the falls is named Blood Rock for a reason.

Big Falls tumbles down San Bernardino Peak into Falls Creek (sometimes referred to by the repetitive name "Falls Creek Falls").

Miles and Directions

0.0 Start at the trailhead in parking lot.

0.2 Ford Mill Creek to trail split; take trail up and right.

0.3 Gated viewing platform. (At times the area behind here is closed to visitors.)

0.4 Rough, rugged, rocky, steep, loose use trail leads to bottom of falls. Do not attempt to climb any farther. Return the way you came.

0.8 Arrive back at the trailhead.

43 Fuller Mill Creek Falls

It's a short walk to this picturesque falls set in a shady hillside. It's only accessible for four months of the year, so plan your trip accordingly.

Height: About 10–25 feet
Beauty rating: ★★★★
Distance: 0.5 mile out and back
Elevation gain: 100+ feet
Difficulty: Easy
Best season: Winter
County: Riverside
Trailhead amenities: About 10 parking spots, information kiosk

Land status: San Bernardino National Forest
Maps: Tom Harrison San Jacinto Wilderness; USGS Lake Fulmor, San Jacinto Peak
Trail contact: San Bernardino National Forest, San Jacinto Ranger District, 54270 Pine Crest, PO Box 518, Idyllwild 92549; (909) 382-2921 (voice); www.fs.usda.gov/main/sbnf/home
Fees and permits: Display Adventure Pass

Finding the trailhead: Google Maps: Fuller Mill Creek Picnic Area. From I-10 East, exit 100 Eighth Street/CA 243 for Idyllwild for 16.9 miles. The picnic area and parking is near marker 243 RIV 12.01.
GPS: N33 47.520' / W116 44.511'

The Hike

This beautiful and peaceful falls is not far from the road, but feels a world away. Set against granite boulders in a shady forest not far from a former picnic area, it is home to another endangered species—the southwest arroyo toad, one of the rarest amphibians in the world (see sidebar in the Upper Buckhorn Falls hike for more info). Found only in southern California, in recent times its favorite spawning grounds were getting trampled by human visitors to this (and other) waterfalls. To help protect what chance this species has left for survival, this trail is only open from November through February. But if the weather is warm during the winter months, these falls are worth the trip as you're driving into the mountain town of Idyllwild.

At the parking area numerous signs warn of the creek's closure to protect the arroyo toad. Read them and make sure you understand the current regulations, as closure dates and regulations can change. If you are visiting during the proper months when the creek and trail are open to visitors, carefully cross CA 243 toward the creek.

On either side of the creek, more signs warn that the area is closed during the non-winter months. If your timing is correct, proceed on the trail on the right (east) side of the bank (it's easier to follow). You hike through oak forest with pine trees. It's shady and cool in here. The trail turns into an old, wide road. At first you won't see the creek. Near a large ponderosa the area widens and you can spot the creek below. Numerous signs warn about getting close to the creek during toad season.

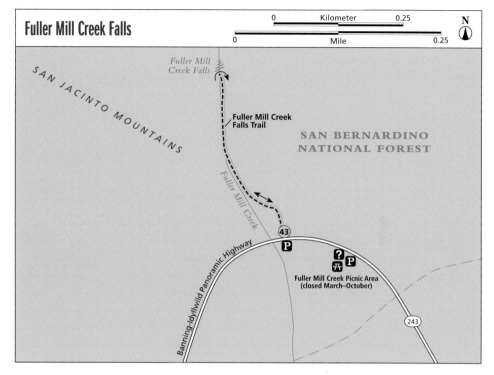

Fuller Mill Creek Falls

0 — Kilometer — 0.25

0 — Mile — 0.25

N

Fuller Mill Creek Falls

SAN JACINTO MOUNTAINS

Fuller Mill Creek Falls Trail

SAN BERNARDINO NATIONAL FOREST

Fuller Mill Creek

Banning-Idyllwild Panoramic Highway

43

P

Fuller Mill Creek Picnic Area (closed March–October)

243

After 0.15 mile the trail becomes more obscure. Though trails go up the bank to the cliff side away from the water, your best bet is to stay closer to the water (only when it isn't toad season) until you reach a 10-foot waterfall. Scramble along rocks as the creek turns a corner slightly to the right. The main 25-foot plunge is nestled in a cliff of granite boulders. It's easy to see why folks who mistakenly take one of the use trails higher on the cliff miss the falls. It's hidden in a granite alcove.

Fuller Mill Creek has National Wild and Scenic River status here before it tumbles on the other side of CA 243 into the North Fork of the San Jacinto River.

A nice sitting ledge is on the east side of the creek. It's a peaceful place, and feels like you should have to travel much farther in the backcountry for this experience. You're near the edge of Mount San Jacinto State Park, and the same cool air and alpine atmosphere is on the other side of the boundary line. Enjoy your time here and the satisfaction knowing that, for most of the year, this is a place visited only by toads.

Miles and Directions

0.0 Start in parking area.

0.1 Trailhead (open seasonally).

0.25 Base of falls. Return the way you came.

0.5 Arrive back at the parking area.

◄ *Although only accessible for a few months, Fuller Mill is worth visiting on a winter day.*
BRIAN DAVIDSON

Desert

E ncompassing parts of San Diego, Riverside, and Inyo Counties, the desert region is geologically and ecologically separate from the other regions in this book and in California. Water is found in this dry area along fault lines where subsurface water is able to rise to the surface via springs. The water supports vegetation including the California fan palm (*Washingtonia filifera*), the only palm native to the state. Plant ecologists suspect the palm is a relic of when this part of California was semi-tropical. Others think the native people who lived here cultivated the palms for food and shade. The Indian Canyons on the Agua Caliente Reservation have more native palms than any other oasis, with trees estimated to be 2,000 years old.

Three of the hikes in this section are in the Agua Caliente Band of Cahuilla Indians Reservation. There are opportunities to learn about the history and present-day life of American Indians in this region. Waterfalls and perennial streams were of particular importance to the people who lived here (and still are). The Indian Canyons Outpost and Tahquitz Visitor Center both have guided hikes and opportunities to learn from Native American rangers and guest hosts.

The Colorado and Mojave Desert areas represented in this section of the book are dry and can get hot. Borrego Springs, the closest city to Hikes 47 and 48, recorded temperatures of 122°F in June 2016. Death Valley National Park consistently beats records for hottest spot in the Lower 48. No matter how much water you carry for the other hikes in this book, when you visit the desert, always bring more. Exercise specialists suggest 1.5 liters of water for every hour you plan to be out. Others suggest 1 gallon of water no matter the distance of your hike. Start early and wear a brimmed hat, sunscreen, and loose clothing.

44 Tahquitz Canyon Falls

Unlike almost everything else in Palm Springs, this well-managed hike through a desert park-like canyon is a family-friendly tourist attraction that is actually worth your time (and entrance fee). This beautiful, educational hike is well worth a visit if you're in the area.

Height: About 50-60 feet
Beauty rating: ★★★★★
Distance: 1.7-mile loop
Elevation gain: 300 feet gain/200 feet loss
Difficulty: Easy
Best season: Winter, spring
County: Riverside
Trailhead amenities: Parking lot has about 50 spots, visitor center, restrooms, water, trash cans

Land status: Agua Caliente Band of Cahuilla Indians Reservation
Maps: Park map provided with entrance fee
Trail contact: Agua Caliente Tahquitz Visitor Center, 500 W. Mesquite Ave., Palm Springs 92264; (760) 416-7044; www.tahquitz canyon.com/canyon
Fees and permits: Entrance fees for adults and children; 6-month and annual passes available. $12.50 adults/$6 kids

Finding the trailhead: Google Maps: Agua Caliente Tahquitz Visitor Center. From Palm Springs, take Palm Canyon Drive/CA 111 and turn right onto Mesquite Avenue. Drive 0.5 mile to the Tahquitz Visitor Center. The parking lot is at the end of the road. To access the trailhead, walk through the visitor center, pay the entrance fee, and exit through the back door. Free guided tours are at 8 a.m., 10 a.m., noon, and 2 p.m.
GPS: N33 48.378' / W116 33.047'

The Hike

In a hidden canyon near Palm Springs, Tahquitz Canyon Falls is home to a dark legend.

Tahquitz (pronounced Tawh-quits, despite some locals calling it Tawh-keets) is named after an Agua Caliente Band of the Cahuilla tribe shaman—the first created by Mukat, Creator of All Things. Tahquitz was the guardian of shamans, but he turned evil and corrupted. Banished from his tribe, he was forced to live in Tahquitz Canyon (named after him). Variations of the legend say that when his tribesmen came to the canyon to bring him food, he would kill and eat them. The situation took a turn for the worse when Tahquitz killed a delegation including the chief's son. After a year of training, the chief confronted Tahquitz and killed him, burning his body. But his evil spirit escaped and still haunts the area, manifesting himself variously as a green fireball, tumbling boulders, visions to people in Palm Springs, or earthquakes.

If you're still intrigued by promises of a 60-foot waterfall in the desert, the Tahquitz Canyon Falls is (in my opinion) the best thing to do in Palm Springs; it is a highly visited site and popular hiking trail. Tahquitz Falls is fed by snowmelt from the nearby San Jacinto Mountains, but also by natural springs, so it flows year-round.

Like Disneyland you can only access these falls after paying an entrance fee at the visitor center, getting a wristband, and visiting during operating hours. The Agua Caliente Band of the Cahuilla Indians who own and manage this land have good reason for this system: The canyon was closed after decades of abuse from vandals and squatters in the 1960s and 1970s. Now it's pristine and park-like (again, like Disneyland). It's hard to believe that decades ago this canyon once held graffiti, broken glass, and litter. With a donation from the Spa Resort and Casino, the Agua Caliente Band of the Cahuilla built a sparkling visitor center, opened in 2001. There's a small exhibit on desert flora and fauna, rock art, rock shelters, and how Native Americans live(d) in this climate.

The guided hikes are led at 8 a.m., 10 a.m., noon, and 2 p.m. during peak months. Otherwise, you can visit yourself anytime between 7:30 a.m. and 5 p.m. The loop hike is almost 1 mile to the falls, and the trail is well maintained and marked, so it's suitable for kids, although folks with knee issues should know it has 12- to 18-inch steps.

Along the way you pass interpretive signs that correspond to a free map you can get from the visitor center. In addition to showing the path, it also has interpretive information about Native American rock art, irrigation systems, and the village that used to be in this canyon. The trail travels between large boulders. The legend holds that Tahquitz himself dislodged them from the canyon's cliff sides in a fit of anger after his banishment.

Start at the visitor center and walk out the back door. After about 200 feet you reach the loop hike. Most people start the loop to the right/counterclockwise (though if you start clockwise in the morning, you can take advantage of the shade from the canyon). This isn't so much a loop hike as a "barbell"-shaped hike. It has two loops with shared trail in the middle. Whichever route you take, the trail is clearly marked and corresponds with your visitor's map.

Here we describe it as we hiked it (clockwise): Turn left at the loop intersection and walk down stone steps, following on the left (upper) side of the canyon. The trail ascends right against the tall, red canyon walls and fragrant creosote and mesquite. After about 0.25 mile, descend to the creek, crossing a stone bridge along the way. Notice how the vegetation along the creek is different with sycamores. On the cliff side above, you may spot a barrel cactus.

The trail is the same here, regardless of which direction on the loop you're going. Climb from the creek with a crossing on another stone bridge. You'll meet another junction with a sign pointing right.

Go up the stairs (which are tall) and pass an old copper pipe that follows the trail for hundreds of feet. Pass a USGS gauging station that measures water flow from the creek and a sign that says "No Entry." Right below it is a small waterfall. When we visited we overheard another hiker tell her hiking partner, "Um, seriously?" Be warned the real Tahquitz Canyon Falls is higher up the canyon trail.

The 60-foot falls is framed by a grotto with a large boulder and plunge pool at the bottom. It stays shady almost the whole day, perfect for picnicking. There

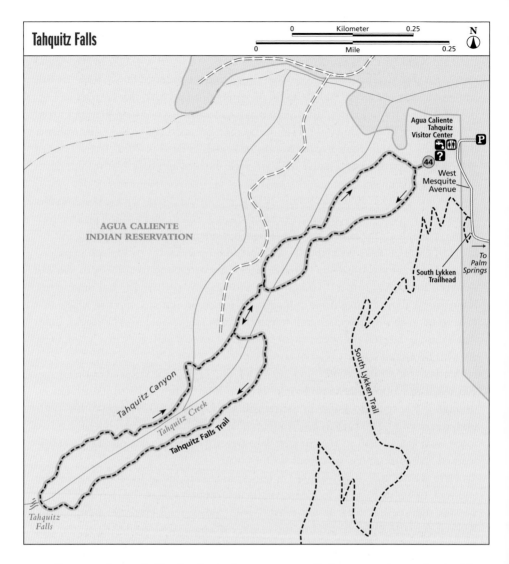

are ferns on the rock. During busy times you may find a ranger here who is able to answer questions about the natural and cultural history of the falls and area. The water comes from Tahquitz Peak, one of the many peaks on Mount San Jacinto.

For the return part of the loop, take a rock bridge to follow Tahquitz Creek downstream on the higher of the two banks on large steps. The loop trail meets the main trail at the arrow sign before breaking off again and descending toward the visitor center. Whichever direction you descend, you'll get expansive views over Palm Springs and the windmills beyond.

Miles and Directions

0.0   Start at the visitor center.

0.25 Left and right trail meet and share trail.

0.45 Trail forks to create second loop. Both left and right go to falls.

0.65 USGS gauge and small waterfall (if on the right trail).

0.85 Base of "real" falls.

1.7   Arrive back at the visitor center.

45 Murray Canyon Falls

Murray Canyon has more than 1,000 native California fan palms, among the most populous groves in the state.

Height: 15-20 feet
Beauty rating: ★★★★
Distance: 4 miles out and back
Elevation gain: 400 feet gain/90 feet loss on descent (one-way)
Difficulty: Easy (but heat can make it more difficult)
Best season: Late fall, winter, early spring
County: Riverside
Trailhead amenities: 2 port-o-potties

Land status: Agua Caliente Band of Cahuilla Indians Reservation
Maps: Indian Canyons map available at visitor center; USGS Palm Springs
Trail contact: Agua Caliente Indian Canyons Visitor Center, 38500 S. Palm Canyon Dr., Palm Springs 92264; (760) 323-6018; www.indian -canyons.com/indian_canyons
Fees and permits: Entrance fees for adults and children; 6-month and annual passes available. $12.50 adults/$6 kids.

Finding the trailhead: Google Maps: Andreas Canyon Trailhead. From Palm Springs, take Palm Canyon Drive/CA 111 and turn right at a Y intersection. Drive to the Murray Canyon entrance station. (**Note:** There can be a long line of cars [30 minutes or more] on busy weekends and holidays.) About 0.1 mile after the entrance kiosk, turn right for Murray Canyon. After a mile the paved road turns into a dirt parking lot complex for the Andreas Canyon trailhead. Turn left into this lot, following signs to the Murray Canyon Picnic Area at the end of the dirt road, about 0.2 mile from where the road becomes dirt.
GPS: N33 45.361' / W116 32.552'

The Hike

Leave Palm Springs for a true desert oasis full of fan palms, barrel cactus, and red rock. Although this hike is well marked, it feels more like an adventure than the nearby Tahquitz Canyon Falls. Unlike its neighbor, Murray Canyon Falls doesn't have bridges over stream crossings, and you'll be making more than ten crossings in the short season when water levels are high enough.

The canyon is named after botanist Dr. Welwood Murray, who built a health resort (the Murray Hotel) popular among the literary figures who turned Palm Springs into a destination. Nearby Andreas Canyon was named for a Cahuilla chieftain who lived in the late 1800s. This area was the summer retreat for the Agua Caliente Band of the Cahuilla, who would spend the winter in the too-hot-for-summer Coachella Valley. They built complex communities in this canyon, growing melons, squash, beans, and corn, and gathering plants for food, medicine, and baskets. The Agua Caliente were deeded 31,500 acres of their homeland by the US government in the 1880s, 6,700 acres of which are within Palm Spring city limits.

The trail starts at the eastern part of the palm-treed Murray Canyon Picnic Area behind a wooden information kiosk. Near the trailhead are grinding rocks once used by the Cahuilla. Follow signs for Murray Canyon/Seven Sisters/Coffman Trail/West Fork Trail. Descend southeast on sandy trail—well packed by horses and visitors—and away from the fan palms of the picnic area. You'll see horse droppings, at least at the beginning.

It's hard to imagine this dry beginning is the start of a hike to a waterfall. Wide-open desert is filled with cholla and burrobush with views of the Santa Rosa Mountains straight ahead. While this stretch is exposed and can be toasty during the day, it does give you a chance to appreciate views of the San Jacinto Mountains looming above.

After 0.25 mile, turn right at a signed junction. The trail flattens and is wide and sandy. It braids into several parallel trails here, all within sight of one another. Pick one and continue on. After 0.5 mile you get your last views of the town and windmills. Turn a corner to the right and descend toward the fan palms and your first ford of Murray Creek.

Right after the first crossing, stay right (west) at a signed intersection near a solar-powered gauging instrument. Continue following Murray Creek upstream among its forested palms. The fan palms, willows, cottonwoods, and mesquite here are prime habitat for wildlife, including birds such as the purple Costa's hummingbird. The deeper you get in the canyon, the more robust the stream becomes. The canyon twists and turns often, and has more than a dozen crossings. The crossings are often over stone steps you can rock-hop (if they aren't underwater).

Throughout the hike, helpful wooden confidence posts let you know how far into the hike you are and that you're headed toward the Seven Sisters and Coffman Trails.

After 1.2 mile, stay left (straight) at a post directing hikers and horses on different routes through the canyon. As the canyon narrows, there are numerous braidings of the trail along the creek. These are horse trails, meant to keep the animals safe from bouldery terrain. Others are meant to keep you drier or to circumvent the minor cascades (5 to 10 feet in height) along the route. When confused, keep heading upcanyon.

Farther up the canyon you encounter reeds, willows, and even wild grapes. The rangers say there are over 1,000 fan palms in Murray Canyon alone. As the canyon narrows, it towers above you in striped cliff-band formations 100 feet tall and a deep

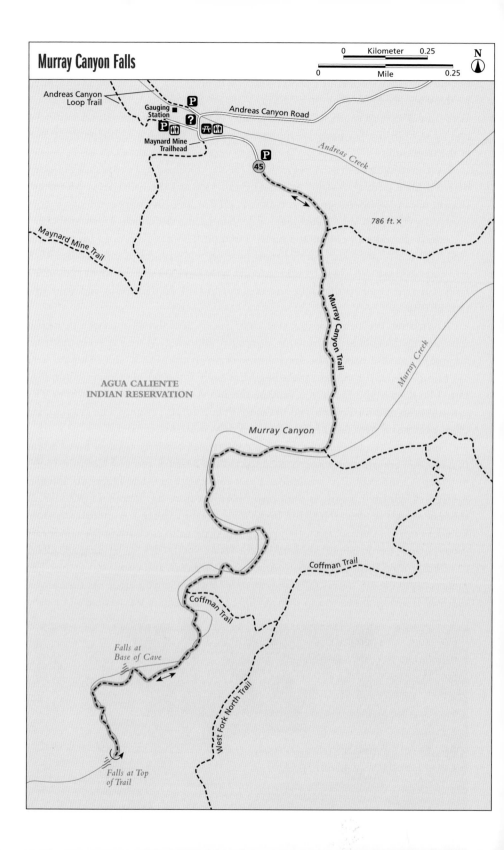

Murray Canyon Falls

0   Kilometer   0.25

0   Mile   0.25

N

Andreas Canyon
Loop Trail

Gauging
Station

P

Andreas Canyon Road

P

?

Maynard Mine
Trailhead

P
45

Andreas Creek

Maynard Mine Trail

786 ft. ×

Murray Canyon Trail

Murray Creek

AGUA CALIENTE
INDIAN RESERVATION

Murray Canyon

Coffman Trail

Coffman Trail

Falls at
Base of Cave

West Fork North Trail

Falls at Top
of Trail

red in color. Keep your eyes peeled for bighorn sheep, which live on the ridgetops and hillsides of this canyon. When we last visited, we saw a mother bighorn sheep with her baby high on the ridge.

At 1.4 miles reach an intersection with the Coffman Trail, which goes off to the left and climbs toward a notable triangular rock. Instead, stay straight. You pass a hitching area indicating the trail upstream is closed to horses.

It becomes clear why the next section is for human feet only: At 1.7 miles you have to scramble and climb up stone-carved stairs along a cliff. This steep climb takes you on the canyon walls on the left to skirt around the first of the waterfalls.

There is a more low-key option if you're feeling hot or tired or want to avoid more exposed areas. Right before the trail has you climb stairs, you can see the first of the "Seven Sisters" waterfalls. Take a side trail on the opposite side of the creek from the stone "stairs" and follow the creek upstream for less than a minute. In a boulder-lined cove is a 10- to 15-foot plunge falls. We would argue that, depending on the season, this falls is more spectacular than the one at the end of the canyon. However, accessing it may be trickier in higher water levels when the smooth rocks are wet.

If you want to see more, go back to the main trail and head up the stone-carved steps to a narrow trail carved out of the cliff on the left side of the canyon. It will take you above the first falls, but you can't see it from here, so there's no point in risking going anywhere near the edge. Descend a 30-foot section of stone slab with a drop-off on the right. It can feel exposed, and we watched several people crawl across on all fours.

Continue on the trail as it crosses back and forth over the creek. Follow the trail around a bend until you find a sign that marks the end of the hiking trail and requests hikers go no farther. At the end of the trail is a block-style waterfall that is sometimes split by a boulder (in high water the boulder gets subsumed). There's a small pool suitable for wading (depending on current park regulations). Depending on your angle, you can also see a plunge falls above it. Above that are even more cascades. This is why people (and signs along the route) refer to Murray Canyon Falls as the "Seven Sisters."

Miles and Directions

0.0 Start at the trailhead kiosk in picnic area.

0.25 Turn right at signed junction.

0.5 Cross creek and turn right at signed junction.

1.2 Horse trail up Murray Canyon splits.

1.4 Stay straight at junction with Coffman Trail and horse hitching post.

1.7 Side trail to first waterfall right before a rocky climb.

2.0 End of trail at waterfall. Return the way you came.

4.0 Arrive back at the trailhead.

46 West Fork Falls

This short hike gives you a taste of the joy of seeing waterfalls in the desert without requiring the time or scrambling. Even though it's a highly seasonal falls, this is one of the most fun and well-designed trails of its length I've seen. It's twisty and curvy, leaving you in mystery until the end. The same could be said of the drive to get to the panoramic trailhead.

Height: 5–15 feet
Beauty rating: ★★★★★
Distance: 0.3 mile out and back
Elevation gain: 65 feet gain/55 feet loss
Difficulty: Easy
Best season: Winter, spring
County: Riverside
Trailhead amenities: Ranger and information, trading post, outhouses
Land status: Agua Caliente Band of Cahuilla Indians Reservation

Maps: Indian Canyons map available at visitor center, USGS Palm View Peak
Trail contact: Agua Caliente Indian Canyons Visitor Center, 38500 S. Palm Canyon Dr., Palm Springs 92264; (760) 323-6018; www.indian -canyons.com/indian_canyons
Fees and permits: Entrance fees for adults and children; 6-month and annual passes available

Finding the trailhead: Google Maps: Indian Canyon (gets you to the entrance kiosk). From Palm Springs, take Palm Canyon Drive/CA 111 and turn right at a Y intersection. Drive to the Indian Canyon entrance station. After paying the fee, drive 6.1 miles on S. Palm Canyon. Parking lot at the Trading Post by Palm Canyon.
GPS: N33 44.165' / W116 32.196'

The Hike

This is the perfect 0.3-mile hike, even if the waterfall isn't running. The trail is designed so well, you won't want it to end. In its short distance it manages to twist and turn and keep you in suspense. It gives you a taste of the beauty of the can-yon, the surrounding mountains, and the nearby fan palms and red rocks. There are numerous caves, cubbies, and holes along the hike for kids and adults to play in (but watch for snakes).

Near the Trading Post restrooms, look for a wooden sign near a picnic table for West Fork Falls Trail. Follow the wide, sandy trail, heading west around a bend as the trail descends toward West Fork Creek. Along the way you pass under an overhanging boulder that almost creates a tunnel over the trail. Turn a corner and pass under the arch of a tree branch over the trail. After 250 feet you reach the sandy creek bed near West Fork Creek. Follow the trail ascending a "hallway" between two slabs of rock.

To get right to the base of the falls, look on the right for two boulders by the side of the creek near a double palm tree. Between the boulders is a needle-like eye—a

Even when it isn't flowing, it's worth viewing the beautiful polished rock of the seasonal West Creek Falls.

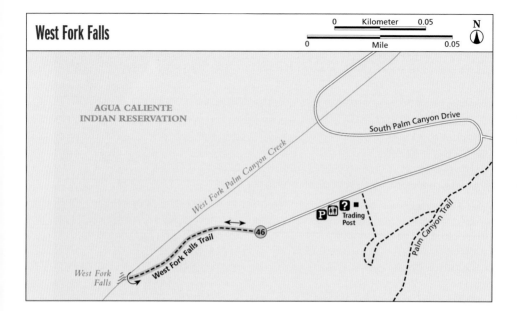

AGUA CALIENTE
INDIAN RESERVATION

South Palm Canyon Drive

West Fork Palm Canyon Creek

Trading
Post

West Fork Falls Trail

46

Palm Canyon Trail

West Fork
Falls

hole you can crawl through. There are three constructed stone steps designed to lead you to this hole, though they blend in so well they almost don't look human-made. If you scramble between, you'll be at the base of the upper and middle tier of the three-tiered West Fork Falls.

The falls descends about 30 feet across a polished gray and white rock slab. In high water a pool sits below. Above, a house-sized boulder forms a "roof" over the pool on the right side. A local tour guide told me that after a recent major flash flood, the house-sized boulder moved several inches.

Return the way you came. If you have more energy, explore the Palm Canyon Trail, which is accessible from the same Trading Post parking lot. There's no waterfall, but it's one of the most classic hikes in Southern California.

Miles and Directions

0.0 Start at the trailhead near the Trading Post.

0.15 Base of falls. Return the way you came.

0.30 Arrive back at the trailhead.

47 Borrego Canyon Falls (Borrego Palm Canyon Trail)

This Anza Borrego classic nature trail leads to the third-largest palm oasis in California. Borrego Canyon is prime bighorn sheep territory. This easy-to-follow trail is one of the best oasis waterfall hikes—even if the waterfall isn't running.

Height: About 15 feet
Beauty rating: ★★★★★
Distance: 2.9 miles out and back
Elevation gain: 371 feet ascent/443 feet descent
Difficulty: Easy to moderate (in heat)
Best season: Winter, spring
County: San Diego
Trailhead amenities: About 40 parking spots (plus more closer to the campground), water spigot, picnic tables, shade, campground, women's restroom with running water and flush toilets but no roof (!), men's restroom farther out, trash cans, amphitheater nearby, interpretive maps, AT&T cell reception; no dogs
Land status: Anza-Borrego Desert State Park
Maps: USGS Borrego Canyon
Trail contact: Anza-Borrego Desert State Park Visitor Center, 200 Palm Canyon Dr., Borrego Springs 92004; (760) 767-4205; www.parks.ca.gov/?page_id=638
Fees and permits: Day-use fee

Finding the trailhead: Google Maps: Borrego Palm Canyon Campground. From Christmas Circle in Borrego Springs, stay east on Palm Canyon Drive for 1.5 miles. Turn right following signs for Borrego Palm Canyon Campground for 1.0 mile to an entrance fee kiosk. Drive through a kiosk. Follow signs to "trailhead," which is located at the end of the campground. **GPS:** N33 16.131' / W116 25.046'

The Hike

In 1921 Borrego Palm Canyon was the first site designated to be part of Anza-Borrego Desert State Park. It's easy to see why.

Even the parking lot of the Borrego Springs Canyon hike is impressive. Here you'll find a small pond and interpretive exhibit about the endangered desert pupfish, an incredible small fish that lives in desert springs. There are smaller California fan palms here, giving you a taste of what lies ahead.

Before starting this hike, make sure you have plenty of water. Anza-Borrego Desert State Park recommends 2 gallons per person. We suggest starting this hike early in the morning or later in the afternoon after the heat has cooled. Make sure you have a hat, sunglasses, and sunscreen. This canyon has little shade. As multiple signs near the trailhead warn you, people have died here.

Dogs are not allowed on this trail. Endangered Peninsular bighorn sheep live on steep mountainsides in either direction. You increase your chances of seeing them by being quiet and looking for white rumps against the brown rock. They're most often spotted when they're running.

Pick up a paper trail guide available at the trailhead kiosk. The well-marked trail is lined with posts that correspond to numbers marked in the interpretive pamphlet.

Several trails leave from the parking lot. Here we describe an out-and-back hike on the main trail. An alternate return is a loop marked with signs for the amphitheater or posts for the alternate trail. The featured main trail starts at the information signs on a wide, well-marked trail. It's easy to follow: lined with rocks or palm wood logs with interpretive posts as confidence markers.

Not far from the trailhead, look for beavertail and cholla cactus. Tall ocotillos may be in bloom. They grow leaves any time of year, bursting within 24 hours after a rainstorm. The leaves photosynthesize sunlight to feed the plant, but dry out and fall off after about a month. The cycle repeats with the next rainstorm.

About 500 feet in, you cross what looks like a dry creek bed. This is a desert wash. Flash floods turn this into a temporary stream during monsoon season in July and August, when clouds form over the Sea of Cortez and move north to Anza-Borrego. Flash floods are responsible for carrying the giant boulders you see scattered near the trail down the mountain. In February 2019 they also washed away part of the trail and it closed for a month.

As you continue upcanyon, you pass desert lavender. If you rub the leaves, you'll notice similarities to the European garden varietals. It's a desert pollinator that blooms October through May (likely the time you'll be visiting). Its leaf size corresponds to soil moisture. When there's lots of water around, the plant builds big leaves to maximize photosynthesis. In drier times it creates smaller leaves to reduce surface area and thus moisture loss. During dry times the leaves may grow "hair" to protect against moisture loss, too.

As you continue uphill toward the oasis, you pass the ancient village once inhabited by the Cahuilla Native Americans, who lived here because of the availability of water. The narrowness of the canyon provided shade in the late afternoon and protection from the wind. Cahuilla used willows for building homes and bow-making. Fragrant creosote and brittlebrush are medicinal. Mesquite pods are food.

About 1 mile in, the trail crosses a (often dry) creek bed, giving you your first view of the green, leafy, almost tropical oasis. Signs point toward the oasis to the right. Continue upcanyon on masterfully built stone steps placed by the Civilian Conservation Corps in the 1930s.

Approaching the oasis, the trail becomes less distinctive and more magical as you come to a grove of the rare California fan palm (*Washingtonia filifera*), the only palm native to California. Borrego Palm Canyon is the largest of more than twenty-five palm oases in Anza-Borrego and has over 800 trees.

But the palms aren't doing so well. You can tell by looking at the skirt of fronds, which protect the tree from bugs and water loss. Fires are one reason. You can help preserve the longevity of this canyon by stepping carefully, avoiding areas where there are "seedlings" of fan palms. Groves are fenced off and signed to encourage propagation.

Borrego Palm Canyon

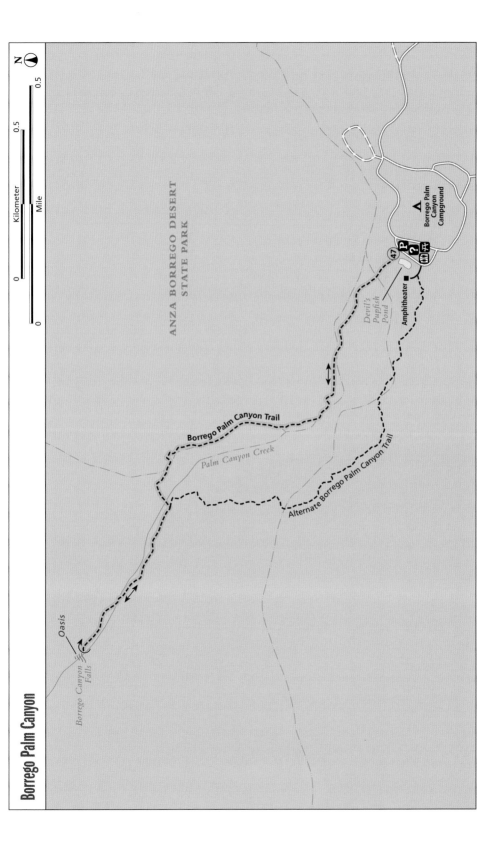

N

0   Kilometer   0.5   0.5

0   Mile   0.5

ANZA BORREGO DESERT
STATE PARK

Borrego
Canyon
Falls

Oasis

Borrego Palm Canyon Trail

Palm Canyon Creek

Alternate Borrego Palm Canyon Trail

Devil's
Pupfish
Pond

47

P

Amphitheater

Borrego Palm
Canyon
Campground

The maidenhair fern–lined falls tumble 15 feet over a boulder. If you're having trouble finding it, keep heading back into the canyon and look for a trail on the right side of the creek (where fewer palm seedlings can be damaged by hikers' feet). It's located about 0.4 mile from the trail junction.

Miles and Directions

0.0 Start at trailhead for the main trail.

0.2 Cross a wash.

1.1 Cross creek and turn right at signed junction with alternate trail.

1.3 Enter oasis.

1.4 Waterfall. Return the way you came.

2.9 Arrive back at the trailhead.

Option: From the trail junction, instead of turning left to return the way you came, go straight on the "alternate route." It'll give you a different view of the canyon and an appreciation for the expansiveness of the desert and how different it is from the oasis you just visited. The alternate route climbs on the return route and is rockier and 0.1 mile longer. It doesn't have posts along the way and isn't as impeccably defined as the main trail. If you're worried about getting lost, 0.6 mile from the falls you can see the campground. At 1.5 miles from the falls, at the paved trail to the amphitheater, turn right to get back to your car.

48 Maidenhair Falls

A long but gentle climb through desert leads to a palm oasis. The waterfall is seasonal, but maidenhair ferns grow year-round.

Height: About 20-30 feet
Beauty rating: ★★★★
Distance: 5.3 miles out and back
Elevation gain: 1,000 feet/descent 25 feet
Difficulty: Easy
Best season: Winter, spring
County: San Diego
Trailhead amenities: Pit toilets, kiosk, shaded bench

Land status: Anza-Borrego Desert State Park and Wilderness
Maps: USGS Tubb Canyon
Trail contact: Anza-Borrego Desert State Park Visitor Center, 200 Palm Canyon Dr., Borrego Springs 92004; (760) 767-4205; www.parks .ca.gov/?page_id=638
Fees and permits: None

Finding the trailhead: Google Maps: Trailhead to Maidenhair Falls. From Christmas Circle in Borrego Springs, take Palm Canyon Drive for 1.3 miles. Turn left on Montezuma Valley Road (S22) heading south for 0.8 mile. Although there is no sign along the road for the Hellhole Canyon trailhead, the parking lot, information kiosk, and pit toilets are visible on your right. The trailhead dirt road pullout is before S22 starts to climb, and it's easy to miss. Should you miss it, there are several pullouts a few minutes up S22 where you can safely turn around.
GPS: N33 14.528' / W116 24.215'

The Hike

The desert of Anza-Borrego Desert State Park seems like an unlikely place for a waterfall, but that just makes the hike to the oasis around Maidenhair all the more special. Maidenhair Falls flows seasonally, but the lush palm and fern haven is worth visiting even when the falls are only a trickle.

Anza-Borrego is the largest state park in California and the second largest in the contiguous United States after Adirondack Park, making it a quiet and wild place for hikers to visit. The hike to Maidenhair Falls takes you through classic desert washes, past colorful rock formations, and through prime endangered Peninsular bighorn sheep habitat. You'll see the best of the Colorado Desert environ of the Sonoran Desert ecoregion. While the elevation gain is not rigorous, it requires hand-over-hand scrambling and rocks can be slippery when wet. This hike can be warm even in January, so bring plenty of water (park signs recommend at least a gallon per person).

From the kiosk at the west end of the parking lot, follow a wide, sandy trail marked as heading to Hellhole Canyon, so-called because of a legend that rancher Wid Helm called this place "one hell of a hole to get cattle out of." You pass cholla, tall ocotillo, fragrant creosote, and desert lavender.

Maidenhair Falls

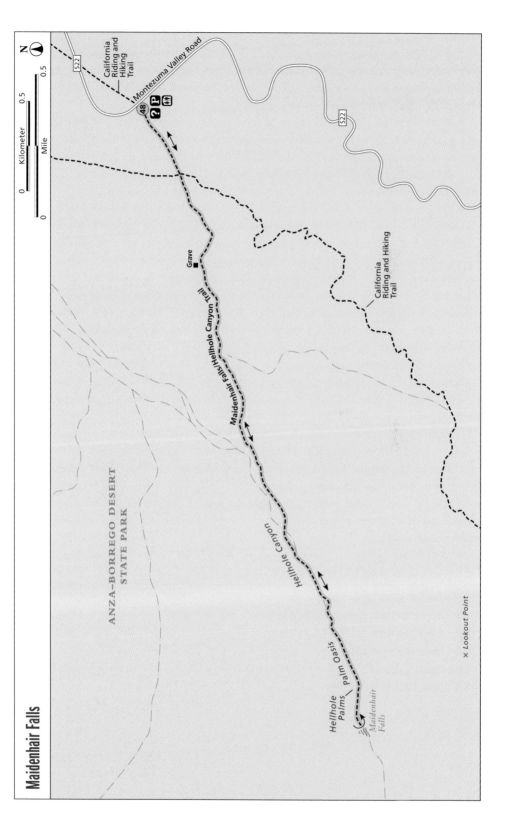

N

Kilometer
0   0.5

Mile
0   0.5

S22

California Riding and Hiking Trail

Montezuma Valley Road

48 ? P 🚻

S22

ANZA–BORREGO DESERT STATE PARK

Grave

California Riding and Hiking Trail

Maidenhair Falls/Hellhole Canyon Trail

Hellhole Canyon

Palm Oasis

Hellhole Palms

Maidenhair Falls

x Lookout Point

You are headed toward the palms and sycamores at the mouth of the left canyon to the west. Stunning views of the sharp crags along Palm Mesa (4,324 feet) unfold to your right. The green-looking town of Borrego Springs is visible below you to the east.

In 0.5 mile reach a signed intersection for the California Riding and Hiking Trail, which climbs a ridge to the left. Stay right, walking toward the mouth of the canyon on a wide alluvial fan. The canyon narrows and the trail twists, heading northwest. At 0.7 mile you pass tall trees and a memorable sign and grave marker indicating: "They didn't bring enough water." (A good reminder: If you don't have enough, turn back.)

After 2.5 miles the canyon narrows and the trail heads into the leftmost drainage of Hellhole Canyon, not the red/purple-rocked canyon to the right. As you look into Hellhole Canyon, you can see the oasis area above. As you approach the oasis, the vegetation changes to mesquite, wildflowers, and beavertail cactus.

The trail narrows, following close to the drainage. You may have your first views of water. From year to year the trail changes after flash floods, but generally you follow the wash on its left side as you head up Hellhole Canyon. In 2018 the trail crossed back and forth over the drainage five times, following along the banks of the wash.

Soon you reach the fan palms, the only palms native to California. Sycamore, cottonwood, and other water-loving trees grow here, too. The lush fan palm oasis is home to wildlife, including bighorn sheep.

Expect to scramble to continue toward the falls. Avoid climbing or walking on wet rock, which is slippery due to algae.

Two falls are in Hellhole Canyon. The area noted as Maidenhair Falls on the map is where you'll find the lower falls. There are three small alcoves with water descending 10 to 15 feet off the top of boulders. In at least one of the alcoves, water pools below even when the falls above is dry.

Follow a rough, rocky path to the right for several minutes to reach the upper falls, which trickles year-round and is covered in maidenhair ferns, as unlikely a sight in the desert as one can imagine.

Miles and Directions

0.0 Start at the trailhead kiosk.
0.5 Intersection with California Riding and Hiking Trail; stay right.
0.7 Grave and signs.
2.5 Lower Maidenhair Falls.
2.65 Upper Maidenhair Falls. Return the way you came.
5.3 Arrive back at the trailhead.

49 Darwin Falls

This Death Valley National Park year-round cascade is unforgettable. The family-friendly (but not dog-friendly) hike is a must-see. Bring water, start hiking at dawn, and carry plenty of sun protection: The average temperature here is 100°F in May.

Height: Upper and lower tier: 80 feet combined (only the lower tier, at 25–30 feet, visible from hike)
Beauty rating: ★★★★★
Distance: 2.2 miles out and back
Elevation gain: 275 feet
Difficulty: Moderate to strenuous (due to heat)
Best season: Fall, winter, spring, summer
County: Inyo

Trailhead amenities: 10 parking spots, plus more along the side of road into parking area (watch for No Parking signs); dogs not allowed
Land status: Death Valley National Park
Maps: USGS Darwin
Trail contact: Death Valley National Park, PO Box 579, Death Valley 92328; (760) 786-3200; www.nps.gov/deva/
Fees and permits: None

Finding the trailhead: Google Maps: Darwin Falls Trail Parking Lot, Old Toll Road, Death Valley National Park, Panamint Springs, CA 92004. From the town of Lone Pine, take I-395 to the Lone Pine Interagency Ranger District (worth stopping by prior to your trip) at the intersection with CA 136 south of town. If you're driving from LA, you'll reach the visitor center before town. There are few services in Death Valley, so best to refuel in Lone Pine first. Turn east on CA 136 for 17.5 miles until it turns into (stay straight on) CA 190 for another 30 miles. Turn right (south) on the unsigned dirt Old Toll Road toward Darwin Falls. It's found 1 mile west before you reach Panamint Springs Resort, where you can get emergency provisions. Take the rough two-wheel-drive-accessible road for 2.6 miles to the trailhead.

Alternatively, from the town of Ridgecrest, take CA 178 for 54.9 miles as it turns into Trona Road and Wildrose Road for Panamint Valley Road for 14 miles. Turn left on CA 190 for 3.6 miles, passing town on the left to reach Old Toll Road toward Darwin Falls.
GPS: N36 19.396' / W117 30.527'

The Hike

Visiting Darwin Falls is one of those trips that can't help but give you hope: To walk and drive through harsh, desolate Death Valley and come to the riparian greenway oasis of Darwin Falls is a reminder that miracles can happen. Darwin Falls is the largest waterfall found on any of the four perennial streams in the 3-million-acre Death Valley National Park (which is the largest national park in the Lower 48).

A common misconception is that Darwin Falls and other landmarks nearby are named for Charles Darwin. They're actually named after Dr. Erasmus Darwin French (1822-1902), a rancher and veteran of the Mexican-American War. He's known for leading several expeditions through Death Valley on unsuccessful searches for silver. Death Valley is the ancestral winter home to the Timbisha Shoshone ("rock paint")

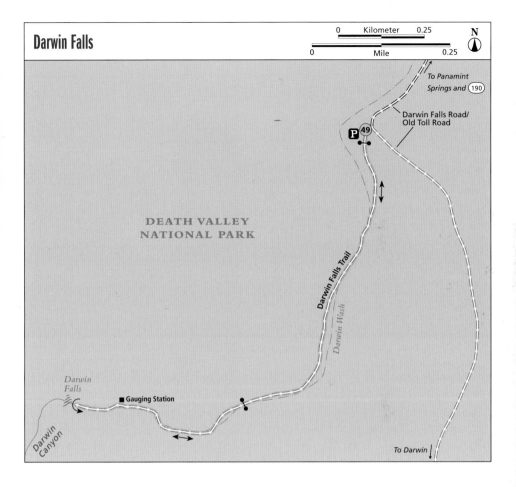

Kilometer 0 0.25

Mile 0 0.25

N

To Panamint
Springs and 190

Darwin Falls Road/
Old Toll Road

P 49

DEATH VALLEY
NATIONAL PARK

Darwin Falls Trail

Darwin Wash

Darwin
Falls

■ Gauging Station

Darwin
Canyon

To Darwin

people, who have been in the area of the park for over a thousand years. Some of their descendants (who call themselves the Nümü Tümpisattsi, "Death Valley people") live in the Death Valley Indian Community within the park near Furnace Creek.

Start on a sandy, dirt jeep track at the mouth of the canyon near a gate. Follow rock cairns and light markings; this trail isn't signed or paved like what you may find in other national parks. At 0.3 mile you pass a metal fence. Follow the mostly dry streambed as you walk up the canyon.

Although the trail is sandy and wide through the wash, the canyon walls work like handrails, boxing you in so you're always headed in the right direction. A water pipe lines the right side of the canyon.

You'll start seeing more vegetation as you approach the falls. It's a surprise to see willows, cattails, and reeds in this lush, green oasis. There are even ferns. Birders claim to have found more than eighty species of birds visiting here, many migrants that have stopped to get water. Quail is native here.

The canyon walls become narrower and arc to the right. The walls are made of intrusive igneous rock called plutonic rock. It appears red, yellow, and orange, contrasting with the green vegetation inside the canyon.

The last 0.3 mile requires hopping across the creek several times through a narrower canyon. This is not to be attempted during flash floods. Take care not to tromp on fish, eggs, or frogs here. They have a hard enough time living in the desert as it is. You pass a USGS gauging station before finding the falls.

Darwin Falls tumbles 30 feet down a rock cliff with an iconic fork two-thirds of the way down. A cottonwood tree grows above it. The nearby Darwin Falls Wilderness (administered by the Bureau of Land Management in the adjacent northern Mojave Desert) protects the source of the falls: Darwin Wash fed by the moon-like volcanic tablelands of Darwin Plateau.

Hikers with rock climbing skills and experience should research the route to the upper falls before visiting. Any technical rock climbing should be attempted at your own risk. But for all, the shade and beauty of this forked falls makes for a good place to pause and contemplate life.

Miles and Directions

0.0   Start at the parking lot.

0.7   Trail and canyons arc to right.

1.0   Base of falls. Return the way you came.

2.2   Arrive back at the trailhead.

Ojai and Sespe Wilderness

Ojai and Sespe–area waterfalls are the most wild and difficult in this book. With the exception of Rose Valley Falls, all the falls in this section require scrambling, off-trail navigation, or at the very least, getting your feet wet. Yet with its wildness comes a beauty and solitude not found elsewhere. Slot canyons, sandstone cliffs, and even a chance to spot an endangered California condor await those with the curiosity, sense of adventure, skillset, and experience to enter the Ojai and Sespe region.

This section is mostly in the 219,700-acre Sespe Wilderness, although it includes a hike in the smaller Matilija Wilderness and the Santa Paula frontcountry as well. Sespe Creek is one of the last undammed streams in Southern California and is designated a National Wild and Scenic River and National Scenic Waterway. It's one of the only streams where one can find southern steelhead trout. It's also home to the endangered southwestern willow flycatcher, least Bell's vireo, California red-legged frog, and the largest population of the arroyo toad. The term Sespe dates to 1791 and refers to a Chumash Indian village, meaning "knee cap" in the Chumash language.

The Sespe Wilderness was established in 1992 and is home to the Condor Sanctuary, which is closed to humans. It's home to among the 200 or so California condors alive in the wild. They're intelligent and curious birds that are attracted to trash and can choke on microtrash. When you visit, please pick up after yourself and consider bringing a trash bag and picking up after others as well.

For those seeking waterfalls and big adventure, the Sespe has swimming holes and waterways worth exploring. Lion Canyon holds multiple falls. Backpacking Indian Creek in the nearby Dick Smith Wilderness is worth researching for intrepid waterfall explorers. Other falls have been closed to further protect condor habitat.

In 2017 the Thomas Fire became the largest wildfire in California history (in 2018, it was surpassed). The subsequent debris flow in early 2018 destroyed the trails in the area. While traveling here, take care for branches and loose snags.

50 Santa Paula Falls and Punchbowl

These falls flow into a famous swimming hole, though the trail is not always as clear as you would think given the popularity. It can be enjoyed as a backpacking trip with a camp not far from the falls.

Height: About 25–30 feet
Beauty rating: ★★★★
Distance: 7.4 miles out and back
Elevation gain: 800+ feet
Difficulty: Moderate to strenuous
Best season: Fall, winter, spring, summer (beginning can be hot)
County: Ventura
Trailhead amenities: About 15 parking spots, 8 spots along road within sight of the gate, more farther out; dog-friendly, watch for vandalism at trailhead
Land status: Los Padres National Forest
Maps: Tom Harrison Sespe Wilderness; USGS Santa Paula Peak, Topatopa Mountains
Trail contact: Los Padres National Forest, Ojai Ranger District, 1190 E. Ojai Ave., Ojai 93023; (805) 646-4348; www.fs.usda.gov/main/lpnf/home
Fees and permits: Display Adventure Pass

Finding the trailhead: Google Maps: Santa Paula Canyon. From Ojai, travel east on CA 150 for about 11 miles. Park at a dirt pullout on the north side of CA 150, east of the entrance of Thomas Aquinas College. Cross the bridge over Santa Paula Creek, turn right into the Thomas Aquinas campus, and follow signs for trails. This parking lot is known for vandalism. Do not leave valuables in car.
GPS: N34 25.348' / W119 05.218'

The Hike

Santa Paula Falls is famous for its punchbowls, swimming holes carved into the rock bed of the canyon. With the Topatopa Mountains above and nestled between Big Cone Camp and Cross Camp, two Los Padres National Forest primitive backcountry camps, there's a lot of fun to be had here. Post–Thomas Fire debris flow and erosion have impacted the trail, as have graffiti and litter, though not as bad as in the past.

The downside is the road walk through the college, avocado farm, and oil wells required to enter the national forest. While navigating the roads through the private property can seem intimidating, it's well marked and signed.

This area was near where the Thomas Fire started in fall 2017 (the "Thomas" in its name refers to Thomas Aquinas College), but the Forest Service had opened and cleared the trail by the time we visited in March 2019. You may notice charred trees on the drive to the trailhead, but most of the hike appears unscathed or is already growing back green.

Start at the parking lot on CA 150 in the town of Santa Paula, east of the entrance to Thomas Aquinas College. From the parking area cross the highway, then turn left and walk west to cross a bridge over Santa Paula Creek.

The colorful hills of Santa Paula Canyon are starting to rebound after the Thomas Fire of 2017 and subsequent debris flow of 2018.

Enter Thomas Aquinas College through a green gate via a paved road to the right of the stone arch. Less than 0.1 mile later, make another right onto a road, following signs that say "Hiking Trail." When walking here, please be respectful of the school and stay on the paved road instead of cutting across the campus. The road curls around the east side of the college campus and has excellent views of Our Lady of the Most Holy Trinity Chapel and other neo-Spanish campus buildings set against the landscape of the Topatopa Mountains.

As you walk toward the punchbowls, you'll pass the summer home of infamous tycoon Edward Lawrence Doheny. He owned the oil fields here, as well as discovered the La Brea Tar Pits in 1892. His name was synonymous with oil and graces Southern California on college buildings, beaches, and the Graystone Mansion in Beverly Hills. Doheny was later implicated in the 1923 Teapot Dome Scandal and was the inspiration for the character in Upton Sinclair's novel *Oil!* In the 2007 film *There Will Be Blood*, Daniel Day Lewis won an Oscar for his portrayal of a character based on Doheny. To get out of the scandal's spotlight, Doheny built Ferndale Ranch; Thomas Aquinas College sits on part of its former land here. The dean of Thomas Aquinas College lives in Doheny's old hacienda.

In 0.6 mile, turn right uphill on a paved side road, following signs for "Hiking Trail." In less than 0.1 mile, go through a gate and enter Ferndale Ranch. In September 2018 the college acquired the ranch's charred land and reassembled the historic Doheny property. After the gate, bear left at the fork following signs downhill on an olive tree–lined road. In 0.8 mile, at a three-way fork in the road, follow signs to stay right on the main road.

At 1 mile you reach the grand entrance gate of Rancho Rucuerdo, the avocado farm. Despite numerous No Trespassing signs and an absence of the "Hiking Trail" signs you've seen at every intersection up until now, this is indeed your route. Resist the temptation to pick avocadoes while walking through here. Numerous signs warn they are protected, and it's a crime with up to a three-year jail sentence.

After the gate, stay right on a paved road, following trail signs (they appear again!). At 1.25 miles the road dead-ends at chain-link-fenced oil derricks, but the trail continues skirting the left side of the fenceline.

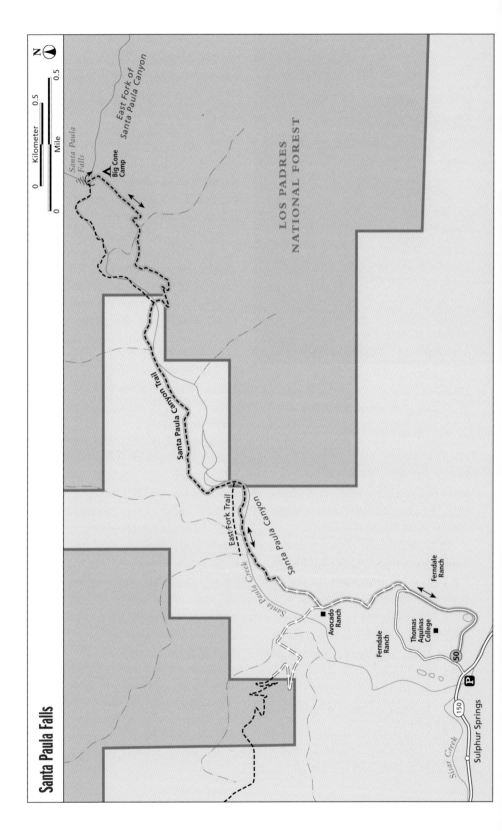

Santa Paula Falls

Santa Paula Falls

East Fork of
Santa Paula Canyon

Big Cone
Camp

Santa Paula Canyon Trail

East Fork Trail

Santa Paula Canyon

Santa Paula Creek

LOS PADRES
NATIONAL FOREST

Avocado Ranch

Ferndale
Ranch

Ferndale
Ranch

Thomas Aquinas
College

Sissar Creek

Sulphur Springs

N

Kilometer
0   0.5

Mile
0   0.5

At 1.45 miles you reach Santa Paula Canyon Trail, aka East Fork Trail (FR 21W11). Now cross the wide Santa Paula Creek—you can often find crossing logs here. Once on the opposite side, follow a narrow path upstream through riparian woodland. Erosion, especially after the fire, has taken out this and other sections of trail. Finding the right trail at this part is a common complaint among hikers, but here are a few tips: You are fenced in on the left by the avocado farm and on the right by the creek. The trail is blazed (for better or worse) with spray-painted green, blue, or orange dots. When you see a road to your left, don't take it; instead, stay on the trail that hugs the creek.

In 1.8 miles the trail draws farther from the creek and you may hear frogs. You reach a wide, rock-lined trail, and views open up of the Topatopa Mountains ahead. Ceanothus (California lilac), yerba santa, black and white sage, wild cucumber, and chemise grow here, unscathed by the fire.

At 2.5 miles, right after a log "bench" under a tree branching over the trail, you reach an important intersection. Turn right across the creek at a large, colorful arrow painted on a rock. Follow the trail on the other side. There's a path continuing straight along the creek, but it degenerates into a scrambling path that eventually leads to the waterfalls, albeit on much tougher terrain.

At 2.7 miles the trail splits uphill on an eroded embankment. Head right and uphill here, away from the creek. In another 0.25 mile, reach another split and bear right again. Continue climbing on trail with excellent views of the canyon, although be aware that portions have eroded. At 3.6 miles you switchback to Big Cone Camp, on a terrace above the creek.

The trail descends to a trail junction with a trail marker (and painted markers, too). The trail on the left returns to Santa Paula Creek and up the side canyon to the base of the falls. The junction on the right takes you to the top of the punchbowl, a swimming hole on top of the falls. For those looking for more walking, the Last Chance Trail continues up the canyon to even more falls.

Miles and Directions

0.0 Start at parking area, cross CA 150 and a bridge, and enter Thomas Aquinas College.

0.1 Turn right on road and continue, skirting the college campus on its east boundary.

0.6 Turn right and uphill onto side road to Ferndale Ranch.

1.0 Go through gate to Rancho Recuerdo (avocado farm), staying right on paved road.

1.25 Road ends at oil pump and trail continues as dirt path along fenceline.

1.45 Reach Santa Paula Canyon Trail and cross creek, following path upstream.

2.5 Cross creek.

2.7 Stay right at junction.

3.0 Stay right, continuing up side of canyon.

3.6 Big Cone Camp.

3.7 Junction to base of falls or top of punchbowl. Return the way you came.

7.4 Arrive back at the trailhead.

51 Rose Valley Falls

A short family- and dog-friendly hike starting at a campground leads to one of the largest falls in Southern California.

Height: 300 feet in 2 tiers (100-foot lower falls visible from this hike)
Beauty rating: ★★★★★
Distance: 0.7 mile out and back
Elevation gain: 140 feet ascent/25 feet descent (one-way)
Difficulty: Easy
Best season: Fall, winter, spring, summer (but falls are seasonal)
County: Ventura
Trailhead amenities: 20 parking spots in a small lot along road, 9 campsites available, privies outside and in campground, trash/recycle bins
Land status: Los Padres National Forest

Maps: Tom Harrison Sespe Wilderness; USGS Lion Canyon
Trail contact: Los Padres National Forest, Ojai Ranger District, 1190 E. Ojai Ave., Ojai 93023; (805) 646-4348; www.fs.usda.gov/main/lpnf/home
Fees and permits: Day-use fee if you park in the Rose Valley Campground, or free (no Adventure Pass required as of the writing of this book) to park outside the campground and walk in, which adds about 0.2 mile round-trip. Rose Valley Campground is managed by the Parks Management Company (https://campone.com) for the US Forest Service.

Finding the trailhead: Google Maps: Rose Valley Campground. From Ojai, drive 15 miles north on CA 33, climbing into the mountains. At the Sespe Road turnoff, follow signs for Rose Valley Campground. Take this road for 3 miles and turn right on Chief Peak Road, following signs for Rose Valley Campground again (may be closed if the road is damaged). The gate to the campground is sometimes closed during high water due to a shallow seasonal creek that occasionally flows over the road (logs over the creek allow foot traffic to pass without wet feet). **GPS:** N34 31.572' / W119 10.565'

The Hike

One route report describes this hike as Yosemite-esque. We were doubtful, until we visited the falls after a big storm. Found in the western part of the Topatopa Mountains, Rose Valley sees moderate traffic despite being considered one of the better attractions to the already-interesting Ojai area. Suitable for families and dogs on a leash, the hike is worth the long but scenic drive from town.

As you turn toward the campground on the road, you can see the impressive upper falls dropping 300 feet over two tiers. The falls are best viewed in the winter when the water level is high and vegetation is low. This hike takes you to the base of the smaller, lower falls—which itself is one of the more impressive falls in Southern California.

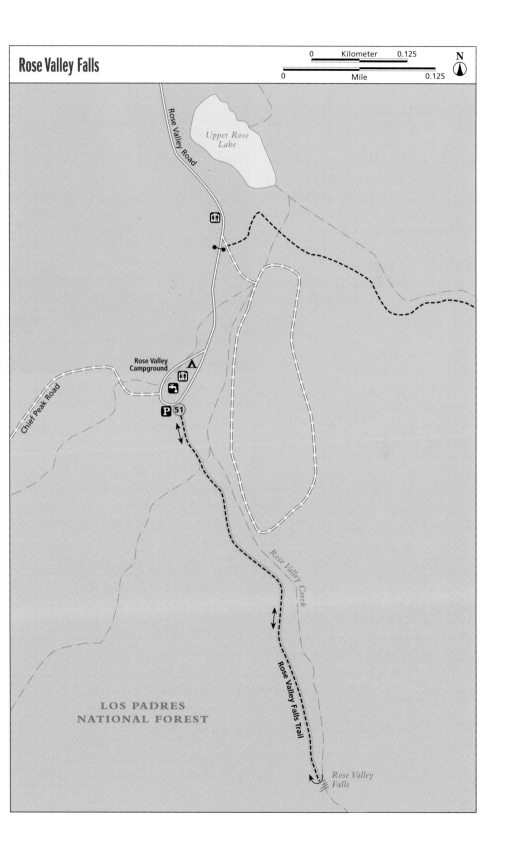

Rose Valley Falls

0 Kilometer 0.125

0 Mile 0.125

N

Rose Valley Road

Upper Rose Lake

Rose Valley Campground

Chief Peak Road

P 51

Rose Valley Creek

Rose Valley Falls Trail

LOS PADRES NATIONAL FOREST

Rose Valley Falls

From the back of the campground near site 4, follow a straightforward path (FR 22W15). Even after the Thomas Fire, which burned the area, the trail is in impeccable shape thanks to the US Forest Service and volunteers. In order for vegetation to regenerate after the fire, seeds and soil need to be given space and time to heal. Please stay on the main trail when visiting and resist the temptation to take use trails off the main trail.

Cross a tributary of Rose Valley Creek at 0.1 mile, which flows to Rose Valley Lake (you perhaps noticed it on the drive here). The trail gradually ascends on the right side of the creek, with stunning views of the upper falls almost the whole way. You travel through bay trees and oaks already growing from what was left after the Thomas Fire.

A stone stair trail goes down to a cascade on the creek. That's a fine place to get away from the crowds, but the real showstopper is ahead.

If you're able to visit in the winter or spring, the family-friendly hike to the base of Rose Valley Falls can be one of the most magical waterfall hikes described in the book.

The lower falls are in a small grotto tumbling down a cliff. You can walk right to its base and get a shower. The moss and molten lava–looking rock reminds waterfall chasers of Nojoqui Falls, Limekiln Falls, or even Escondido Falls. This area is notable for arkosic sandstone cliffs, which are rich in feldspar. The most notable arkose formation is Uluru in Australia. Here at Rose Valley there's limestone under the moss. If visiting in winter, there may even be icicles.

Miles and Directions

0.0 Start at trailhead behind campsite 4.

0.1 Cross creek.

0.35 Base of falls. Return the way you came.

0.7 Arrive back at the trailhead.

52 Potrero John Falls

This short wilderness hike, which can be done as a backpacking trip, requires faith, patience, navigation, and bushwhacking to accomplish.

Height: About 70 feet
Beauty rating: ★★★★
Distance: 5.6 miles out and back
Elevation gain: 900 feet
Difficulty: Moderate to difficult navigation
Best season: Winter, spring
County: Ventura
Trailhead amenities: Parking along windy road: 4 spots nearby, another 8 farther out

Land status: Los Padres National Forest, Sespe Wilderness
Maps: Tom Harrison Sespe Wilderness; USGS Wheeler Springs
Trail contact: Los Padres National Forest, Ojai Ranger District, 1190 E. Ojai Ave., Ojai 93023; (805) 646-4348; www.fs.usda.gov/main/lpnf/home
Fees and permits: None

Finding the trailhead: Google Maps: Potrero John Trailhead. From the intersection of CA 150 and CA 33 in Ojai, take CA 33 north for 20.9 miles, passing Wheeler Springs and Rose Valley Road along the way. The trailhead is marked with a brown sign you can see from the road right after you cross the bridge over Potrero John Creek at mile marker 32.10.
GPS: N34 35.058' / W119 16.075'

The Hike

These elusive, rugged wilderness falls are seasonal and require navigation, scrambling, and bushwhacking skills to reach. Expect more than a dozen creek crossings during springtime (though even when the Forest Service was reporting the nearby Sespe River Trail had waist-deep crossings, Potrero John Creek was calf-deep at most). The first mile along the trail leads to a primitive backcountry campsite. Afterward, the trail becomes muddy, overgrown, and harder to follow—the route was much easier to follow before the fires and debris flow. The last 0.7 mile of trail can be difficult to follow through thick brush, and it's easy to resign yourself to walking right in the creek (or turning around before the falls). As a result the trail doesn't see much traffic relative to others in the area.

Start on the clear, signed trail near the vehicle bridge over Potrero John Creek. It's named for John Power, a turn-of-the-twentieth-century resident. Potrero is a loanword from Spanish for "meadow." It means long mesas with slopes on one end with higher terrain, often referencing an open range used to graze horses.

Within 500 feet of starting, climb over a short rockfall section. The trail starts in a pleasant, narrow canyon. Sandstone cliff towers rise hundreds of feet on both sides of the creek. Trees grow at odd angles on strangely sloped geologic upheavals. It reminds me of the Gila Wilderness in New Mexico more than Southern California.

Continue to follow the creek upstream with creek crossing after crossing. This is a hike where you should expect to get your feet wet in winter or spring. Large cedars keep the trailside shady.

Cross into the signed Sespe Wilderness, designated in 1992 and the fourth-largest roadless area in the Lower 48. The Sespe is the largest wilderness near a major city in the United States.

You're among oaks, cedars, and large cottonwood trees. Mountain mahogany, yerba santa, manzanita, and sagebrush line the trail. The farther you get up the trail, the more it feels like you are in a tunnel of vegetation. After 1 mile the canyon opens up. Bigcone Douglas fir grows along the east slope. You may notice signs of a fire that burned here in 2003, but the vegetation has come back.

The trailhead up the sandstone cliff lined canyon that holds Potrero John Creek.

The trail heads northwest at 1.3 miles with views of the aptly named Pine Mountain ridge ahead with heights of more than 7,000 feet. The trail climbs gently. For about 0.5 mile you stay within earshot but not within view of the creek. At 1.9 miles the trail drops close to the creek. Now the navigation gets trickier. A use trail here goes almost all the way to the falls, but there are also use trails that go nowhere.

Although the final section is only for those with the skills and patience to navigate, here's tips to find the correct use trail: You may see a confluence with a tributary from a canyon that joins from the east. Do not go up this canyon. Instead, stay on the same creek you've been following. On the right side of the creek, you may find a lone cottonwood tree growing over a campfire pit. Cross the creek back to its left (west) bank, where the trail stays until almost the end.

The canyon narrows with steep sandstone walls. The cascades on the creek become larger and the nearby walls steeper. While this looks like a good spot for a waterfall, you still have about 0.5 mile to go. If you find the correct trail, it should be relatively easy going. You pass two rugged campsites with fire pits. For the next 0.5 mile, the use trail stays about 20 to 40 feet above on the left (west) bank of the creek, contouring above the creek—not often within sight of the water and often within the trees. If you can't find the trail, you can walk in the waterway, but it's slower, slippery, and loose.

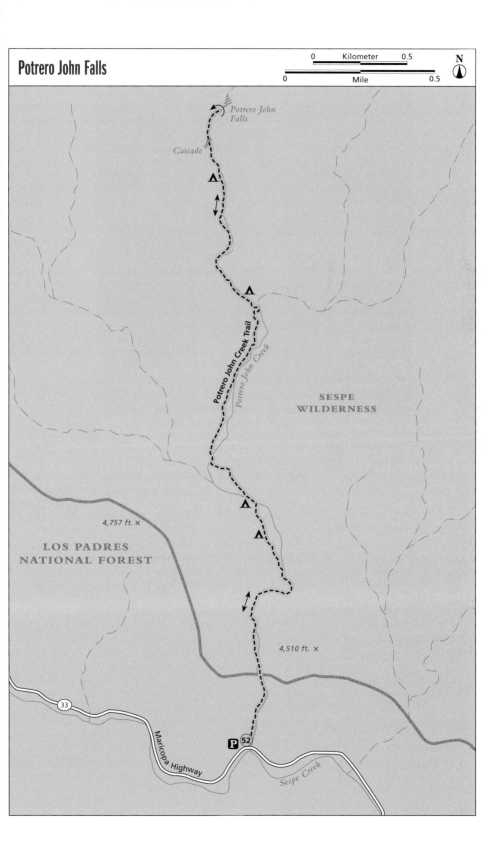

Potrero John Falls

Potrero John Falls

Cascade

Potrero John Creek Trail

Potrero John Creek

SESPE WILDERNESS

4,757 ft. ×

LOS PADRES NATIONAL FOREST

4,510 ft. ×

Maricopa Highway

Sespe Creek

N

Kilometer
0   0.5

Mile
0   0.5

33

P 52

It can feel like a lot of work to get to Potero John Falls if you get off route, but I assure you that it exists!

When the water channel narrows and turns into a gully of blue water with its tallest cascade about 10 feet high, continue up the creek without trail for about 0.2 more mile, scrambling at the end.

The falls tumbles in two tiers, improbable and surprising to find in this gentle canyon and wild place. The surrounding cliffs and the narrow gorge make this hike feel like one of the wildest and most remote in this book—which it is!

Miles and Directions

0.0 Trailhead.

0.25 Wilderness boundary sign.

1.0 Large primitive camp to left of trail.

1.1 Another camp.

1.75 Canyon widens.

2.25 Another small camp.

2.5 Large primitive camp in trees.

2.6 Cascade.

2.8 Waterfall. Return the way you came.

5.6 Arrive back at the trailhead.

53 Matilija Falls

Public access to this trail was the subject of a recent win for hikers. This rough use trail was damaged by the debris flow of 2018, but leads to more than three falls and a famous swimming hole. It requires navigation skills, stamina, patience, and physical ability, but can be done as a backpacking trip.

Height: About 25 feet
Beauty rating: ★★★★
Distance: 8 miles out and back
Elevation gain: 800+ feet
Difficulty: Strenuous and difficult navigation, especially post-fire and debris flow
Best season: Spring, summer, fall
County: Ventura
Trailhead amenities: About 30 parking spots including along dirt road, dog-friendly

Land status: Los Padres National Forest, Matilija Wilderness
Maps: Tom Harrison Sespe Wilderness; Bryan Conant Matilija and Dick Smith Wilderness
Trail contact: Los Padres National Forest, Ojai Ranger District, 1190 E. Ojai Ave., Ojai 93023; (805) 646-4348; www.fs.usda.gov/main/lpnf/home
Fees and permits: None

Finding the trailhead: Google Maps: Matilija Trail–Trailhead. From CA 150 in Ojai, take CA 33 north toward Maricopa for 5 miles. Turn left up the steep, once-hidden Matilija Road/FR 5N13. Drive for 5 miles on narrow dirt road until you reach a dirt parking area/trailhead. Landslides and floods happen often, and the road may be closed in winter or after rain.
GPS: N34 30.184' / W119 22.290'

The Hike

Matilija Falls was among the worst hit by the Thomas Fire and subsequent debris flow. Yet the falls, swimming pools, and wilderness backdrop make it worth a visit. The Los Padres Forest Association spent much of 2018–2019 rebuilding the trail and campsites; this century-old area can now be enjoyed again.

If you choose to hike within the burn area, beware of unstable loose soil and rocks. Boulders and entire trees were uprooted in the debris flow of 2019. Even before the fire, parts of this route required scrambling and following the creek without trail. If you visited prior to 2018, the landscape has changed.

There are free, primitive, undeveloped camps near the route, making this well suited to be enjoyed as a backpacking trip.

From the trailhead and parking, follow Matilija Canyon Road/FR 5N13, built by the CCC during the Depression, through the gate toward the Matilija Canyon Wildlife Refuge. Your route follows the Middle Fork of Matilija Creek and is surrounded by private property until you reach the 29,600-acre Matilija Wilderness, which was established in 1992 by the Los Padres Condor Range and River Protection Act. Old Man Mountain (5,500 feet) dominates the skyline.

A VICTORY FOR PUBLIC ACCESS TO PUBLIC LAND

Under California law, the public has the right to use historic trails if an area was accessed prior to 1972 and was used by the public for five or more continuous years, as long as someone who hiked the trail before 1972 testifies as proof. As time passes, these hikers are becoming rarer, and advocates are working to get the law to apply to coastal access as well. Matilija Falls is an excellent example of how rights-of-way can be established in federal court to allow future generations access to public land.

The Middle Fork Matilija Creek Trail winds through a checkerboard of public and private lands to ultimately end in the federally designated Matilija Wilderness in Los Padres National Forest. When landowners barred access in 2009, Keep Sespe Wild and Los Padres ForestWatch successfully sued for public access in 2016. Regardless of the condition of the trail, there is now permanent, public access to this special place via a 10-foot-wide easement maintained by the Ojai Valley Land Conservancy. There is also a public easement access on Matilija Canyon Road. Part of the agreement requires conservation groups to reconstruct trail. Please be respectful of private property as you hike this route.

Matilija Sandstone is only found in Santa Barbara and Ventura Counties. You'll pass notable formations on the hike up Matilija Creek. Matilija (Mah-til-luh-hah) is named after a Matâ'ilha, a Chumash village in the area and Chief Matilija, who may have fought against the Spanish at Mission Buenaventura in 1924.

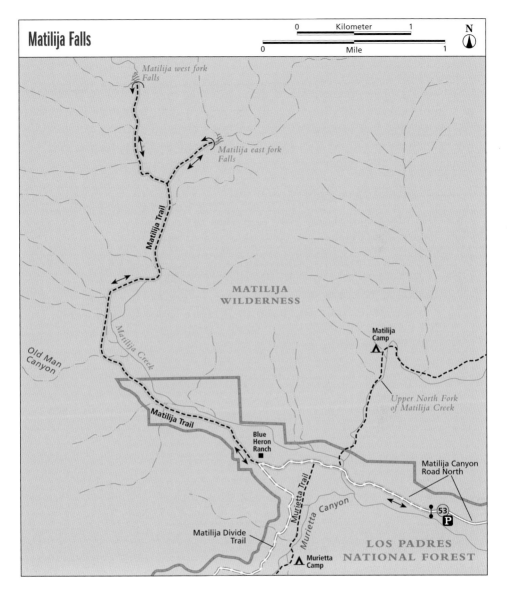

After about 0.6 mile on the road, a trail on the right leads to the North Fork Matilija Trail, which goes up the canyon on your right for 0.7 mile to Matilija Camp. Continue up the road for another 0.1 mile; Murietta Canyon and the Murietta Canyon Trail are on your left, named for an infamous nineteenth-century Mexican bandit. A camp is located 0.5 mile south of here. Continue straight/right on a public access easement through the private historic orchards of Blue Heron Ranch, leaving the Murietta Divide Road/Trail at 1.1 miles.

After the orchards the navigation gets rougher but the geology more interesting. You're in the Sespe formation, a purple and red erratic vaulted strata of rocks.

Pass Matilija Camp. It was covered in boulders during the debris flow, but used to have numerous swimming holes where you could spot native trout or the rare western pond turtle. As you continue the rough journey upstream, look for Old Man Canyon on your left.

About 1.25 miles after Old Man Canyon, reach the confluence of the West Fork of Matilija Creek and the main East Fork. Turning left leads you in 0.25 mile to the falls on the West Fork of Matilija Creek, which is two-tiered in a cove of sandstone cliffs. Taking the trail to the right leads 0.5 mile later to the falls on the East Fork of Matilija Creek, which tumbles off calcite into a blue-green pool and a cave.

Miles and Directions

0.0 Start at the parking lot trailhead and head up the road.

0.6 Upper North Fork Matilija trailhead on right.

0.75 Murietta Canyon trailhead on left.

1.1 Junction to cross through easement across Blue Heron Ranch.

2.3 Old Man Canyon joins on left.

3.5 Confluence of West Fork of Matilija Creek and East Fork. Choose a direction to head to a waterfall.

4.0 Waterfalls. Return the way you came.

8.0 Arrive back at the trailhead.

54 Piru Falls

If you enjoyed the navigation and wilderness of Potrero John and Matilija Falls, consider them a warm-up to this difficult and strenuous canyon—which you may prefer to tackle as a backpacking trip. These ephemeral falls may last only weeks, but though incredible, are just part of what makes this hike memorable. It requires a car shuttle or pickup.

Height: About 30–50 feet

Beauty rating: ★ ★ ★ ★ ★

Distance: Approximately 22 miles one-way (distance depends on your own cross-country route; requires car shuttle or pickup)

Elevation gain: 400 feet gain/2,200 feet loss (but due to cross-country travel, is much more difficult than an on-trail version with similar statistics)

Difficulty: Extremely strenuous; extremely difficult micro-navigation

Best season: Spring (call ranger district for water level and trail conditions)

County: Los Angeles and Ventura

Trailhead amenities: About 50 parking spots, outhouse (may be locked), dogs ok but not recommended

Land status: Starts in Angeles National Forest, ends in Los Padres National Forest at the Lake Piru Recreation Area

Maps: Tom Harrison Sespe Wilderness; USGS Whitaker Peak, Cobblestone Mountain; recommended to look at the satellite view before you go

Trail contact: Los Padres National Forest, Ojai Ranger District, 1190 E. Ojai Ave., Ojai 93023; (805) 646-4348; www.fs.usda.gov/main/lpnf/home

Fees and permits: Day-use parking fee at Piru Lake National Recreation Area. Gates locked at night. As the area is remote without cell service and almost no other foot traffic, it's essential to call the Los Padres Ojai Ranger District to learn about conditions and flooding before you go. There are sections that are narrow, and high flow could be dangerous or deadly.

Finding the trailhead: South end (for car shuttle): Google Maps: Lake Piru Recreation Area. From I-5 North, take CA 126 west for 11 miles into the town of Piru, following signs to the Lake Piru Recreation Area 7.2 miles later. Pay the day-use fee at the entrance station (only accessible sunrise to sunset) and drive 2.3 miles up Piru Canyon Road to the Juan Fernandez Boat Launch, the last parking lot before the locked gate.

North end (start of hike): Google Maps: Frenchmens Flat Picnic Area, Castaic 91384 (the actual destination is beyond). From I-5, take the Templin Highway/Golden State Highway exit and turn left under I-5. Turn right onto the Golden State Highway (a frontage road). At 2.2 miles past Oak Flat Campground, park in a wide lot along the road before a locked gate.
GPS: N34 36.590' / W118 44.376'

Note: The last 6 miles of the hike are on a paved road. Some hikers decide to leave a locked bike nearby to make the hike out shorter.
GPS: N34 28.322' / W118 45.379'

The seasonal and highly ephemeral waterfall in Piru Creek in the narrows section of the canyon is just one of the many splendors on this challenging but deeply rewarding bushwhack, swim, and hike down Piru Canyon. It may take a lifetime of skills, experience, practice, and the right conditions and hiking partners to make it down Piru and is not to be attempted lightheartedly.

The Hike

Skilled hikers who want a challenging approach to a waterfall can visit Piru Canyon—a remote area of Los Padres National Forest. Though short, seasonal, and not a waterfall on a named creek, the overall quality makes it worth a visit, even if the falls aren't running. Expect sun and slow, rough bushwhacking and difficult micro-navigation finding your way around vegetation and logjams. While backpacking in can help cut down your daily mileage, you'll likely be swimming for portions of the trip and must pack accordingly. Consider leaving your phone at home lest it get wet and fail to function afterward (my hiking party knows from experience). Start early, wear protective clothing and sturdy shoes, and bring emergency supplies.

Although not technical, at times this hike feels more like canyoneering than hiking. There's almost no trail, lots of riverbank walking, snakes, ticks, and possible swimming. Once you're in the twisted canyon, the only way out is backward or forward. With all the rock scrambling and logs here, one foul step could lead to a busted ankle or worse. There are no bailout points, so those who attempt it must be committed. Call the ranger first, and leave an itinerary and emergency instructions with loved ones. There's no cell reception for the entire length of the hike, so consider carrying a satellite SOS messenger or PLB. After calling the ranger station, postpone your trip if Piru Creek is flowing too fast or high (people can kayak this creek). However, when water levels are low, like in the autumn, the waterfall probably won't run.

Start at the parking area for Frenchmens Flat, following Piru Creek southwest and then west through thick cottonwood and willow. There may be remnants of a rough, narrow trail through house-sized boulders here and evidence of anglers' camps from those seeking trout. It's not long before your feet get wet. You'll crisscross, wade, and swim through the creek for much of the hike.

At 5.3 miles in, North Fork of Fish Creek joins from the right (northwest). Check how long it took you to get here and consider it a possible turnaround point, as the route gets more difficult due to increased vegetation and logjams. Otherwise, continue following Piru Creek as it now heads south, and keep an eye out for rattlesnakes.

The farther you hike, the more the canyon walls rise above you. At times they can be hundreds of feet high with striations of different-colored rock ranging from 600 million years old (Precambrian metamorphic rocks) to tens of millions of years old (Eocene sedimentary rocks).

The highlight of the trip is 9.5 to 10 miles in at the Narrows of Piru Gorge, a slot canyon that can hold significant water and may require swimming. The conglomerate rock here looks carved as if by a large-scale abstract sculptor. About 0.3 mile into the heart of the narrows where it widens, but approximately 0.4 mile north of the confluence with Ruby Canyon, the falls joins on the right (west). With a backdrop of the tall walls of the slot canyon and the curved lines of the rock, it feels unlike anything outside of Utah. Linger here and marvel, picnicking on the sandy ground around its base.

The canyon widens after this, though your walking-in-water days are not over yet. As the canyon opens, you may notice Ellis Apiary Camp (1,240 feet). This turn-of-the-twentieth-century beekeeping area has no facilities other than abandoned historic stoves. For those backpacking, ending here at 11.75 miles into the hike will feel like a full day. Although the topo map shows falls up Turtle Canyon, the route hasn't been maintained and isn't recommended.

You may find bits of trail through here that'll keep you away from the creek (and into the grass—check for ticks), but soon the canyon becomes narrow, surrounded by walls of a Juncal formation filled with cobbles in sandstone. Here you return to walk in the rocky water. At the confluence of Michael and Piru Creeks, you leave the Sespe Wilderness.

At around 13.5 miles the creek joins and follows remnants of an at-times-flooded dirt road. Take this road. After crossing Agua Blanca Creek near its confluence with Piru Creek, another dirt road (Agua Blanca Trail/FR 19W10) on your right leads to Devils Gateway. The route passes through a gate before reaching the Whitaker Ranch. Please respect private property here and leash your dog.

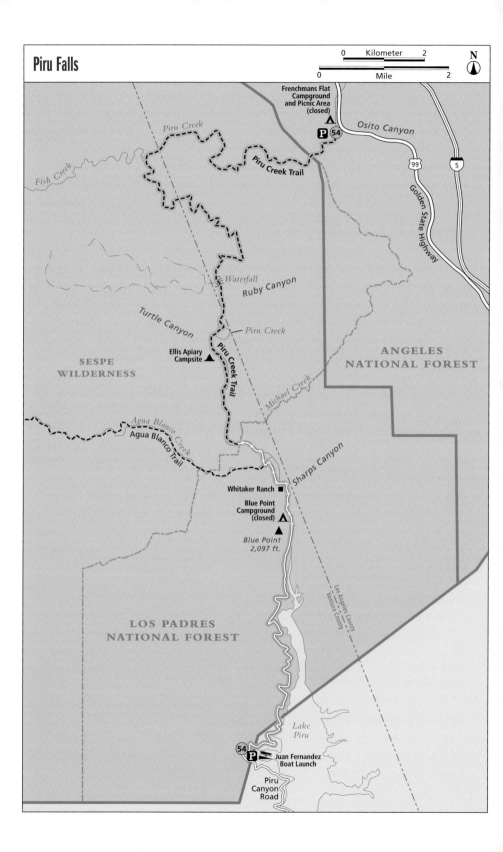

Piru Falls

0   Kilometer   2

0   Mile   2

N

Frenchmans Flat
Campground
and Picnic Area
(closed)

P 54

Osito Canyon

99

5

Piru Creek

Fish Creek

Piru Creek Trail

Golden State Highway

Waterfall

Ruby Canyon

Turtle Canyon

Piru Creek

**ANGELES
NATIONAL FOREST**

Ellis Apiary
Campsite ▲

Piru Creek Trail

**SESPE
WILDERNESS**

Michael Creek

Agua Blanco Creek

Agua Blanco Trail

Sharps Canyon

Whitaker Ranch ■

Blue Point
Campground
(closed) ▲

▲

Blue Point
2,097 ft.

Los Angeles County
Ventura County

**LOS PADRES
NATIONAL FOREST**

Lake
Piru

54 **P** ⚓ Juan Fernandez
Boat Launch

Piru
Canyon
Road

Piru Canyon is arguably the most difficult hike in this book, but the views and experience reward the experienced and skilled hikers who visit.

A mile and a half later, reach the Blue Point Campground, closed in 1999 to protect the arroyo toad. Blue Point refers to the serpentine rock outcrop (2,097 feet tall) above the Sespe formation sandstone to the west.

The last 6 miles are on a hilly paved road closed to cars at the request of the Department of Water. You drop to the boater- and picnicker–surrounded Lake Piru, built in 1955 and held up by the Santa Felicia Dam, before reaching your car.

Miles and Directions

Note: As the route description is "forge your own route" downstream, mileage may vary depending on your route-finding. Mileage here is approximate based on my experience.

0.0 Frenchmens parking area.

5.3 Confluence of North Fork Fish Creek.

9.5–10.0 Narrows and waterfall.

11.75 Ellis Apiary Camp.

13.75 Cross Agua Blanca Creek.

16.0 Closed Blue Point Campground.

22.0 Piru Lake parking.

Santa Barbara Area and the Central Coast

Los Padres National Forest was named for the padres who built the mission here in Santa Barbara. It's the second-largest US Forest Service unit in the state. Established as part of the US Forest Service system in 1905, it includes slot canyons and sandstone geology. Over half the forest is wilderness.

Summers are hot and waterfalls may be dry. But in winter and spring, there are beautiful falls surrounded by wildfires and swimming holes. The western Santa Ynez Mountains in the frontcountry are mostly made of Miocene-era sedimentary geology.

This is the ancestral home of the Chumash people. A coastal tribe who lived between Malibu and San Luis Obispo, they were skilled in seafaring before disease and conscription into the mission system reduced their populations. Many of the falls are associated with Chumash legends. For example, Nojoqui Falls may be associated with star-crossed lovers who may have leapt from the top.

Many of the hikes in the Santa Barbara area were impacted by the 2017 Thomas Fire and subsequent debris flow in 2018. Through herculean efforts by volunteers, nonprofits, and the Forest Service, many of the trails have been restored. Check the Resources section at the back of this book for more on how to get involved in trail building and maintenance in this region. Because so many trails were impacted, call the ranger station and check for conditions prior to your trip.

55 San Ysidro Falls

This impressive falls tumbles over a sandstone composite cliff and is among the only falls in the area accessible completely by trail. Unlike other falls impacted by the post–Thomas Fire landslides, San Ysidro is open to visitors, easy to access, and on excellent trail.

Height: 40-60 feet
Beauty rating: ★★★★★
Distance: 3.6 miles out and back
Elevation gain: 800+ feet
Difficulty: Easy to moderate (last 0.1 mile requires navigating around a washout)
Best season: Fall, winter, spring
County: Santa Barbara
Trailhead amenities: About 100 parking spots, dog-friendly, free maps at information kiosk

Land status: Between parts of Los Padres National Forest
Maps: USGS Carpinteria, Santa Barbara; Bryan Conant's Matilija and Dick Smith Wilderness
Trail contact: Los Padres National Forest, Santa Barbara Ranger District, 3505 Paradise Rd., Santa Barbara 93105; (805) 967-3481; www.fs.usda.gov/main/lpnf/home
Fees and permits: None

Finding the trailhead: Google Maps: San Ysidro Trailhead. From US 101 North, exit 93 for San Ysidro, continuing right on San Ysidro Road for 1 mile. Turn right onto East Valley Road for 0.9 mile. Turn left onto Park Lane, which turns into East Mountain Drive, for 0.6 mile. The trailhead is on the right between two houses at the end of the road before crossing the creek. **GPS:** N34 26.456' / W119 37.201'

The Hike

The town of Montecito, San Ysidro Creek, and its canyon were devastated following the Thomas Fire in 2017 and debris flow on January 9, 2018. But by early 2019 when we visited, the trail was in excellent shape thanks to volunteer groups like the Montecito Trails Foundation.

The trail starts on the right at the end of the road before the creek by a sign between two houses marked "San Ysidro Trail." Follow the trail between the fences of two homes for 500 feet until you reach a wooden "Montecito Trails" sign. Follow the trail signs indicating you should turn left onto pavement, walking West Park Lane uphill through the neighborhood until the end of the road (no parking allowed here). The gorge created by Montecito Creek is below to your left, an impressive testament to the power of water.

A quarter mile into the hike, turn left at a Y onto a dirt trail. Signs indicate you turn left with a gate and Private Property sign keeping you away. Continue on the trail to the right. Just 0.1 mile later you're on the same road on the other side of that gate. It seems petty, but the owners ask that you stay on the dirt trail around the gate instead.

On the upper part of this paved road, turn left to rejoin the road for a few feet until it becomes a dirt road at a signed junction with the Old Pueblo Trail. Stay straight, through a gate, and downhill on the Edison Catwalk dirt road, following signs for the San Ysidro Trail. Follow the creek upstream past cascades. This wide dirt road was recently regraded and is in excellent condition, with incredible views of how large the creek can get.

Half a mile in, ignore a signed junction for the McMenemy Trail to the left, which crosses the creek. Stick to your wide, easy-to-navigate dirt fire road. As you ascend, notice the impressive rock cliffs on the opposite side of the creek. Below, San Ysidro Creek forms a narrower, but deep chasm with cascades. At 0.75 mile into the hike, a creek crosses the trail. Ignore a fire road that joins above from the right.

After another dry creek crosses the road, reach a signed junction for the San Ysidro Trail at 0.9 mile. Follow it uphill to the right on singletrack through an oak forest. You may see wild cucumber and views of the ocean far below.

San Ysidro Creek turns to the right and so does the trail. The area you're walking did not burn in the Thomas Fire, but many nearby hillsides did. After a rain the soil smells of ash, and a dark layer can be seen in some of the soil.

At 1.3 miles into the hike, the trail ascends. Below, the creek has 15-foot cascades. Newly rebuilt and reinforced trail leads up stone steps and switchbacks. At 1.5 miles a metal bannister along the left separates you from the cliff edge above the creek. You

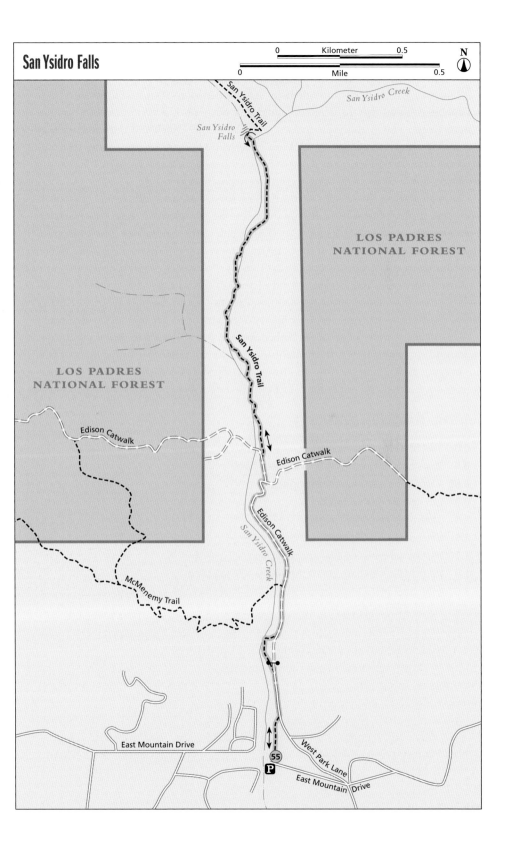

San Ysidro Falls

soon cross under a large overhanging boulder. Stand underneath and listen to it echo the sound of the larger cascades of the creek below.

The trail gets steeper through here up wooden stairs, but you'll notice at 1.7 miles that the trail flattens. Then it "ends" at a washout at a 90-degree bend in San Ysidro Creek. This is also the confluence of San Ysidro Creek and the tributary that is home to this waterfall. It's a confusing "intersection"—to the right is the true San Ysidro Creek, bending to join the creek you've been following. Straight ahead is the tributary, home to the falls, which joins the main creek here.

Your goal is to go straight across San Ysidro Creek and follow its tributary. If you look in that direction, you may even see the top of San Ysidro Falls. Getting there requires crossing San Ysidro Creek right before the confluence. You'll be going straight ahead up the canyon in the same trajectory you've been traveling for a while, north-northwest. Do not turn right (east) up the "true" San Ysidro Creek.

Any evidence of trail on the left side (west) of the tributary has eroded away. As of 2019 there's evidence of the good, reinforced trail up on the hillside straight ahead above the right (east) bank of the tributary. Your goal is to get back up to that trail.

Less than 0.1 mile on good reinforced tread, the trail starts switchbacking up the hillside to the right. But at the switchback before you climb or turn right, the falls are straight ahead. After the fires and landslides, the soils are sensitive, so do your best to stay on the trail and enjoy the falls from this switchback.

Miles and Directions

0.0 Start at trailhead at end of road.

0.5 Stay straight at junction with McMenemy Trail.

0.85 A road joins from above to the right.

0.9 Turn right on San Ysidro Trail.

1.3 Fifteen-foot cascades on creek.

1.5 Metal banister along the side of trail.

1.7 Washed-out creek; creative navigation required.

1.8 View of falls near base of falls. Return the way you came.

3.6 Arrive back at the trailhead.

56 Cold Springs Falls (Tangerine)

The wild-feeling, 150-plus-foot-tall falls gets its name from an orange-ish color to the travertine under the falls. Visible via an easy-to-moderate trail or by a more rugged use trail for the adventurous, wildflower-covered hills, paragliders overhead, and views of the ocean make this an incredible spring hike.

Height: Probably over 150 feet
Beauty rating: ★★★★★
Distance: 1.7 miles out and back (lower viewpoint); 3 miles out and back (upper viewpoint)
Elevation gain: Mostly level
Difficulty: Easy to moderate (first viewpoint); strenuous (second viewpoint)
Best season: Winter, spring
County: Santa Barbara

Trailhead amenities: 20 parking spots in a small lot along the road
Land status: Los Padres National Forest
Maps: USGS Santa Barbara; Bryan Conant's Matilija and Dick Smith Wilderness
Trail contact: Los Padres National Forest, Santa Barbara Ranger District, 3505 Paradise Rd., Santa Barbara 93105; (805) 967-3481; www.fs.usda.gov/main/lpnf/home
Fees and permits: None

Finding the trailhead: Google Maps: Tangerine Falls Trailhead or 960 East Mountain Drive, Montecito, CA. From US 101 North, exit 94A for Olive Mill Road, which turns into Hot Springs Road. Take it for 2.9 miles. Turn right on East Mountain Drive until you reach trailhead parking about 1 mile later.
GPS: N34 27.216' / W119 39.114'

The Hike

Note: The surrounding area burned in the December 2017 Thomas Fire. In January 2018, flooding and debris flows killed at least twenty-one people and destroyed more than one hundred homes in the surrounding area. Although the trail was closed through 2018, its restoration is a priority for the Montecito Trails Foundation and Los Padres Forest Association and it was in passable condition as of late February 2019. Check www.montecitotrailsfoundation.info and the US Forest Service website, and call the rangers to determine conditions.

The Santa Ynez Forest Service was established in 1899, and rangers used the West Fork of Cold Springs Canyon to patrol the backcountry. Finding it difficult to maintain, they built the East Fork of Cold Springs Canyon Trail (which you intersect at 0.5 mile) in 1905.

We split this hike into two parts—the first leads to a safe viewing point of the falls from good trail, while the more difficult part takes a use trail to approach the falls. The use trail can be steep, loose, slippery, muddy, and dangerous when wet, and may require clinging to rocks or branches. There's also poison oak along the way.

Both routes start in an upscale residential neighborhood. East Mountain Drive used to continue over Cold Springs Creek on a concrete ford. In 2018 it was washed away in the debris flows, but in 2019 construction was under way, so this could change. As of 2019 the trailhead starts at a gate that says "Road Closed." From the gate, walk up the road for 0.2 mile until you reach the end of the paved road and the creek.

There are three trailheads in a row here—make sure you take the correct one. At first, the West Fork of Cold Springs Trail parallels the creek on its right (east) side and is the *second* trailhead you encounter. You do not need to hop across the creek (yet). The Ridge Trail to the East Fork (which you do not want) climbs switchbacks and has a wooden sign.

Follow the eroded trail along the right (east) side of the creek for 0.3 mile. This is the confluence of the East Fork and the West Fork. Here, there is an important intersection no longer marked as of February 2019. If you were to continue along the right (southeast) bank straight on the trail, you'd follow the East Fork of Cold Springs. Instead, you need to get to the West Fork. Turn left, wading or hopping across the creek. Cross at a spot where it looks like two creeks are joining and there's an "island" of land in between, near a large boulder with fading blue graffiti.

Good trail continues on the other side. There is no need to follow the West Fork upstream on rough rocks. If you've been doing this and get to a point where you see a suspension "bridge" holding a white pipe over the West Fork, go back downstream and look for the trail.

Once you're gradually ascending on shady, good trail, you pass what looks like miniature caves on the left. The trail follows a 4-inch water pipe. You ascend above the creek on a wide trail. Still, the drop-off can seem high and steep.

The trail has ferns and wild cucumber vines, with views of the creek flowing below. After 0.85 mile you get your first view of the falls hovering above the canyon. For those who prefer a shorter, straightforward hike, this is the best spot to appreciate the falls. You may also see colorful groups of parasailers, who enjoy launching nearby.

For experienced hikers with the energy and skills to navigate rough, eroded, and exposed terrain, continue on the trail. At 0.9 mile you reach a junction marked only by a wooden post. To the left on good trail is the way to the West Fork trailhead on Gibraltar Road (an alternate way of reaching the falls). To continue to the falls, turn right at the post. Follow a narrower, more overgrown trail near two giant boulders. Many hikers, especially those with dogs and children, decide to turn back here.

If you continue on, follow a rusted pipe to a seasonal (often dry) tributary 0.1 mile from the intersection. As of my scouting, the trail was eroded around the embankment, but continues across the tributary following the rusted pipe (it will be on your right). You may need to go down and around to reconnect to the trail.

◀ *West Cold Springs Falls gets its nickname "Tangerine" from the color of the rock. The rough trail to the waterfall's base was washed away in the 2018 debris flow. The route to the viewpoint shown in this photo is sometimes called the "Root Cellar trail" because it goes to the remains of a homestead at the top of the falls.*

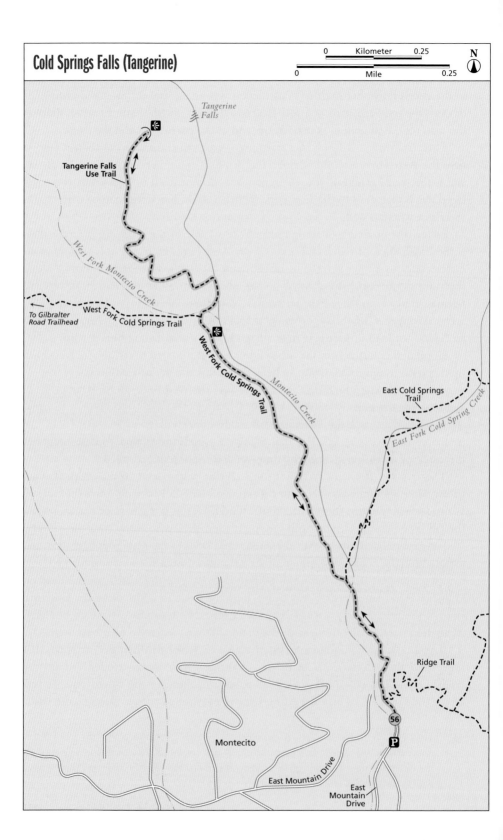

Cold Springs Falls (Tangerine)

0   Kilometer   0.25

0   Mile   0.25

N

Tangerine Falls

Tangerine Falls Use Trail

West Fork Montecito Creek

To Gilbralter Road Trailhead

West Fork Cold Springs Trail

West Fork Cold Springs Trail

Montecito Creek

East Cold Springs Trail

East Fork Cold Spring Creek

Ridge Trail

Montecito

56

P

East Mountain Drive

East Mountain Drive

Continue to follow the pipe on decent trail until you get to switchbacks that lead high up onto the hillside on the left bank of the creek. As of February 2019 a section of the trail had washed into the creek right before the start of the switchbacks. To reconnect to the trail, hop the pipe, scramble 20 feet down to the creek, walk in it for about 50 yards, and scramble 20 feet back up the bank back to the trail.

Don't make the mistake of walking too far upstream. If you see silver piping on the bank to your left (or you get to a 15-foot cascade that looks like a tougher scramble up), you've gone too far. There is what looks like a trail to the left of the cascade, but it goes nowhere.

If you've located the correct trail, switchback up and continue on narrow, over-grown but easy enough to follow trail as it climbs on the hillside to the left of the creek. You'll veer away from the water through a hillside burned in the Thomas Fire. Without the trees it can get hot and exposed. But this ecosystem is resilient, and despite the fire and debris flow, it was covered in wildflowers, wild cucumber, and verdant vegetation a year after the fire.

Certain portions of this use trail are steep and there is climbing. If the trail doesn't have grass growing in it, the dirt is loose and can feel like ball bearings in dry conditions and slippery in very wet conditions.

The primitive trail continues for 0.5 mile, eventually contouring very high above the creek for unobscured views of the falls nestled in the mountainside. The trail continues to a rock outcropping above the falls and eventually contours the hillside and descends gently to the placid streambed before the water falls over the cliff.

Unlike most falls in the Santa Ynez Mountains, the West Fork has an east-west orientation (almost everything else is north-south). Keep this in mind when attempting photography. It can be dangerous to scramble any closer to the falls; hikers have been stranded, injured, and died here. There is no cell reception, and the descent and ascent takes far longer than hiking on a trail. Start early and carry the Ten Essentials.

Miles and Directions

0.0 Start at gate near parking on paved road.

0.2 Start this hike at second trailhead right before the creek.

0.5 Turn left onto West Fork Trail by crossing the creek.

0.85 Lower view of falls from trail.

0.9 Turn right at wooden post for use trail.

1.5 Upper viewpoint for falls. Return the way you came.

3.0 Arrive back at the trailhead.

57 Seven Falls (and Mission Falls)

These falls were a famous and crowded destination hike even before 1900. The hike is exposed, sunny, and can get toasty: all reasons to cool off in the numerous swimming holes afterward. Despite its popularity, the trail is not always as clear as you may think and requires scrambling.

Height: Series of falls, all 15–25 feet
Beauty rating: ★★★
Distance: 2.5 miles out and back
Elevation gain: 350 feet
Difficulty: Easy to moderate (due to exposure)
Best season: Winter, spring
County: Santa Barbara
Trailhead amenities: About 100 parking spots, dog-friendly, free maps at information kiosk

Land status: Los Padres National Forest
Maps: USGS Santa Barbara; Bryan Conant's Matilija and Dick Smith Wilderness
Trail contact: Los Padres National Forest, Santa Barbara Ranger District, 3505 Paradise Rd., Santa Barbara 93105; (805) 967-3481; www.fs.usda.gov/main/lpnf/home
Fees and permits: None

Finding the trailhead: Google Maps: Inspiration Point Trailhead. Park at the Tunnel Trail south trailhead at the end of Tunnel Road. These popular falls can get quite crowded on weekends and holidays. Parking is limited, so expect to add up to 1.5 miles round-trip to the hiking distance to account for having to park up to 0.75 mile away from the trailhead.
GPS: N34 27.538' / W119 42.454'

The Hike

John McKinney, "The Trailmaster," who had a popular *LA Times* hiking column and wrote numerous guidebooks, notes this trail was a destination even before 1900. Now, these seven falls with numerous swimming holes are a popular destination for UCSB students and other young people. The water that feeds Mission Creek to Mission Falls and Seven Falls comes from nearby White Mountain. After the falls the creek goes through the Santa Barbara Botanic Gardens, which you drive past on your way to the trailhead.

Start at a locked gate near a water tower on a paved road. A metal sign on the other side says "Tunnel Trail/Canto Cielo Road 4.5."

Continue up the paved road following an electric line. Across the canyon are the rock towers of Arlington and Cathedral Peaks. Below are the ocean views that make Santa Barbara famous, including the Channel Islands, Arroyo Burro Beach, and the coastal plains. This section is exposed and can be quite hot as you hike uphill through chaparral, including laurel sumac and ceanothus, which blooms in the late winter and early spring. We also spotted the vine-y wild cucumber. In 0.5 mile, where the road splits, turn right and uphill on the better road. The trail/road curves

to the left and downhill toward a bridge over Mission Creek. Below the bridge, picturesque Ferndale Falls tumbles into a pool. Unfortunately, there isn't a great angle to take a photo of this falls—especially for selfies. The bridge and equipment around here is fenced off, which makes the best photo-taking areas off-limits.

Nonetheless, enjoy the beauty of these falls as you descend toward the bridge. Cross the bridge at 0.65 mile. A use trail across the bridge goes down to the pools above the bridge.

Continue uphill again on the paved road. At 0.75 mile you reach a junction where the paved road turns to dirt. There's a sign here for the Tunnel Trail. Stay straight (actually on the Jesuita Trail—its sign is now gone) and keep climbing. Less than 0.1 mile later, reach the narrow, brushy Tunnel Trail to the right. If you were to turn right and follow the Tunnel Trail for 3 miles past the Rattlesnake Connector Trail, you'd cross Mission Creek right above Mission Falls. This 200-foot waterfall is ephemeral and

One of the many falls and sunny swimming holes of Seven Falls. Bring your swimsuit!

doesn't have a great viewing spot unless you want to do sketchy rock scrambling.

To stay on course for Seven Falls, though, stay straight at the intersection. At 0.85 mile a singletrack trail heads uphill to the right. Instead, stay straight on the dirt road.

About 100 yards later you reach a three-way junction. There's no sign at this critical junction, but there are clues to ensure you turn left at the right spot. The closest thing to a sign is a metal post with a triangle sign indicating who yields to whom (bikes to hikers, everyone to horses). There's also a tree near the left side of

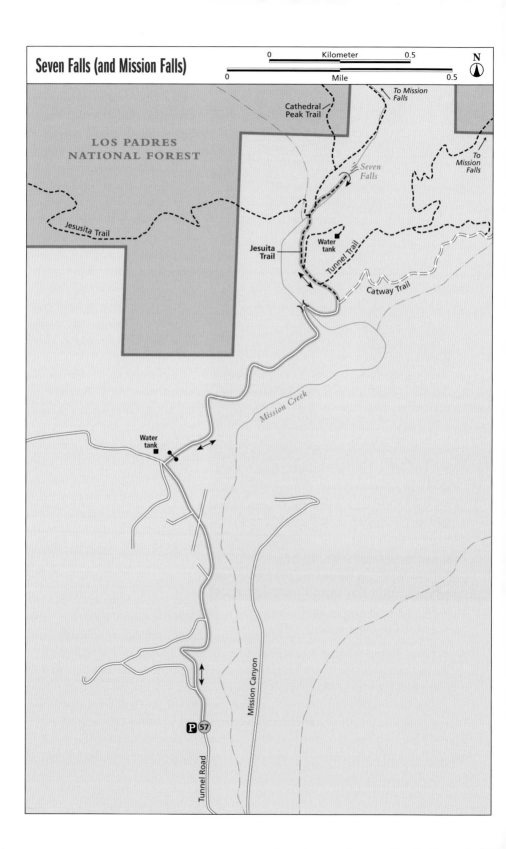

Seven Falls (and Mission Falls)

0   Kilometer   0.5

0   Mile   0.5

N

LOS PADRES
NATIONAL FOREST

Cathedral
Peak Trail

To Mission
Falls

Seven
Falls

To
Mission
Falls

Jesusita Trail

Jesuita
Trail

Water
tank

Tunnel Trail

Catway Trail

Mission Creek

Water
tank

Mission Canyon

P 57

Tunnel Road

the junction that people use to take snack breaks. To the right of the junction is a cement water tank and wooden telephone pole.

Turn onto the trail on the left/straight part of the Y, climbing before descending toward Mission Creek. After 1 mile from the trailhead, switchback down to the creek.

This is the next critical junction. Here you break away from the Jesuita Trail, which goes uphill, turning to the left away from the water. Instead, after crossing the creek, you immediately turn right, scrambling up a small sandstone slab. Now you can walk straight in the water or follow Mission Creek upstream on its left bank via the Seven Falls Trail (which looks more like a use trail).

Both routes require scrambling and special care on wet rocks. From the junction with the main trail, the use trail continues for 0.25 mile. There are several use trail options, and depending how you choose, it can be overgrown and may require hand-over-hand clambering from dirt to rock. Some people prefer to go up the waterway instead of dealing with the tick-ridden high grasses along the trail. Watch for poison oak.

The trail peters out after the first falls. A pool below makes for a decent swimming hole. There are Seven Falls of similar size, although to scramble to each requires skill, dedication, and potentital use of equipment. Mission Falls is even farther upstream and requires significant scrambling and rock climbing skills to view (or taking the Tunnel Trail, which you passed on the way here, uphill).

Miles and Directions

0.0   Start at trailhead at end of Tunnel Road.

0.5   Stay straight (left) on main road, ignoring a side road to the right.

0.6   Bridge over Mission Creek and view of top of Ferndale Falls.

0.75 Stay straight on the Jesuita Trail (continue climbing).

0.85 Stay straight on wider trail, ignoring singletrack to your right.

0.9   Stay straight (left) at important, unmarked intersection.

1.0   Switchback down to Mission Creek.

1.1   Take use trail up the streambed of Mission Creek.

1.25 First of Seven Falls. Return the way you came.

2.5   Arrive back at the trailhead.

58 Nojoqui Falls

A short, family-friendly hike begins in a county park with a playground and leads to a tall falls nestled in a forested hillside.

Height: 100-160 feet
Beauty rating: ★★★★★
Distance: 0.6 mile out and back
Elevation gain: Mostly level
Difficulty: Easy
Best season: Fall, winter, spring, summer
County: Santa Barbara
Trailhead amenities: 50+ parking spots, plus more along the side of road into parking area
(watch for No Parking signs); dogs on-leash allowed
Land status: Nojoqui Falls Park, County of Santa Barbara
Maps: USGS Solvang
Trail contact: Santa Barbara County Parks, 123 E. Anapamu St., 2nd floor, Santa Barbara 93101; (805) 568-2460; www.countyofsb.org/parks/
Fees and permits: None

Finding the trailhead: Google Maps: Nojoqui Falls Park. From US 101 North at Gaviota State Park, continue north for 6 miles, over Nojoqui Summit, and exit at Old Coast Highway following signs for Nojoqui Falls Park. Continue for 1 mile and turn left at Alisal County Road. The park is on your right. Trailhead parking is at the far southern part of the park, 0.2 mile from its entrance. **GPS:** N34 31.580' / W120 10.357'

The Hike

Note: Because mudslides and erosion happen in this narrow canyon, the county often closes the trailhead after rains—sometimes using security guards to ensure there is no public access. We visited the trailhead three times over three different weekends before finding it open. If traveling from a distance, call ahead (the website is rarely updated).

Nojoqui Falls (pronounced Nah-hoh-wee) was formed where the shale in the lower canyon meets the sandstone of the upper canyon. Calcium from the upper canyon built (and continues to build) up the falls into many layers. This is in contrast to most falls, which are eroded away by water over time. The stream originates in the Santa Ynez Mountains near Gaviota Peak, part of Los Padres National Forest. It is fed by springs and is located in one of the wettest parts of the county.

While the word "Nojoqui" is Chumash in origin, linguists debate over the meaning. Some say it is named after a Chumash village "Naxuwi" (meaning "meadow") that was located here. Others say it means "nighthawk" or "honeymoon" after a legend of star-crossed lovers who leapt from the falls. Starting in a shady oak grove, begin on a wide trail following peaceful Nojoqui Creek gently upstream. Pass 200-year-old California laurels, whose fragrance dominates this cool canyon.

While the word "Nojoqui" is Chumash in origin, linguists debate over the meaning. Some say the falls are named for a Chumash village "Naxuwi" (meaning "meadow"). Others say it means "nighthawk" or "honeymoon" after a legend of star-crossed lovers who leapt from the falls. ISTOCK

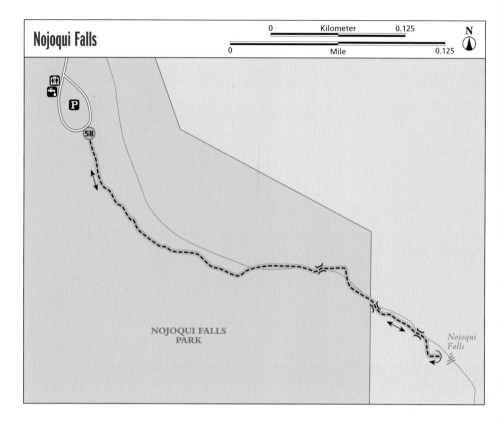

At 0.2 mile reach a bridge (there's even a trash can here). The trail narrows to a box canyon but is fenced off to reduce human-caused erosion.

Cross bridges two more times. At the last bridge you can see the falls around a corner to the left. It's huge and tumbles down a green moss-covered travertine slope. It seems unlikely here, minutes from a grassy county park. You may spot Venus maidenhair ferns. They require lots of moisture and acidic, calcium-rich soil—a rarity in Santa Barbara County's arid coastal climate.

The last hundred feet to the falls may be fenced off with signs indicating security cameras can detect you if you hop the fence. There's not a great place to take a photo of the entire falls without being blocked by vegetation, but the peace comes from enjoying it free of the need to capture its image.

Miles and Directions

0.0 Start at the trailhead.

0.2 First bridge.

0.3 End of trail near base of falls. Return the way you came.

0.6 Arrive back at the trailhead.

59 Little Falls

This is a low-trafficked hike to a little-known wilderness area filled with spring wildflowers, trout, and shady inviting pools. Little Falls' flow is better than nearby Big Falls' later in the season, making it a worthy destination by itself.

Height: About 50 feet

Beauty rating: ★★★★

Distance: 8.4 miles out and back; 14 miles as Little Falls–Big Falls Loop variation, 1 mile out-and-back from Lopez Canyon Trailhead (4WD)

Elevation gain: 700 feet down/800 feet up (one-way just to Little Falls)

Difficulty: Moderate to strenuous

Best season: Winter, spring

County: San Luis Obispo

Trailhead amenities: 50+ parking spots, plus more along the side of road into parking area

(watch for No Parking signs); dogs on-leash allowed; no camping allowed at trailheads or in the wilderness

Land status: Los Padres National Forest, Santa Lucia Wilderness

Maps: USGS Lopez Mountain

Trail contact: Los Padres National Forest, Santa Lucia Ranger District, 1616 N. Carlotti Dr., Santa Maria 93454; (805) 925-9538; www.fs.usda.gov/main/lpnf/home

Fees and permits: None

Finding the trailhead: Google Maps: Rinconada Trailhead, Santa Margarita. From US-101 N in San Luis Obispo, take Exit 211 east onto CA-58 toward Santa Margarita for 1.7 mile. Turn right to stay on CA-58 for 1.5 mile. It turns into W. Pozo Road, which you take for 9.5 mile to the trailhead on the right.
GPS: N35 17.240' / W120 28.287'

The Hike

The little-known Santa Lucia Wilderness was established in 1978 by the Endangered American Wilderness Act and now has 20,412 acres of pristine riparian vegetation, oak forests, and rugged terrain.

The wilderness is bordered on the west (lower valley) and east (closer to the tops of the ridges) by two roads. Santa Lopez Canyon Road is a publicly accessible, high-clearance dirt road that is crossed by Lopez Creek many times. By starting at the trailhead to Big and Little Falls on this road, you can shorten the distance you have to hike to get to each waterfall. But since most folks don't have access to high-clearance vehicles, here we describe the scenic, longer hiking route from the east via the Rinconada trailhead, which can be accessed by the paved Pozo Road.

This hike is best visited in winter or early spring as it can get quite hot and there is little shade on the ridgetops. Once you head into the canyons, there are more than a dozen creek crossings. Bring water shoes or prepare for wet feet.

From the trailhead, follow the Rinconada Trail, which starts by a big trail information sign and horse corral/water. The next 0.25 mile is shady, can be muddy, and is well traveled. The trail climbs up switchbacks, ascending about 500 feet until it widens to an old dirt road. Intersections with the remnants of other dirt trails are marked with metal signs with arrows pointing in the correct direction.

At 1.3 miles in, reach a gate with a grand view to the east. Shortly you come to a grassy open ridgetop with views in all directions. You can see Morro Rock and the Seven Sisters hills of San Luis Obispo. This open area is also an important unmarked intersection. Turn right toward a broken carbonite (a flat pole made of plastic-like material) trail sign and rock piles (cairns) marking the trail.

Descend on steep, rocky trail for 0.2 mile. On your left is a cement circular water tank on Little Falls Spring. A side trail leads to the water, which is there for wildlife use. A sign indicates that rocks, logs, and mesh in the tank are ramps and perches to help smaller wildlife access the water.

Continue on the main trail downhill. To your left the creek from the spring flows through a grassy meadow. At 1.75 mile contour above a dirt road. Take an unmarked route on a short, steep, rocky trail down to the (closed to traffic) Hi Mountain Lookout Road. On the road, reach the sign for the Rinconada Trail.

At the road, turn right downhill and away from the cement tank, following the trail signs. At 1.8 miles, reach a signed trailhead and the Santa Lucia Wilderness sign to your left. Take the trail to the left past a big metal sign and head downhill on a narrow, brushy trail located on a former road, exposed to the sun.

The Santa Lucia Wilderness is so pristine that it is habitat to amphibians, reptiles, and many rare flowers and plants.

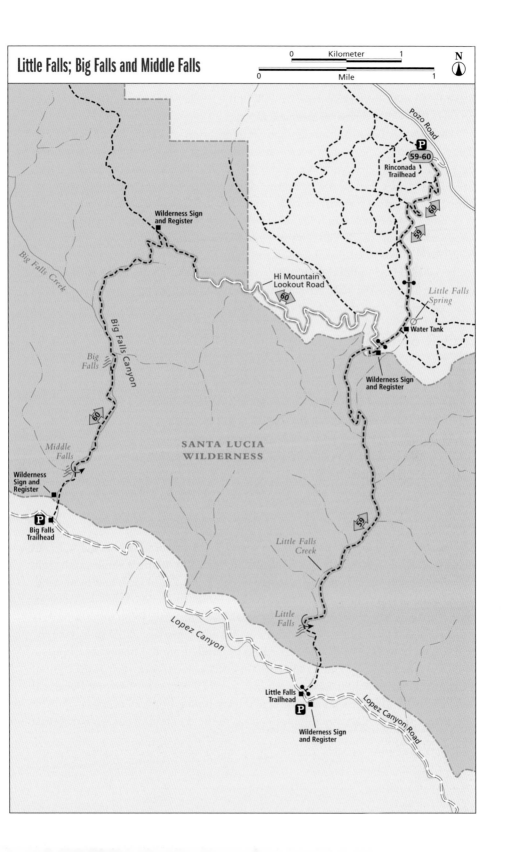

Little Falls; Big Falls and Middle Falls

0 Kilometer 1

0 Mile 1

N

Pozo Road

P 59-60
Rinconada
Trailhead

60

59

Wilderness Sign
and Register

Big Falls Creek

Hi Mountain
Lookout Road
60

Little Falls
Spring

Big Falls Canyon

Water Tank

Big
Falls

Wilderness Sign
and Register

60

SANTA LUCIA
WILDERNESS

Middle
Falls

Wilderness
Sign and
Register

P
Big Falls
Trailhead

59

Little Falls
Creek

Little
Falls

Lopez Canyon

Little
Falls

Little Falls
Trailhead

P

Lopez Canyon Road

Wilderness Sign
and Register

At 2.55 miles you cross the water. A small cascade may flow to your left after a rain. For the next 0.75 mile, you'll cross it several times. At 3.25 miles the canyon becomes so narrow you may have to walk in the creek. Soon you pass a bearing tree on your left with a yellow metal marker.

The forest is beautiful through here, though brushy with plenty of poison oak. The trees are big: oaks, maples, sycamores, and fragrant bays. Cross the creek multiple times before the trail ascends high above the water with views of the canyon, which has widened. At 4.2 miles the trail drops closer to the creek and is marked with carbonite signs. Look for a small cascade where the trail bends to the left.

Cliffy rows of rock bands are above you. The trail contours the hillside and is level with the top of the falls. This is a good viewpoint to see the falls. If you want to get to the base, continue downhill for about 0.2 mile past impressive rock slabs to the creek. Head uphill through the creek for about 0.1 mile until you reach the limestone base of the falls. Maidenhair and prehistoric-looking giant *Woodwardia* ferns are found along the edge of the pool.

Miles and Directions

0.0 Start at the Rinconada trailhead.

1.3 Gate.

1.4 Turn right down rocky trail at open grassy area/unmarked junction.

1.6 Little Falls Spring and junction to cement water tank on left.

1.75 Unmarked junction down to Hi Mountain Lookout Road.

1.8 Turn left at trailhead for Little Falls/Santa Lucia Wilderness sign.

4.0 See falls from above.

4.2 Cross creek. Junction to base of lower falls (0.3 mile farther). Return the way you came.

8.4 Arrive back at the trailhead.

Option: Big Falls Loop (14 miles): In the spring this is one of the most enjoyable and under-trafficked loop trails I've ever hiked. Continue descending 0.5 mile on the trail toward the trailhead at Lopez Canyon Road. At the road, turn right and head uphill for 2.2 miles. The road may have many creek crossings and mild traffic from residents and off-roaders. When the road ends, you reach the signed Big Falls trailhead. Make a sharp right and cross a creek to reach the wilderness boundary in 0.2 mile. Take the trail to ascend to Middle Falls and Big Falls (0.8 mile from the trailhead). Continue uphill past the falls for 1.5 miles to reach a wilderness sign. Turn right at the sign on a narrow, brushy trail. In 0.3 mile, reach the closed Hi Mountain Lookout Road and turn left. In 1.5 miles, reach the same signed intersection for the Rinconada Trail you saw at mile 1.75 (it indicates it's 2 miles back to the trailhead). Take the Rinconada Trail back to your car.

60 Big Falls and Middle Falls

In the little-known Santa Lucia Wilderness lies a pristine waterfall with salamanders, turtles, and butterflies. Start in moss-covered oak forest and descend to a fern-lined limestone canyon that almost looks tropical.

See map on page 233.
Height: Big Falls: close to 80 feet, Middle Falls: about 30 feet
Beauty rating: ★★★★★
Distance: 12.2 miles out and back for Big Falls and Middle Falls; 2 miles out and back from Santa Lopez Canyon Road; 14-mile loop when combined with Little Falls
Elevation gain: 400 feet gain/90 feet loss from Santa Lopez Canyon Road; 1,000 feet gain/1,600 feet loss from Santa Lopez Canyon Road (remember you have to climb back out on your return); 2,600 feet gain and loss on loop
Difficulty: Easy
Best season: Fall, winter, spring, summer

County: San Luis Obispo
Trailhead amenities: 50+ parking spots, plus more along the side of road into parking area (watch for No Parking signs); dogs on-leash allowed; no camping allowed at trailheads or in the wilderness
Land status: Los Padres National Forest, Santa Lucia Wilderness
Maps: USGS Lopez Mountain
Trail contact: Los Padres National Forest, Santa Lucia Ranger District, 1616 N. Carlotti Dr., Santa Maria 93454; (805) 925-9538; www.fs.usda.gov/main/lpnf/home
Fees and permits: None

Finding the trailhead: Google Maps: Rinconada Trailhead, Santa Margarita. From US-101 N in San Luis Obispo, take Exit 211 east onto CA-58 toward Santa Margarita for 1.7 mile. Turn right to stay on CA-58 for 1.5 mile. It turns into W. Pozo Road, which you take for 9.5 mile to the trailhead on the right.
GPS: N35 17.240' / W120 28.287'

The Hike

Big Falls is the main attraction in the remote and little-known Santa Lucia Wilderness. For more about this wilderness and the many ways of accessing it, read the Little Falls route description.

If you're planning to start at the Rinconada trailhead, we recommend visiting Big Falls as part of the Little Falls–Big Falls Loop described at the end of the Little Falls hike. It's best to do the loop clockwise (start with Little Falls) for a gentler, shadier climb on the return trip.

To reach Big Falls from the Riconada Trailhead, follow the route description for Little Falls past Little Falls Spring (1.6 miles in). Continue downhill to Hi Mountain Road, which you reach at a sign for the Rinconada Trail.

Big Falls is a multi-tiered fall that outshines the lower Middle Falls in height.

At the road, turn right downhill and away from the cement tank, following the trail signs. At 1.8 miles, reach a signed trailhead for Little Falls and the Santa Lucia Wilderness sign to your left. (**Option:** You can reach Little, Middle, and Big Falls via a scenic 14-mile loop by turning left and following the route description variation listed at the end of the Little Falls route description. To go directly to Big Falls, stay straight (northwest) on the dirt Hi Mountain Lookout Road.

Take this dirt road as it swirls around the oak-covered hillsides. The road ends at a noticeable flat area and low point between hills. Before the end there's a hard-to-spot trail on your right. It's in the brush and marked only by a brown carbonite.

Take this narrow, brushy trail for 0.4 mile until it opens up to wide views of the entire range and the valley below. At 4.1 miles you reach the Santa Lucia Wilderness trail sign and a register. Turn left and downhill here, descending on the picturesque open, grassy hillside filled with butterflies and wildflowers.

Follow a seasonal tributary downhill among moss-covered oaks. The tributary ultimately joins Big Falls Creek, and you may notice the confluence 0.6 mile later. Your trail descends toward the main creek. The water here is pristine enough that you may spot a salamander, considered an indicator of water quality.

When you reach Big Falls Creek 0.3 mile later, it's strikingly wide and placid. It's difficult to imagine such a flat, peaceful area is so near any falls. Picnic on a creekside limestone slab.

The trail takes you from the lazy creek above Big Falls to across from the edge of the falls itself. The trail here is wide, but a steep drop-off may concern those with heights issues. From where you see Big Falls, turn right on a short use trail to reach its base and the shallow pool underneath.

To see Middle Falls, return to the intersection with the use trail and descend the main trail for 0.8 mile. The trail is wider and less brushy than before. There are several creek crossings. The plant ecosystem here has fewer moss-covered oaks. It's chaparral with oak, toyon, and mountain mahogany.

At 0.4 mile from Big Falls, climb from the creek to the north bank (right as you're descending), passing a white quartz cliff. For a few hundred feet, the trail bed is made of white quartz gravel. After 0.2 mile, descend on switchbacks to the water and falls, another 0.2 mile later.

About 500 feet before the falls, you'll have a view of the upper part of the two-tiered Middle Falls. The upper chute is at a lower angle. The steeper, bigger lower tier is best seen by descending to the creek, crossing, and taking a use trail up its northern bank (left as you're ascending toward the falls) for about 200 feet.

It's worth continuing down the trail from Middle Falls for another 0.2 mile to see the creek become a narrow, limestone canyon. There are numerous swimming holes and water-carved caves. Western pond turtles sun themselves along the banks. The gorge looks almost tropical, like something you'd see in Thailand instead of outside San Luis Obispo. When you've had enough time basking in the sun, return the way you came or continue as a reverse loop with the Little Falls Trail (though we think starting with Little Falls is more enjoyable).

Miles and Directions

0.0 Start at the Rinconada trailhead.

1.4 Turn right down rocky trail at open grassy area/unmarked junction.

1.8 Stay on Hi Mountain Lookout Road with Little Falls junction on left.

3.7 Hi Mountain Lookout Road turns right on narrow dirt trail.

4.1 Santa Lucia Wilderness sign and register; turn right, downhill.

5.1 Reach Big Falls Creek confluence after following a seasonal eastern tributary

5.3 Junction with side trail to base of Big Falls.

5.5 Pass under quartz cliff.

6.1 Side trail to base of Middle Falls.

10.6 Return the way you came.

12.2 Arrive back at the trailhead.

Big Sur

Whether you like blue water on rugged coastline, redwood rainforests, or the steep Santa Lucia Mountains, there's something in Big Sur for everyone. Home to one of the most photographed falls in the state, Big Sur has been called the longest undeveloped coastline in the Lower 48.

It receives similar visitorship as Yosemite National Park, but without the developed campsite amenities. Big Sur is also home to the 1960s "new age" movement, including the Esalen Institute, which was named after the Native Americans who were drawn to the hot springs nearby.

Big Sur's name comes from the Spanish *el pais grande del sur* or "big country of the south." It's home to numerous state parks, and hikes in this book visit Limekiln State Park, Julia Pfeiffer Burns State Park, and Pfeiffer Big Sur State Park as well as private land, Los Padres National Forest, and California Coastal public land.

Waterfalls abound in Big Sur for those willing to backpack farther into the Santa Lucia Mountains or Silver Peak or Ventana Wildernesses. Most notably, Pine Falls was a pleasant backpacking trip along what used to be one of the most popular trails in Big Sur, the Pine Ridge Trail. The trail closed after the Soberanes Fire in 2016, and other access points require a high-clearance vehicle to enter via a seasonally closed road.

In 1972 California voters passed Proposition 20 for a coastal trail system. In 2001 SB 908 passed, giving the California Conservancy responsibility to complete a continuous trail. The California Coastal Trail is designed to run from Oregon to Mexico and is about 60 percent complete. For more information, see the book *Hiking the California Coastal Trail*.

Big Sur is notorious for lacking public restrooms. According to one count, there are only sixteen available along the entire coast to accommodate 5 million visitors. Be sure to use the facilities before you leave state park facilities.

For more waterfall hikes in the northern Big Sur area, see the companion guide to this book, *Hiking Waterfalls in Northern California* by Tracy Salcedo-Chourré.

61 Black Swift Falls (Ragged Point Falls)

This seasonal four-plus-tiered falls tumbles 300 feet from a coastal bluff to the ocean. When it's flowing, it's reminiscent of the famous McWay Falls up the coast, but with fewer crowds. If you catch this falls after a good rainstorm, it may become your favorite falls yet. Even when the waterfall is not running, hiking to a hidden ocean cove is a worthy experience.

Height: At least 100 feet

Beauty rating: ★★★★★ (if flowing)

Distance: 0.6 mile out and back

Elevation gain: 325 feet loss/95 feet gain

Difficulty: Moderate to strenuous (short hike, very steep)

Best season: Winter, spring

County: San Luis Obispo

Trailhead amenities: Hotel, coffee shop, burger stand, trash/recycle bins, restrooms, water, 100+ parking spots

Land status: Coastal access granted by the Ragged Point Inn and California Coastal Commission

Maps: USGS Burro Mountain

Trail contact: Ragged Point Inn and Resort, 19019 Hwy. 1, Ragged Point 93452; (888) 584-6374; www.raggedpointinn.com; California beaches are public according to the California Coastal Act

Fees and permits: None

Finding the trailhead: Google Maps: Ragged Point Inn. From San Luis Obispo, take CA 1 north for 56.5 miles. The inn complex is on your left.

GPS: N35 46.493' / W121 19.489'

The Hike

Don't be intimidated that these falls start at the Ragged Point Inn. While this route starts on private land, the owners kindly allow coastal access to visitors (in fact, they're hoping you'll stay for a sandwich afterward). Nonetheless, be aware that the landowners can revoke access at anytime and to anyone.

The hike down to the coast is short, but very steep. Children and those with knee issues will want to take care deciding whether this hike is for them. This is a good trail to bring hiking poles. But even if steep isn't your kind of hike, the view from the trailhead at the top of the bluff is something everyone should see (the paved trail is wheelchair friendly). However, from the trailhead, you can only see the coast, not the falls, which are hidden around the corner in the gully.

The trail is clear, but like California coastal soil, it can be as loose as walking down ball bearings unless there has been a rain recently. Moisture solidifies the soil and makes the walking much easier—and ups the chances the falls will run.

If you time your visit to right after a good winter or spring downpour, you'll find one of the most memorable waterfalls in this book. If you get here in summer, the hike down to the protected cove is still nice, but there won't be a waterfall.

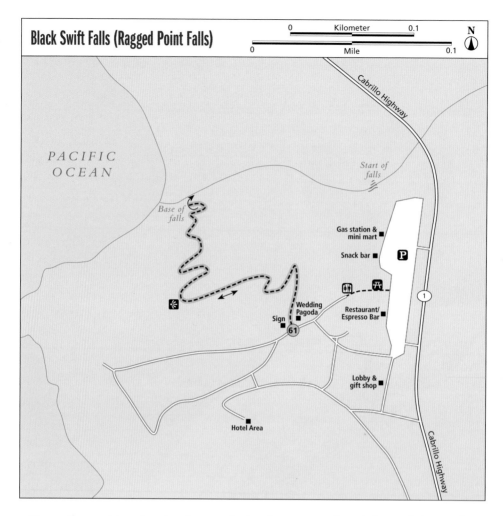

Kilometer 0
0.1

Mile 0
0.1

N

PACIFIC
OCEAN

Start of
falls

Base of
falls

Gas station &
mini mart

Snack bar

Cabrillo Highway

Wedding
Pagoda

Sign

Restaurant/
Espresso Bar

61

Lobby &
gift shop

Hotel Area

Cabrillo Highway

From the parking lot, head toward the burger stand and beyond it to the restrooms. A wooden sign indicates to continue down the paved path toward the "Trail." Walk past a wedding gazebo toward a large wooden sign that indicates you are allowed access to the beach by Ragged Point Inn and to enter at your own risk.

Descend wooden stairs to the trail. There are grand views of the beach cove below. Take your time descending switchbacks steeply down loose trail. Sweetgrass and non-native but still pretty nasturtium and ice plant abound on the slope. About 200 feet in, turn left, continuing on switchbacks at a Monterey cypress tree (ignore a side trail that goes to the right).

About 0.1 mile from the westernmost point of the switchback, you may have a view of a falls tumbling from the northern part of the gully (if there has been recent rain). While this is a tall falls, the best is yet to come.

Switchback around a very windblown California bay tree and continue down toward the beach. This slope can erode, so the trail may change from year to year (you may notice the remnants of a trail bridge abandoned and inaccessible along the slope). The trail switchbacks steeply, but there are occasional undulations.

At 0.3 mile from the gazebo, you reach the near end of the trail before it hits the rocky beach via downclimbing a large, steep, and wet and slippery boulder (not recommended). However, right before this point, take a short side path headed to the water and the base of a 30-foot falls. From the rocks you can see the tier of falls above it, the falls right below it, and even the bottom of the grand tier at the very top.

For those who are skilled and experienced in scrambling, you can ford or rock-hop the creek at this point to get a better view. Do so at your own risk. While the remnants of a wooden footbridge are strewn on a lower boulder, best to find a safer spot to rock-hop across.

The four-plus-tiered falls drops at least 100 feet, appearing to go from the Pacific Coast Highway at an elevation of about 300 feet to the ocean. Coastal wildflowers bloom in the spring. It's picturesque to see this falls when it's flowing, but the season is short.

Miles and Directions

0.0 Start at wooden sign.

0.3 Base of lowest tier of falls. Return the way you came.

0.6 Arrive back at the trailhead.

62 Salmon Creek Falls

After a big rainstorm, these double falls with a hill in the middle are reminiscent of waterfalls with a Yosemite dome. A short walk from the road, Salmon Creek is a must-see if you're driving the Pacific Coast Highway.

Height: 120-150 feet
Beauty rating: ★★★★★ (if flowing)
Distance: 0.6 mile out and back
Elevation gain: 180 feet gain/125 feet loss
Difficulty: Easy (but it has uneven and muddy ground and should be taken slowly due to less sure footing)
Best season: Winter, spring
County: Monterey
Trailhead amenities: 50+ parking spots in dirt lot; Salmon Creek ranger station nearby; dogs allowed

Land status: Los Padres National Forest, Monterey Ranger District
Maps: Tom Harrison Silver Peak Wilderness; USGS Burro Mountain
Trail contact: Los Padres National Forest, Monterey District Office, 406 S. Mildred, King City 93930; (831) 385-5434; www.fs.usda .gov/main/lpnf/home
Fees and permits: None

Finding the trailhead: Google Maps: Salmon Creek Trailhead, California 1, Big Sur. From Ragged Point, take the Pacific Coast Highway (CA 1) north for 3.7 miles. You'll see the parking lot when the road makes a tight leftward bend immediately before the permanently closed US Forest Service Salmon Creek Station and past mile marker 1 MON 51.00.
GPS: N35 48.568' / W121 21.316'

The Hike

Start at the large, dirt parking lot on the right side of the PCH (as you're headed north).

From the parking lot, carefully head south on a use trail behind the metal bannister to the official Salmon Creek trailhead behind a brown Forest Service sign. Ascend a short switchback heading east toward the falls and climb for another 0.1 mile before descending. In 0.1 mile you reach a trail junction.

Stay straight, following signs to the falls.

The trail continues past a field of house-sized boulders. They're cave-like and could be a fun place for kids to play (if they watch out for poison oak in the area).

The trail descends again toward the southern edge of Salmon Creek. The trail is braided in here. Choose the path requiring the least scrambling. At 0.3 mile from your car, you arrive at the base of the impressive lower falls. Two branches drop 120 feet with a hill behind it rising like a Sierra dome.

The force of Salmon Creek Falls after a winter storm can be overwhelming.

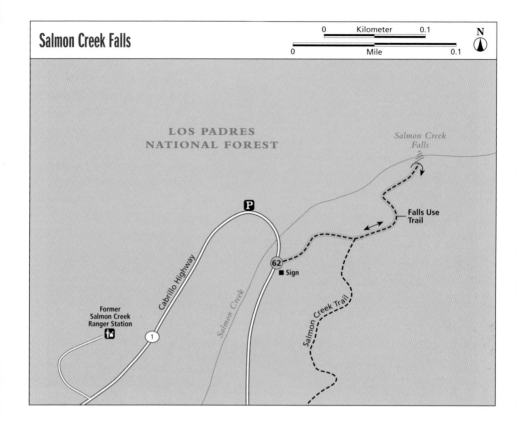

Salmon Creek Falls

LOS PADRES
NATIONAL FOREST

Salmon Creek
Falls

Falls Use
Trail

Cabrillo Highway

Salmon Creek

Salmon Creek Trail

Sign

Former
Salmon Creek
Ranger Station

Miles and Directions

0.0 Start at trailhead behind sign.

0.1 Stay straight at junction.

0.2 Rock garden.

0.3 Base of falls. Return the way you came.

0.6 Arrive back at the trailhead.

63 Limekiln Falls

Travel through a park that encompasses microclimates, from coastal sequoia red-woods forest and ferns to tall, fan-shaped falls. This mild-temperature hike ventures through magical forest to a tall, year-round falls in a state park with beach access. It's worth a visit on your Big Sur road trip.

Height: 100 feet
Beauty rating: ★★★★★
Distance: 1.2 miles out and back
Elevation gain: 250 feet gain
Difficulty: Easy to moderate (hand-over-hand scrambling and wet feet when visiting outside of peak season)
Best season: Winter, spring, fall, summer
County: Monterey
Trailhead amenities: Camping, potable water, flush toilets, trash/recycle bins, hot showers (for camping guests). The rangers sell hot coffee in winter. Parking is limited (the rangers at the entrance station will tell you where to park or if there is parking available). Park has beach access.
Land status: Limekiln State Forest
Maps: Park map available at ranger station; USGS Lopez Point
Trail contact: Limekiln State Park, Highway 1, Big Sur 93920; (985) 434-1996 or (805) 434-1996; www.parks.ca.gov/?page_id=577
Fees and permits: Day-use entrance fee; allows access to all California state parks until sundown. Camping on-site (reservations recommended).

Finding the trailhead: Google Maps: Limekiln Campground, Limekiln Creek, Big Sur. (**Note:** The Google Maps for Limekiln State Park does not take you to the correct entrance area for this hike.) No cell reception at park or nearby on PCH. From Ragged Point, drive 23.7 miles north on the Pacific Coast Highway (CA 1) past Kirk Creek and Lime Kiln Campground. Entrance fee station is on your right 0.2 mile down a narrow paved road. If you cross a bridge over Limekiln Creek or drive through a tunnel, you've gone too far.
GPS: N36 00.385' / W121 31.058'

The Hike

From the day-use parking by the campground shower house, walk on a road through the campground for 0.1 mile until you reach a wooden bridge and a trail sign.

Cross the bridge and continue on a wide, clear trail until you reach a signed junction. Head left, following signs to the falls. You pass a bench and a named grove of sequoias.

In 0.3 mile cross another wooden bridge. Reach another bench with a John Muir quote and a named grove. Then, a trail junction appears on the right. If you head straight, you'll reach the lime kilns for which this park gets its name. For the falls, head down wooden stairs to the right toward the water.

Until now the trail to the falls is idyllic, wide, and safe for kids and a wide variety of skill levels. After this, it can become more difficult, especially in high water. When we visited in February 2019 right after a storm, there were four creek crossings, up

Limekiln has a noticable split.

to my knees through swift-moving water. In summer or lower water, it's possible for folks with good balance to rock-hop or cross logs, and the rangers create seasonal bridges. On a hot day you may even find crossing the creek to be refreshing. In the wet season you may find bits of the trail to be narrow or require using your hands to get around logs or downed trees. The rangers try to stay on top of keeping the trail clear during peak season, but be prepared.

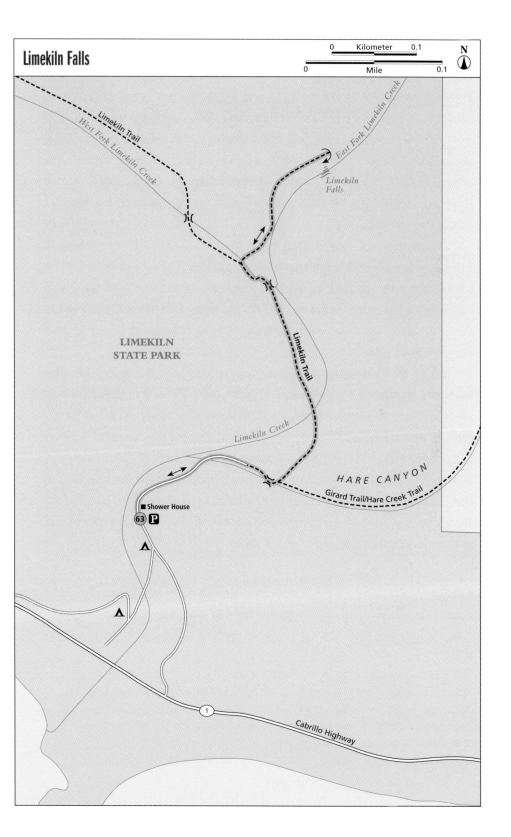

Limekiln Falls

Limekiln Trail

West Fork Limekiln Creek

East Fork Limekiln Creek

Limekiln Falls

LIMEKILN
STATE PARK

Limekiln Trail

Limekiln Creek

HARE CANYON

Girard Trail/Hare Creek Trail

Shower House

63 P

Cabrillo Highway

1

A SHORT HISTORY OF LIME KILN PARK

Archaeological evidence found in the Big Sur area suggests the ancestors of today's Salinan, Esselen, and Ohlone people lived here for thousands of years. They fished and hunted, gathered seeds and grasses, and traded with other tribes who lived inland. When the Spanish and Mexicans came, the people were forced into the mission system and suffered from new-world diseases to which they were not immune. Through violence and treaties with the federal government, settlers took the native people's land for fishing, agriculture, and industries such as lime extraction.

Situated where the redwood forest meets the ocean, Limekiln State Park is home to diverse plants and wildlife including over 200 bird species. This geologically young (2.5 million years) park is part of the Santa Lucia Range, which runs south to San Luis Obispo (also found in the Little Falls and the Big Falls and Middle Falls hikes). The park boasts that it is "one of few places on earth where fog-loving redwoods thrive not far from drought-tolerant yucca."

In 1887 the Rockland Lime and Lumber Company extracted and processed lime from this canyon, establishing four stone-and-iron furnaces (which are worth visiting as an add-on trip to your waterfall hike). The redwood forest was cleared for lumber and to fuel the furnaces, so most of what you see here is second growth. Lime was then hauled out in barrels to the nearby Rockland Landing and shipped to be turned into concrete. After three years, lime and trees were running out and the venture was no longer profitable. One hundred years later, in 1994, Save the Redwoods League and the American Land Conservancy protected and restored the area. The California Conservation Corps built the hiking trails and campgrounds so future generations can enjoy this magical place.

After 0.3 mile from the junction and four creek crossings, climb up a wooden trail reinforcement to the base of the double falls. It's an impressive sight hidden in this verdant gully surrounded by sequoias. The falls itself drops 100 feet.

Miles and Directions

0.0 Start at day-use parking by the shower house.

0.1 Cross bridge at end of campground. Turn left at signed junction with Hare Creek Trail.

0.4 Cross bridge over Limekiln Creek and follow trail up West Fork of Limekiln Creek to a junction. Turn right toward falls, down wooden stairs, and cross creek.

0.6 Base of falls. Return the way you came.

1.2 Arrive back at the trailhead.

64 McWay Falls

An essential stop along any drive of the California coast, McWay Falls is among the most iconic waterfalls in California. It tumbles 80 feet off an ocean bluff to the sea with a sand beach, secluded cove, and even a sea tunnel right at its base. Take a well-marked, well-maintained crushed granite trail to an overlook.

Height: About 80 feet
Beauty rating: ★★★★★
Distance: 0.8 mile out and back
Elevation gain: Mostly level
Difficulty: Easy
Best season: Winter, spring, fall, summer
County: Monterey
Trailhead amenities: 100+ parking spots
Land status: Julia Pfeiffer Burns State Park

Maps: USGS Partington Ridge; park map at entrance station or downloadable from park website
Trail contact: Julia Pfeiffer Burns State Park, Big Sur Station #1/47555 CA 1, Big Sur 93920; (831) 649-2826 or (831) 667-1112; www.parks.ca.gov/?page_id=578
Fees and permits: Day-use entrance fee; allows access to all California state parks until sundown

Finding the trailhead: Google Maps: Julia Pfeiffer Burns State Park. From San Luis Obispo, take CA 1 north for 93.8 miles to the park.
GPS: N36 09.320' / W121 40.092'

The Hike

Note: The Julia Pfeiffer Burns State Park information/ranger station and parking lot were damaged by landslides in 2018. Check regulations to determine whether it's open before going. Even when closed, the falls are always visible from the PCH.

McWay Falls is one of the most photographed and famous falls in California. It's the only waterfall in this book that goes directly into the Pacific Ocean. McWay Falls tumbles to McWay Cove.

Start at the parking lot following signs for the Waterfall Overlook Trail. The well-marked, crushed granite trail starts across from the restrooms. Climb wooden stairs or take the wheelchair-friendly route. After 0.1 mile, pass through a tunnel under CA 1. Once across, a path with "kid-proof" railing keeps everyone safe as you enjoy the view.

Along the hike are interpretive signs highlighting local history. You pass the ruins of the Waterfall House, owned by Lathrop and Helen Hooper Brown. They purchased what was then the Saddle Ranch in 1924, and built the house and a funicular rail line to get there. In 1962 Helen gave what is now Julia Pfeiffer Burns State Park to California, requesting it be named in memory of her good friend, Big Sur pioneer and cattle rancher, Julia Pfeiffer. Of the 280 state park units, it's one of four

Despite its not-so-memorable name, McWay Falls is one of the most visited and photographed falls in this book.

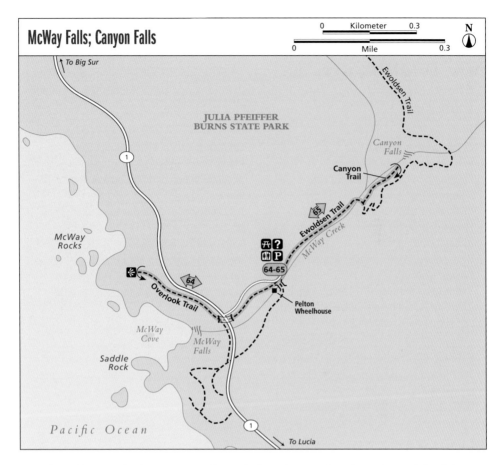

exclusively named after a woman (Benicia State Recreation Area, Emma Wood State Beach, and Forest of Nisene Marks State Park being the others).

Prior to 1983, McWay Falls dropped right into the ocean. But in 1983 the size of the beach "increased" when a landslide deposited soil and sand into the pocket cove.

As much as we hikers would like to go down to the pocket beach, there isn't access. You'll have to enjoy the falls from above.

Miles and Directions

0.0 Start at the trailhead at parking lot.

0.1 Pass through pedestrian tunnel.

0.4 Reach overlook. Return the way you came.

0.8 Arrive back at the trailhead.

65 Canyon Falls

A pleasant add-on to McWay Falls when visiting Julia Pfeiffer Burns State Park, Canyon Falls gives you a taste of the redwood coast on a much less crowded waterfall trail.

See map on page 253.
Height: About 60–80 feet over 3 tiers; lower tier (visible from trail) about 30 feet
Beauty rating: ★★★★★
Distance: 1.2 miles out and back
Elevation gain: 50 feet one-way
Difficulty: Easy
Best season: Winter, spring, fall, summer
County: Monterey
Trailhead amenities: 100+ parking spots, restrooms, potable water, trash bins, information, picnic areas, camping.

Land status: Julia Pfeiffer Burns State Park
Maps: USGS Partington Ridge; park map at entrance station or downloadable from park website
Trail contact: Julia Pfeiffer Burns State Park, Big Sur Station #1/47555 CA 1, Big Sur 93920; (831) 649-2826 or (831) 667-1112; www.parks.ca.gov/?page_id=578
Fees and permits: Day-use entrance fee; allows access to all California state parks until sundown

Finding the trailhead: Google Maps: Ewoldsen Trailhead. From Ragged Point, take the Pacific Coast Highway (CA 1) north for 37.5 miles. The Julia Pfeiffer Burns State Park entrance station is to your right.
GPS: N36 09. 364' / W121 40.068'

The Hike

Note: This area was subject to landslides in 2018, and the Julia Pfeiffer Burns State Park information/ranger station and parking lot were damaged. Check regulations to determine whether it's open before going.

McWay Creek is home to two waterfalls: the famous McWay Falls (Hike 65), and its less famous upstream sister: Cousin Falls. Start at the parking lot on the side closest to the forest, signed for the Canyon and Ewoldsen Trails. Your trailhead is across the lot from the more popular Waterfall Overlook Trail.

Walk among coastal redwoods and ferns through the picnic area and past a large boulder to signs for the Ewoldsen Trail. Considered to be the finest day hike in Big Sur, this 4.3-mile, 1,600-foot-gain lollipop loop is worth completing in full if you have the time and energy.

Continue along McWay Creek into McWay Canyon. In 0.25 mile, at a Y junction, cross over McWay Creek. Boards keep your feet dry. Cables show the route you'll take, switchbacking up the bank of the creek but generally still heading upstream.

At 0.4 mile you reach an intersection with the Ewoldsen Trail. Turn left, following signs for the Canyon Falls Trail. A little more than 0.2 mile later, after a series of steep switchbacks and a drop to the base of the falls, you reach the end of the trail and canyon. Here you can see 30 feet and two tiers of the falls nestled against a fern-covered rock in a narrow gorge.

Miles and Directions

0.0   Start at the uphill/inland part of parking lot, following signs for Canyon/Ewoldsen Trails. Pass through picnic area.

0.25 At Y intersection, cross stream on boards following cables as trail switchbacks up bank from the creek.

0.4   At junction with Ewoldsen Trail, turn left toward Canyon Falls Trail.

0.6   After switchbacks and a drop, reach base of falls. Return the way you came.

1.2   Arrive back at the trailhead.

The Big Sur redwood ecosystem.

66 Pfeiffer Falls

Take a wide, well-signed and maintained trail through redwoods and oaks to a multi-tiered waterfall.

Height: About 60 feet over 2+ tiers
Beauty rating: ★★★★★
Distance: 2 miles out and back
Elevation gain: 400 feet
Difficulty: Easy to moderate
Best season: Winter, spring
County: Monterey
Trailhead amenities: 100+ parking spots, restaurant, lodge, campground, gift shop, nature center, information.

Land status: Pfeiffer Big Sur State Park (not to be confused with Julia Pfeiffer Burns State Park to the south)
Maps: USGS Big Sur; map in park brochure and downloadable from park website
Trail contact: Pfeiffer Big Sur State Park, 47225 CA 1, Big Sur 93920; (831) 667-1112 or (831) 649-2836; www.parks.ca.gov/?page_id=570
Fees and permits: Day-use entrance fee; allows access to all California State Parks until sundown

Finding the trailhead: Google Maps: Big Sur Lodge (Google Maps to Pfeiffer Big Sur State Park does not direct you to the correct trailhead). Do not confuse this park with the similarly named Julia Pfeiffer Burns State Park. From Ragged Point, take the Pacific Coast Highway (CA 1) north for 48.2 miles to the park.
GPS: N36 15.079' / W121 47.023'

The Hike

Not to be confused with Julia Pfeiffer Burns State Park, Pfeiffer Big Sur State Park is a busy and popular place, especially when Julia Pfeiffer Burns State Park is closed. It has a restaurant, lodge, campground, gift shop, nature center, and all the amenities you would expect to find in Yosemite Valley (minus the bus).

Big Sur is home to many microclimates, and this waterfall hike (especially if done with the Valley View Trail) lets you experience the sequoia redwoods found in coastal foggy ravines as well as the oak woodland and chaparral filled with manzanitas, coyote brush, buckeyes, and colorful poison oak.

Start at the signed trailhead by the Big Sur Lodge, following pavement across a park road. In 0.2 mile, reach the official trailhead, with a signed information board, and follow a wide dirt trail. Follow Pfeiffer Creek upstream on its way to the Big Sur River (which you passed on the road to the parking area). You are traveling through one of the oldest groves of redwood sequoias in Big Sur. Redwood sorrel, looking like an oversized clover, makes up the understory.

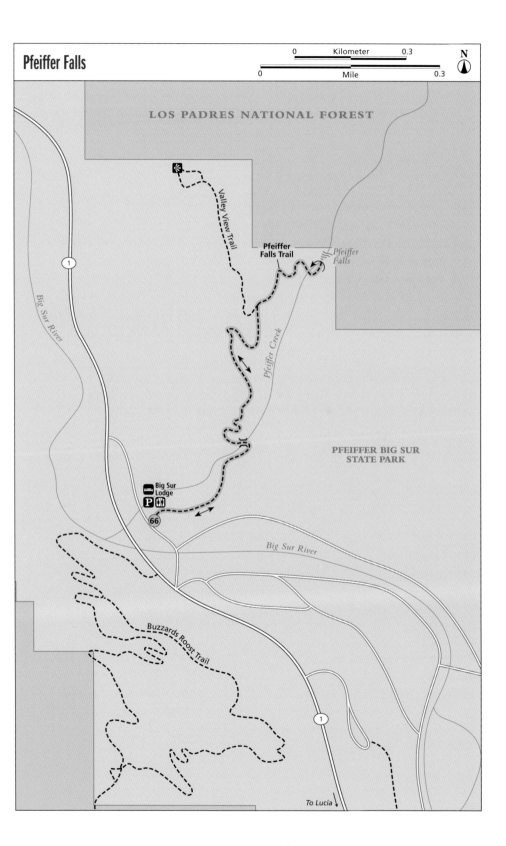

Pfeiffer Falls

LOS PADRES NATIONAL FOREST

Valley View Trail

Pfeiffer
Falls Trail

Pfeiffer
Falls

1

Big Sur River

Pfeiffer Creek

PFEIFFER BIG SUR
STATE PARK

Big Sur
Lodge

P

66

Big Sur River

Buzzards Roost Trail

1

To Lucia

Stairs along the route ease the ascent into the canyon. At the top of the climb, 0.8 mile in, reach the intersection with the Valley View Trail. Here, turn right following signs to Pfeiffer Falls. Views extend inland to the slopes of the Santa Lucia Mountains.

After switchbacking down to a bridge and back into the redwoods, Pfeiffer Creek drops in two cascades, falling 60 feet over a granite base. A wide and shallow pool sits at the base in a grotto surrounded by ferns.

Miles and Directions

0.0 Start at signed trailhead next to Big Sur Lodge restaurant.

0.2 Official trailhead; follow wide, dirt trail into the forest.

0.8 Valley View Trail rejoins; turn right on Pfeiffer Falls Trail.

1.0 Base of falls. Return the way you came.

2.0 Arrive back at the trailhead.

Option: Take the Valley View Trail on the way back to the nature center. Climb through oak and chaparral to a dead-end overlook bench with views to the Big Sur coast, Santa Lucia Mountains, and the ocean.

Sequoia, Kings Canyon, and Southern Yosemite

Within a reasonable drive from Southern California, the western slope of the Sierra abounds with waterfalls, rivers, and swimming holes. Sequoia National Park is the second-oldest national park. San Joaquin farmers urged its creation to protect water supplies. Within the space of this book, it's not possible to document all the wonders of the Sierra. Instead, this chapter highlights some of the must-see waterfalls in the national parks along the western slope. These falls are easy to access and offer a superior balance of beauty to physical effort required to reach the falls while also offering developed trailhead amenities to make executing your hike easier. The western slope also abounds with drive-up falls, notably in Sequoia National Forest. The hikes in this chapter are designed to get you out exploring the most scenic and popular parts of these national parks.

For those interested in further exploring waterfalls here, we suggest reading this book's two companion guidebooks: *Hiking Waterfalls Yosemite National Park: A Guide to the Park's Greatest Waterfalls* by Suzanne Swedo and *Hiking Waterfalls in Northern California* by Tracy Salcedo-Chourré.

67 Grizzly Falls

This limited mobility-friendly waterfall route starts at a picnic area and leads to the base of a tall and scenic waterfall.

Height: 75–150 feet
Beauty rating: ★★★★★
Distance: 0.2 mile out and back
Elevation gain: Mostly level
Difficulty: Easy
Best season: Late spring, summer
County: Fresno
Trailhead amenities: Pit toilet, trash/recycle bins, picnic tables, benches, parking, viewable from a wheelchair-friendly area
Land status: Giant Sequoia National Monument, Sequoia National Forest

Maps: Tom Harrison Sequoia Kings Canyon; park map available at visitor center and online; USGS Cedar Grove
Trail contact: Sequoia National Forest, Hume Lake Ranger District, 35860 E. Kings Canyon Rd., Dunlap 93621; (559) 338-2251; www .fs.usda.gov/main/sequoia/home
Fees and permits: Vehicle pass required to pass through Sequoia Kings Canyon entrance station, valid 1–7 days; annual passes available

Finding the trailhead: Google Maps: Grizzly Falls Picnic Area. This road is open generally from the last Fri in Apr until mid-Nov. From the Big Stump entrance to Sequoia National Park, take CA 180 for 30 miles, exiting the park by following signs to Cedar Grove. Continue on CA 180 up and then down Kings Canyon. Before entering Kings Canyon National Park, look for a sign on the left for Grizzly Falls Picnic Area, which is about 6 miles before the intersection leading to Cedar Grove Visitor Center and Village. There's a cramped parking area with room for about 10 cars and parking along the road.
GPS: N36 48.107' / W118 44.374'

The Hike

Grizzly Falls is a beautiful year-round falls visible from the road in northern Giant Sequoia National Monument. Designated in 2000, the monument protects the *Sequoiadendron giganteium*, the world's largest tree, which grows more than 250 feet tall and more than 20 feet in diameter. The tree grows naturally only on the western slopes of the Sierra Nevada in a narrow 60-mile strip.

Grizzly Falls is on the banks of the South Fork of the Kings River in the heart of Kings Canyon. The falls is visible from the road and makes for a pleasant picnicking area. Grizzly Falls is along Grizzly Creek, which starts along the southeastern slopes of Mount Harrington (10,630 feet) and is fed by snowmelt from the Eagle Peaks. Backpackers can visit the headwaters near Grizzly Lake via a trail starting at Deer

This year-round fall is family-friendly and visible from the road or a short trail.

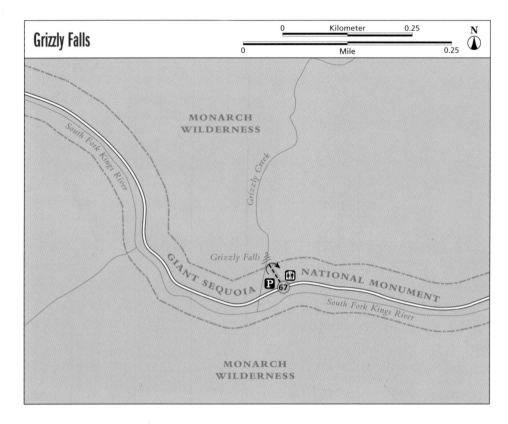

Grizzly Falls

Cove trailhead nearby. On the other side of the road from the parking lot, Grizzly Creek meets the South Fork of the Kings River.

Grizzly Falls is visible from the road. Start at a trail sign near the pit toilet on the eastern side of the lot. The trail is paved for 50 feet. To get closer, the path turns to dirt, which may be less wheelchair friendly. The well-defined trail to the left toward an information sign leads to benches and loops back to the western end of the parking lot. The "trail" to the base of the waterfall is obvious and straight ahead, but involves minor steps and is not paved, so may not be suited for those with limited mobility. There is ample room at the base for group photos or setting up a tripod to get a perfect shot.

You can return the way you came or make a lollipop loop by turning right toward the information sign. There are picnic tables and shady benches at which you can rest, snack, and reflect on the beauty of these falls.

Miles and Directions

0.0 Begin in parking area for the Frank and Bess Smithe Grove. Cross highway to bridge spanning Dora Creek and head up overgrown path on the right (south) as you face the ravine.

0.1 Reach base of falls. Return as you came.

0.2 Arrive back at the trailhead.

68 Roaring River Falls

Choose to take a streamside hike or a short, paved route to this impressive falls in a granite alcove. This waterfall has a route that is wheelchair and limited mobility friendly.

Height: About 15 feet
Beauty rating: ★★★
Distance: 4 mile adventure out and back; 2.1 miles with a car shuttle; 0.4 mile wheelchair accessible out and back (from Roaring Fork trailhead)
Elevation gain: 150 feet ascent/400 feet descent (one-way for the adventure route)
Difficulty: Moderate
Best season: Late spring, summer, fall
County: Fresno
Trailhead amenities: Pit toilet, trash/recycle bins, picnic tables, benches, parking

Land status: Kings Canyon National Park
Maps: Tom Harrison Sequoia Kings Canyon; park map available at visitor center and online; USGS The Sphinx
Trail contact: Sequoia Kings Canyon National Park, 47050 Generals Hwy., Three Rivers 94271-9700; (559) 565-3341; www.nps.gov/seki
Fees and permits: Vehicle pass required to enter the park, valid 1–7 days; annual passes available

Finding the trailhead: Google Maps: Roaring River Trailhead Parking (wheelchair-friendly route) or Zumwalt Meadows Trailhead (longer route). This road is open generally from the last Friday in Apr until mid-Nov. From the Big Stump entrance to Sequoia National Park, take CA 180 for 36.6 miles, following signs to Cedar Grove. Pass the intersection to Cedar Grove Visitor Center and Village. Immediately after crossing the Roaring Fork bridge, the parking lot to Roaring River Falls to access the paved and accessible version of this hike. If you plan to do this trip as a one-way journey, leave a car here. For the longer route, continue on CA 180 for 1.1 miles, crossing two bridges over the South Fork of the Kings River. The parking area for Zumwalt Falls is on the right, 0.1 mile after the second bridge.
GPS: N36 47.017' / W118 37.197' (Roaring River trailhead parking) or N36 47.375' / W118 35.541' (Zumwalt Meadows trailhead).

The Hike

This Kings Canyon National Park waterfall is shady and feels secluded, despite being a popular spot for park visitors. Most visitors take the wheelchair-friendly route, but we also describe the longer route so you can see more of the park.

Starting at the parking lot for Zumwalt Meadows trailhead, head south toward the Roaring River Trail information kiosk. Follow a wide trail toward a nearby sign for the trail for Zumwalt Meadows and a warning about the river. (*Option:* Take this trail for 0.25 mile before breaking off after the bridge (or add it on as a side trip before heading to the waterfall.)

If you look behind you toward the parking lot, you can see the grandeur of North Dome (8,717 feet) towering above.

Roaring Fork Falls can be visited via a paved, accessible trail or a longer dirt path along the river.

After crossing the bridge, you reach a signed T intersection. Turn right, following the sign toward Roaring River Falls on a good, but narrower dirt trail. This shady trail follows the river downstream through dense forest of oak, cedar, white pine, and sequoia.

The river is almost always in sight or audible along this trail. In 0.75 mile the trail is routed between giant house- and car-sized boulders that are a reminder of this area's geologic past. On either side of the canyon, you get views of the granite cliffs to the right and left. Early in the season you may even see waterfalls cascading off the edges of these cliffs.

After descending a rockier area, the road and a parking area become visible on your right. Stay on the trail, which widens and becomes sandier. A short, gradual climb up rock steps leads to a signed intersection with the paved trail. Turn left and the waterfall is less than 0.1 mile away.

You can return the way you came back to the Zumwalt Meadows parking lot or make the trip into a one-way journey by staying on the paved trail for 0.1 mile to the Roaring River Trail parking lot.

Miles and Directions

0.0   Start in parking area for Zumwalt Meadows Trail.

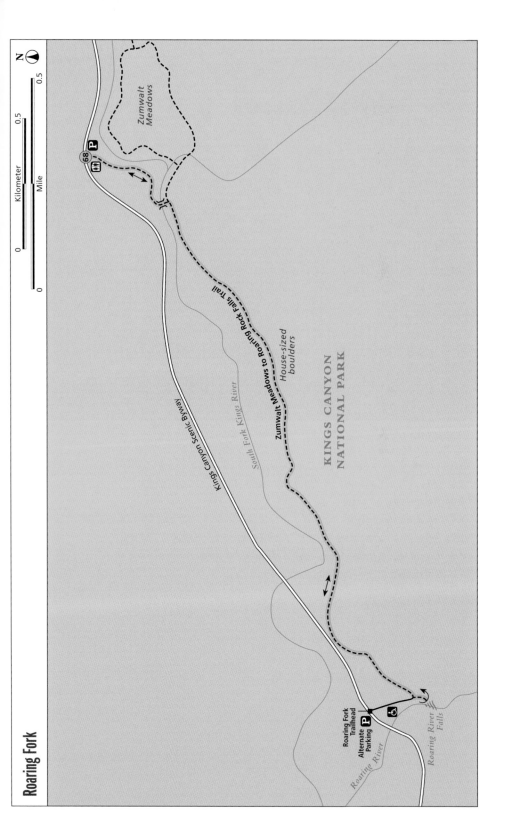

Roaring Fork

N

Kilometer
0   0.5   0.5

Mile
0   0.5

Kings Canyon Scenic Byway

South Fork Kings River

Zumwalt Meadows

68

Zumwalt Meadows to Roaring Rock Falls Trail

House-sized boulders

**KINGS CANYON
NATIONAL PARK**

Roaring Fork Trailhead
Alternate Parking

Roaring River

Roaring River Falls

The view from the bridge on the hike downriver to Roaring Fork Falls.

0.25 Bridge over the South Fork Kings River.

0.5 Turn right at T intersection, following Roaring River Trail downstream.

0.75 House-sized boulders.

1.5 Road visible on right.

1.9 Intersection with paved Roaring Fork Trail; turn left to falls.

2.0 End of trail at base of falls. Return the way you came.

4.0 Arrive back at the Zumwalt Meadows trailhead.

69 Mist Falls

Climb through canyons of grand granite domes to a wide and robust waterfall on Woods Creek on one of the most popular hikes in this part of Kings Canyon National Park.

Height: About 45 feet
Beauty rating: ★★★★★
Distance: 8.2 miles out and back
Elevation gain: 680 feet gain/80 feet descent one-way
Difficulty: Moderate
Best season: Summer, fall
County: Fresno
Trailhead amenities: Ranger station, pit toilets, trash/recycle bins, picnic tables
Land status: Kings Canyon National Park

Maps: Tom Harrison Sequoia Kings Canyon; park map available at visitor center and online; USGS The Sphinx
Trail contact: Sequoia Kings Canyon National Park, 47050 Generals Hwy., Three Rivers 94271-9700; (559) 565-3341; www.nps .gov/seki
Fees and permits: Vehicle pass required to enter the park, valid 1–7 days; annual passes available

Finding the trailhead: Google Maps: Roads End Wilderness Permit Station. This road is open generally from the last Fri in Apr until mid-Nov. Check CALDOT for information. From the Big Stump entrance to Sequoia National Park, take CA 180 for 36 miles, exiting and reentering the park by following signs to Cedar Grove. Continue straight on CA 180, following signs to Roads End, which is about 6 miles past the intersection leading to Cedar Grove Visitor Center and Village. Roads End is a loop with three large parking areas, but it can get crowded during the summer. The first parking lot on the right has a sign for day users and is the closest to the trailhead.
GPS: N36 47.408' / W118 34.587'

The Hike

Roads End is a grand start to a waterfall hike, with impressive granite domes and cliffs to your left and right. Even if there wasn't a waterfall at the end, this trail is worth hiking for the classic views of looming Sierra granite domes.

From the east end of the first (day-use) parking lot, follow signs for Bubb's Creek/ Mist Creek/Paradise Valley. Cross a small bridge and pass a ranger station (cabin) on the left, continuing 100 feet to an information board for "Wood's Creek and Bubb's Creek Trails." The first mile of this trail offers views of the mouth of Kings Canyon with North Dome (8,717 feet) to the northwest and the Grand Sentinel (8,518 feet) to the south.

Continue straight on a wide, sandy, well-defined trail through a mixed forest. Admire giant boulders that fell randomly into this valley during the last 100,000 years.

After 1.8 miles the trail narrows and makes a short, rocky descent to the right. The forest becomes thicker with fewer oaks, more conifers, and even ferns and reeds. You can hear the roaring river, even late in the season. To the south are views of pinnacle and famous alpine rock climbing destination The Sphinx next to Avalanche Peak (10,007 feet).

After 2 miles, reach a well-signed junction of two trails that appear to parallel one another. Take the Paradise Valley trail to the left (which goes up), not the Bubb's Creek trail going straight and then crossing a bridge to follow Bubb's Creek. The Mist Falls Trail curls to the north with Buck Peak high above to your left. Walk through shady forest filled with ferns.

The trail drops to the banks of the South Fork of Kings River, where you can dip your toes or refill a filtered water bottle.

After a gradual rocky ascent, you are above the river. A moraine of rocks is to your left and grand views of the domes are to your right.

Descend and soon see the first views of white water cascading off a granite slab. If the water is low enough, there is even a swimming hole with a cascade running into it (but do not attempt this if water is running fast and high, as people have drowned in these waters).

Some people simply stop here, mistaking the nearby cascades for Mist Falls. While the last bit of the hike involves climbing and can be confusing, Mist Falls

The wide Mist Falls tumbles off granite slab into a pool along the popular Paradise Valley Trail.

makes these cascades look miniature. The trail follows along the right edge of a flat, granite slab. It should be marked with smaller rocks along the edges. If you lose the trail, take about 60 steps up the canyon on the slab to rejoin a well-marked dirt trail. After this, follow good dirt trail up a short switchback and until you hit more granite slab. There may be small cairns nearby or other rocks lining the path in the right direction. If you can't find it, walk about 60 steps from where the dirt trail "ends" up the slab toward a large ponderosa tree with the top knocked off. The dirt trail is well marked again there.

The trail goes back to follow the river on flatter trail. You emerge at a view of the falls, which has a sign marking "Mist Falls." A fallen log blocks access to the water, but when the water is low enough, a use trail to the right curls around and provides access to the small sandy shore and base of the falls. The trail you were on continues to Paradise Valley and up via Woods Creek to the John Muir Trail/Pacific Crest Trail and beyond.

The wide Mist Falls pummels off a granite slab and drops into a clear pool. From the base it's difficult to see the true top. Indeed, if you continue on the trail toward Paradise Valley, you can observe that the waterfall drops from a low-angled granite slab. It's hard to say where the waterfall truly begins. The slabs and rocks near the waterfall can be slippery, flooded, and dangerous, especially early in the season, so use caution.

Miles and Directions

0.0 Start by heading east on wide, flat, sandy trail.

0.2 Cross a footbridge.

0.3 Cross a log bridge (or ford).

1.8 Drop down a short switchback as trail narrows.

2.0 Climb left at junction with Bubb's Creek Trail, following signs to Mist Falls and Paradise Valley.

2.5 Rocky point with view of Sentinel Dome.

3.0 Trail parallels water near pools.

3.6 Cross slab; trail continues upcanyon.

4.1 Reach sign for Mist Falls near its base. Return the way you came.

8.2 Arrive back at the trailhead.

70 Tokopah Falls

At 1,200 feet tall, Tokopah is considered to be the tallest waterfall in Sequoia and Kings Canyon National Parks and is the tallest in this book. The falls is a must-see for anyone visiting the area, and the hike is easy and popular. Expect wildlife, wildflowers, grand views, and (in low water) swimming holes along the way.

Height: 1,200 feet
Beauty rating: ★★★★★
Distance: 3.6 miles out and back
Elevation gain: 600 feet one-way
Difficulty: Easy to moderate
Best season: Spring, summer
County: Tulare
Trailhead amenities: Camping, info, visitor center, water, toilets, trash/recycle bins
Land status: Sequoia National Park

Maps: Free NPS park map with entry, at the visitor center, or download at www.nps.gov/seki; Tom Harrison Sequoia Kings Canyon; USGS Lodgepole
Trail contact: Sequoia Kings Canyon National Park, 47050 Generals Hwy., Three Rivers 94271-9700; (559) 565-3341; www.nps.gov/seki
Fees and permits: Vehicle pass required to enter the park, valid 1–7 days; annual passes available

Finding the trailhead: Google Maps: Lodgepole Campground Upper Loop or Tokopah Trailhead. From Fresno, take CA 180 east for 55 miles to the Big Stump entrance of Kings Canyon National Park. After 1.5 mile, turn right on CA 198 (the Generals Highway) toward Sequoia National Park. After 25 miles, follow signs to the Lodgepole Campground. After 0.65 mile, go to the Log Bridge area of Lodgepole Camp, parking in a lot before the bridge heading north over the river.
GPS: N36 36.176' / W118 43.265'

The Hike

The Tokopah Valley—like Yosemite Valley—was carved by glaciers and a river running through it. That's one reason this hike is one of the most popular in Sequoia and Kings Canyon National Parks. If you want to avoid the crowds, come early in the morning or visit on a weekday.

From the Log Bridge parking area of Lodgepole Camp, walk about 500 feet north to a bridge over the Marble Fork of the Kaweah River. The trailhead for Twin Lakes Trail/Tokopah Valley Trail is to the right after the bridge. The Twin Lakes Trail breaks off, heading northwest. Your trail heads east.

Follow the well-marked Tokopah Valley Trail as it follows the Marble Fork of the Kaweah River. You'll walk through classic Sierra habitats: lodgepole pines, granite boulders, and meadows with ferns. There are forty different wildflower species in the 1.8 miles of trail to the falls, best spotted during the late spring and early summer when the falls are also in their prime.

Tokopah Falls

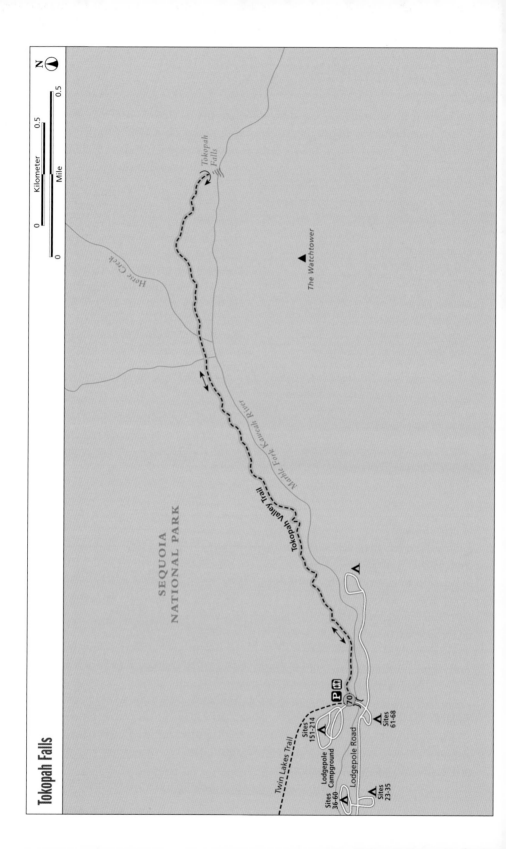

Tokopah Falls is wide and blocky and one of the most popular hiking destinations in this part of the Park.

This is home to bears and deer, which you may see if you are quiet. But the wildlife you're most likely to see are sneaky and tourist-loving squirrels and marmots, who may try to beg snacks from you (please don't feed them).

The highlight of this trip (other than the falls) is the beauty of the Tokopah Valley, with views of the 1,600-foot-tall glacially carved Watchtower (8,973 feet) on the south side of the valley (right as you head to the falls). In low water times and along slow-moving parts of the river, it may be possible to splash around in the river (though care should be taken as accidents often happen, especially to children).

The trail gently travels uphill, occasionally crossing bridges over minor creeks and Horse Creek. After crossing Horse Creek, which joins the Marble Fork from the north, the trail bends southeast, following the natural curve of the river as it flows from Heather Lake to the south.

At 1.5 miles from your car, you can begin to see the giant Tokopah Falls. Like on many Sierra trails, builders blasted into the granite to create a level walkway over the steep slab for hikers. It can feel like walking through a tunnel.

The falls tumbles down granite carved in the classic Sierra U-shape. Your path ends right before the edge of the falls. Numerous signs warn not to get too close, as every year it seems like someone gets into the fast-moving water and is swept over.

Miles and Directions

0.0 Log Bridge parking area.

0.1 Cross bridge and reach trailhead for Twin Lakes and Tokopah Valley Trails; turn right for Tokopah Falls hike.

1.8 Base of falls. Return the way you came.

3.6 Arrive back at the trailhead.

71 Chilnualna Falls

A short, family-friendly hike from the southern entrance of Yosemite National Park leads to the base of Chilnualna Falls—one of the biggest waterfalls in Yosemite outside of the Valley (with fewer crowds, too). It can be extended to a longer trip to the top cascade of the falls.

Height: 695 feet total over 5 tiers over 4 miles; individual falls range 150–250 feet. Visible from the 0.4 mile hike: 30–40-foot cascade.
Beauty rating: ★ ★ ★ ★ ★
Distance: 0.8–8.2 miles out and back
Elevation gain: 200 feet gain one-way to bottom tier of falls; 2,400 feet gain to top of upper tier
Difficulty: Easy to strenuous
Best season: Spring, summer
County: Fresno and Mariposa
Trailhead amenities: Outhouses, bear boxes (to store food away from your cars), dirt parking lot holds about 25 cars

Land status: Yosemite National Park
Maps: USGS Wawona, Mariposa Grove; free NPS park map with entry, at the visitor center, or download at www.nps.gov/yose; Tom Harrison Yosemite National Park
Trail contact: Yosemite National Park, PO Box 577, Yosemite National Park 95389; (209) 372-0200; www.nps.gov/yose
Fees and permits: Vehicle pass required to enter the park, valid 1–7 days; annual passes available

Finding the trailhead: Google Maps: Chilnualna Falls Trailhead. From the southern entrance of Yosemite at Wawona, take CA 41 (Wawona Road) 4.8 miles north toward the Wawona Hotel and Golf Course. Head east 1.7 miles on Chilnualna Falls Road, passing The Redwoods in Yosemite (vacation rentals) along the way. Pull into a large parking lot to the right. If you cross a bridge, you've gone too far.
GPS: N37 32.544' / W119 38.002'

The Hike

When visiting the southern Wawona lowlands of Yosemite National Park, take this short and flat hike to see Chilnualna Creek as it tumbles into the South Fork of the Merced River. Chilnualna Falls itself falls over five cascades over 4 miles, totaling 695 feet of drop!

The Wawona area is known as Pallachum ("a good place to stay") in the Native American Miwok language, which after visiting, you are likely to agree. Strangely, the origin of the word "Wawona" is unknown.

While the Valley gets the glory, Wawona has an important conservation legacy as well. In 1885 Galen Clark, known as the "Guardian of Yosemite Park," lived here. He later proposed legislation to protect the redwoods of Mariposa Grove and what became Yosemite National Park.

Start on paved Chilnualna Falls Road to a signed trailhead on the left. The wide trail splits into a stock trail on the left. Take the foot trail on the right, which narrows. Your route traverses the mountainside through oak above the granite boulder–filled creek.

Reach a staircase. Take a side trail down to a pool below a cascade of 50 feet. Climb stairs to a falls overlook to watch the bottom tier of the falls tumble over room-sized boulders. There are plenty of flat picnicking or hanging-out areas near the base. Return the way you came.

Variation: Take stone stairs to the trail to the top of Chilnualna 3.5 miles away. The trail was built at the turn of the twentieth century by John Conway, famous for the switchbacks to Upper Yosemite Falls, and climbs 2,400 feet, passing into the Yosemite Wilderness. It has numerous flights of stone stairs and climbs gradually from mixed oak to pine. As you climb, you have views of granite Wawona Dome (6,897 feet).

You'll be hiking away from Chilnualna Creek for the next 1.5 miles. About 2 miles from the trailhead, you may catch a view of the many tiers of the falls and the best chance to see the falls at its full height, a view you won't get from the top of the falls. It's a steady climb and often exposed to the sun, without much shade at around 3 miles. Bring enough water, start early, and bring a hat and wear sunscreen. The area toward the top of the falls is a classic Sierra granite, forested landscape with views of the cascades of Chilnualna and the top of the falls.

For people interested in further exploring Yosemite waterfalls, we recommend the partner book to this guide, *Hiking Waterfalls Yosemite National Park: A Guide to the Park's Greatest Waterfalls* by Suzanne Swedo.

The waterfall at the top of the Chilnualna Falls trail.

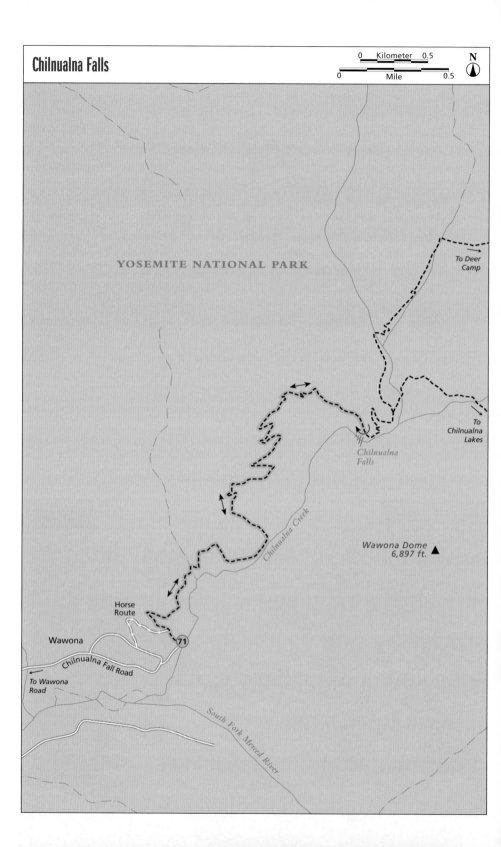

Chilnualna Falls

YOSEMITE NATIONAL PARK

To Deer Camp

To Chilnualna Lakes

Chilnualna Falls

Chilnualna Creek

Wawona Dome
6,897 ft. ▲

Horse Route

Wawona

71

Chilnualna Fall Road

To Wawona Road

South Fork Merced River

Miles and Directions

0.0 Start at the Chilnualna Falls Road trailhead.

0.4 Bottom of bottom cascade.

4.1 Top of falls.

8.2 Arrive back at the trailhead.

The waterfall on the lowest of the Chilnualna Falls.

Mammoth and the Eastern Sierra

The Eastern Sierra is my favorite region in this entire book. Waterfalls abound here, and trying to narrow down which falls should be included in the book was a heart-wrenching process. Those willing to backpack longer distances will find even more beauty in the Sierra's waterways. The falls included in this section are meant to be the beginning of your exploration of Sierra waterfalls. They were chosen because they offer a combination of 1) easy access, 2) high-quality trail, and 3) trailheads with good amenities. They were also chosen because they are among the most iconic waterfalls of the Eastern Sierra.

The waterfalls in this section encompass America's most scenic landscapes including Mount Whitney National Recreation Area, Yosemite National Park, and Devils Postpile National Monument. They almost all venture into federally designated wilderness areas including the John Muir Wilderness, Ansel Adams Wilderness, Hoover Wilderness, and Emigrant Wilderness.

As the region encompasses a large area, you can marvel at the geological interplay between granite carved by glaciers and volcanic activity in this region. Your waterfall hikes will include views of a landscape carved by glaciers, most notably on the hikes in Tuolumne Meadows. Glaciers polished this smooth granite. The craggy peak tops were exposed above so remain jagged. You'll walk past glacial erratics, rocks moved by glaciers long ago and deposited in seemingly "random" spots. Yet, in Devils Postpile, columnar basalt formed less than 100,000 years ago from lava 400 to 600 feet thick. This interplay between the more recent volcanic ridges and peaks and granite can be seen in the Emigrant Wilderness as well as on your drive up US 395.

Portions of the Sierra are free to access. Others require entrance fees and, in the case of Devils Postpile, bus-only access to the park. The area is seasonally covered in snow and roads may be closed. Read the descriptions before going and call to make sure they have not changed.

72 Lone Pine Falls

Whitney Portal is one of the most magical areas in the Sierra. Even the drive through the Alabama Hills (used for many a Western movie set) with views of the Sierra Crest is incredible. Whether you view the falls by pulling up to the picnic area or take the longer hike on a less-crowded Whitney Portal Trail, these two falls give you the Whitney experience without requiring a hiking permit. The longer route, the Whitney Portal National Recreation Trail, is also recognized by the Smithsonian as a National Historic Trail (but don't worry; it's been around for a while but is in fantastic shape).

Height: About 20–50 feet
Beauty rating: ★★★★★
Distance: 0.2 mile for short trip; 4 miles one-way with a two-car shuttle (8 miles out and back)
Elevation gain: Flat (short route) or 2,700 feet gain/150 feet loss (one-way)
Difficulty: Easy for short route; strenuous for longer route
Best season: Late spring, summer, fall
County: Inyo
Trailhead amenities: Lone Pine Campground (lower trailhead): 12 spots, 40 campsites with parking. More parking outside gate. Outhouse, trash, recycling, bear-proof food storage lockers. Mt. Whitney Portal Campground: 100+ spots, campground (reservations required), water, trash/recycling, bear-proof food storage lockers, restaurant, store
Land status: Inyo National Forest, Mount Whitney Ranger District
Maps: Tom Harrison Mt. Whitney Portal; USGS Mount Langley
Trail contact: Inyo National Forest Eastern Sierra Visitor Center, US 395 and CA 136, Lone Pine 93545; (760) 876-6200; www.fs.usda.gov/main/inyo/home
Fees and permits: None

Finding the trailhead: Long route trailhead: Google Maps: Lone Pine Campground. From US 395 in Lone Pine, turn left (west) on Whitney Portal Road for 6 miles to the day-use parking on the east end of the campground. Walk to the Lower Trailhead, found on the west end of the Lone Pine Campground. Upper Trailhead is closed in winter.

Shorter trailhead: Google Maps: Whitney Portal Campground. From the turnoff from Whitney Portal Road to Lone Pine Campground, continue on Whitney Portal Road for 4.5 miles until the road ends. Park in day-use parking near the picnic area and pond, in the far western part of the parking lot loop.

GPS: N36 35.508' / W 118 11.055'

The Hike

Visiting Whitney Portal should be on every Southern California to-do list. Mount Whitney (14,495 feet) is the tallest peak in the Lower 48, and its iconic shape and surrounding valley make it arguably the most beautiful place described in this book. Named in 1864 after California state geologist Josiah Whitney, the Paiute who live(d) in the area have a much older name for Mount Whitney: Tumanguya, meaning very "very old man."

Two falls are described in this hike. The bigger, though lower angle, Upper Falls (technically "rapids" on Lone Pine Creek) can be viewed by walking through a paved picnic area from the Upper Trailhead parking area (8,400 feet). It is a good option if you're looking for a gentle waterfall viewing while still getting the Whitney Portal experience.

Lone Pine Falls is beautiful in the autumn when the leaves turn golden before snows come. iSTOCK

The Lower Falls can be found by starting at the Lower Trailhead (5,900 feet) and hiking the Whitney Portal National Recreation Trail, the route described here. Once part of the official Mount Whitney Trail (constructed in 1904 and financed by the residents of Lone Pine), the trail that is now called the WPNRT was abandoned in 1933 after the Civilian Conservation Corps built the Whitney Portal Road. It was rebuilt as a hiking trail in 1979. It also has National Historic Trail status recognized by the Smithsonian Institute.

To hike the WPNRT, start at the trailhead in the west end of Lone Pine Campground. Follow a well-defined, sandy trail in open sagebrush. As you climb, you have unobstructed views of Mount Whitney Portal, Mount Whitney, and the Eastern Sierra Escarpment.

What makes this hike special is that you climb along the canyon's southern moraine through four ecosystems from the Great Basin Desert (sagebrush) to the pinion pine forest to the riparian zone to the subalpine forest of the Whitney Portal. Your views out to the Inyo Mountains across the Owens Valley give an equal appreciation for the geologic and ecosystem diversity of this special part of California.

This lower-altitude section of the trail can be quite hot during the summer. Start early or time this hike for the fall or late spring, when desert wildflowers bloom. It's open and generally snow-free year-round. The higher-altitude sections of the hike can be 20 degrees colder than the start, so remember to bring plenty of layers. Although much of the trail is shaded, pack plenty of water from the Lower Trailhead.

Follow Lone Pine Creek as the ecosystem transitions in 0.8 miles into a pinion pine forest and, after 2.5 miles, to a riparian canyon with aspens that turn golden in the autumn. The US Forest Service has determined that 8.6 miles of Lone Pine Creek—from its headwaters to the national forest boundary—are eligible for National Wild and Scenic River status. The creek becomes more active. At 1.7 mile at the end of a switchback as the trail goes left and parallels high above Lone pine Creek, you'll see remnants of the old steeper trail before the switchbacks were built. Far below, you'll see a lower gate leading to the switchbacks for Whitney Portal Road. From a coffee table–sized boulder 30 feet off trail, you may see the Lower Falls. If not, don't worry. There are many falls to come.

At 2.5 miles, cross a log under a small waterfall on Meyer Creek with another mini-falls on Lone Pine Creek right after. At 3.1 miles, you'll see the first cabin as the trail turns right into Whitney Portal Campground. From here until the end, you'll be climbing steeply for the next mile with few views of the paved road. Many hikers find the mental challenge of being so close with so much more elevation gain to be a challenge. 0.3 mile later, cross a paved road following signs to the NRT Trail (do not cross the bridge). 0.1 mile later, reach another paved road. Turn right to cross a bridge and immediately turn right, following the creek on its right side. Take a footbridge back to the left side, where you'll stay until the end.

Whether you started at the Upper or Lower Trailhead, the Upper Lone Pine Creek Falls can be viewed from the parking loop. Surrounded by subalpine pines, the falls can freeze as early as October. A rough use trail starting at the southwest corner

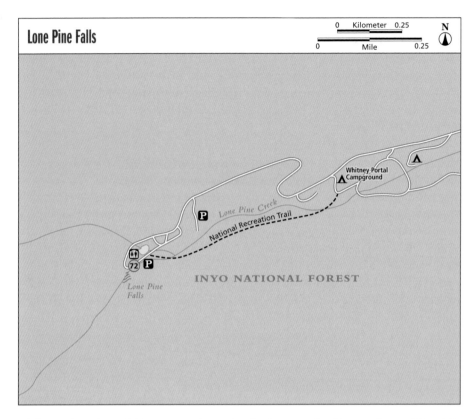

Lone Pine Falls

0   Kilometer   0.25

0   Mile   0.25

N

Whitney Portal Campground

Lone Pine Creek

National Recreation Trail

72

INYO NATIONAL FOREST

Lone Pine
Falls

of the parking loop follows Lone Pine Creek closer to the biggest drop of the falls. You can also see them from the road near the small fishing pond and the picnic area.

Miles and Directions

0.8 Enter Pinon Pine forest

0.9 Trail sign. Head west.

1.0 Trail sign. Head straight.

1.2 Left at trail sign

1.7 Lower Falls visible near a switchback

2.5 Cross Meyer Creek on a log

3.1 First views of cabins

3.4 Cross paved road to continue on trail on left side of creek.

3.5 Take paved road right across bridge, then immediately left on trail along the right bank of the creek.

3.6 Pedestrian bridge

4.1 Wooden pedestrian bridge to parking lot near the fishing pond/Upper Lone Pine Falls

73 Twin Falls

This massive blocky falls tumbles picturesquely into a lake surrounded by mountains. In fall the lakeside aspens are as beautiful as the falls. Enjoyed from a short, wheelchair-friendly road or via a closer view on a rockier trail, this falls is a must-see while in the Mammoth Lakes area.

Height: About 250 feet
Beauty rating: ★★★★★
Distance: 0.8 mile out and back
Elevation gain: Mostly level
Difficulty: Easy
Best season: Fall, winter, spring, summer
County: Mono
Trailhead amenities: 100+ parking spots; this area is very popular and can get crowded

Land status: Inyo National Forest, Mammoth Ranger District
Maps: Tom Harrison Mammoth High Country; USGS Crystal Crag
Trail contact: Inyo National Forest Mammoth Lakes Welcome Center, 2500 Main St., Mammoth Lakes 93546; (760) 924-5500; www .fs.usda.gov/main/inyo/home
Fees and permits: None

Finding the trailhead: Google Maps: Twin Lakes Campground. From the intersection of Lake Mary Road and CA 203 in Mammoth Lakes, continue west on Lake Mary Road. In 2.1 miles, cross a bridge and then immediately turn right on a road. Pass cabins and lodges on the left and a footbridge on the right. Drive past Tamarack Lodge and the cross-country ski area into the campground loop. Follow signs for the day-use/picnic area parking. Road and campground closed in winter and early spring.
GPS: N37 36.582' / W119 00.357'

The Hike

Whether you're camping or on a day trip to Mammoth, the short, awe-inspiring hike to Twin Falls and the surrounding lake basin is not to be missed. It's one of the finest—and physically easiest—outdoor experiences to have in the area.

Mammoth Mountain was created from a series of volcanic eruptions between 50,000 and 200,000 years ago. The earliest evidence of ancestors of Mono Paiutes in the area dates back to 8,000 BCE, summering in the Mammoth area and wintering in the valley. The sharp volcanic obsidian in the area was valued by other tribes on the western slope, where obsidian is rare. In the mid-1800s Euro-American settlers came to the area bringing disease and violence, especially following the discovery of gold and ranching in the area. Summer recreation here became popular around the turn of the century, with resorts popping up in the 1920s and skiing introduced in the 1930s. The establishment of CA 203 sparked the beginning of the ski industry here.

Twin Falls tumbles into Twin Lakes in the late autumn.

From the picnic area (follow signs for parking to the day-use area), take the paved road between the two lakes over a wide bridge. The view of the falls across the Upper Lake will make your jaw drop in any season. In autumn golden aspens dot the lake as the falls starts to take on its first icicles. In early summer the falls rages in an almost unbelievable display from the snowmelt above. Look beyond to the Lower Lake and the peaks protecting this basin. This view is what makes Mammoth Lakes one of the most extraordinary mountain towns in California.

For those who wish to continue to the falls' base, walk across the bridge. Turn left when the campground road forks near site 28. Continue on this paved campground road.

A quarter mile from your car, turn left on a gravel road paralleling the lake. Continue for about 200 feet until you reach a three-way intersection. Take the farthest left (narrowest) of the trails here. There are private cabins along the lake, and the owners ask that you stay on the signed trail instead of their access road.

Following the sign to the public trail, follow the shoreline of the lake between the water and the access road to the cabins, paralleling the road. The path can get muddy or flooded in high water. But it deposits you right at the base of the roaring falls. When snow is melting, the falls is best enjoyed from the sidelines. In autumn or lower water years, it's possible to wade below the falls and look up at the mass of water flowing above.

Although there are use trails all through here, the least brushy way back to your car is to return the way you came.

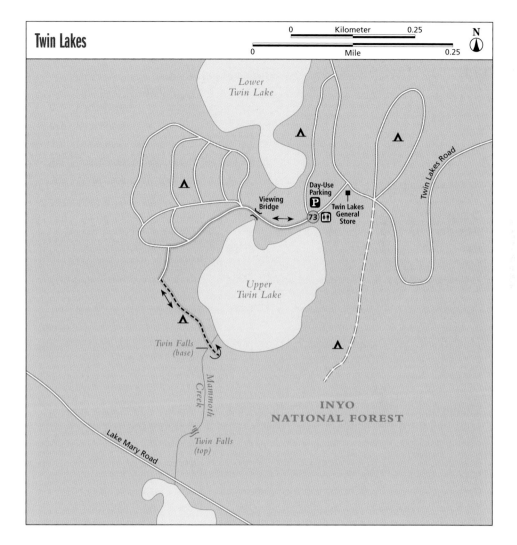

Miles and Directions

0.0 Start at picnic area trailhead.

0.1 Bridge view of falls.

0.25 Turn left out of campground onto dirt road near site 28.

0.4 Base of falls. Return the way you came.

0.8 Arrive back at the trailhead.

74 Rainbow Falls and Lower Falls

This classic must-see waterfall is a major attraction of Devils Postpile National Monument. The trail follows the Middle Fork of the San Joaquin River through volcanic geology. Rainbow Falls has a classic, almost 90-degree drop into a pool below.

Height: Rainbow Falls: about 100 feet; Lower Falls: 30–40 feet
Beauty rating: ★★★★★
Distance: 5 miles out and back
Elevation gain: 500 feet (mostly on the return)
Difficulty: Easy to moderate (due to distance)
Best season: Summer, early fall
County: Mono and Madera
Trailhead amenities: Reds Meadow Bus Stop 10 has a store, restaurant, showers, camping, and cabins (reservations required). Reds Meadow Bus Stop 9 has a ranger station.
Land status: Devils Postpile National Monument; Inyo National Forest, Ansel Adams Wilderness

Maps: Free Devils Postpile maps at ranger station or www.nps.gov/depo; Tom Harrison Mammoth High Country; USGS Crystal Crag
Trail contact: Devils Postpile National Monument, PO Box 3999, Mammoth Lakes 93546; (760) 934-2289; www.nps.gov/depo. Inyo National Forest Mammoth Lakes Welcome Center, 2500 Main St., Mammoth Lakes 93546; (760) 924-5500; www.fs.usda.gov/main/inyo/home.
Fees and permits: With very limited exceptions, all visitors must buy a round-trip shuttle ticket; longer and annual passes are available.

Finding the trailhead: Google Maps: Mammoth Mountain Ski Area. In the town of Mammoth Lakes, turn right (uphill) on Minaret Road (which is still CA 203) past the bottom of the ski resort to the Devils Postpile entrance kiosk. Between 7 a.m. and 7:30 p.m. daily during the summer, purchase an access pass from the Mammoth Mountain Adventure Center. The bus stops throughout the Devils Postpile National Monument. Get off at Bus Stop 9 (Rainbow Falls trailhead). Note that Devils Postpile closes around October 15 as the road is not plowed during the winter. It's still possible to hike into Reds Meadow, but involves adding 4 miles (8 miles round-trip) of hiking over Mammoth Pass from Horseshoe Lake.
GPS: N37 39.030' / W119 02.129'

The Hike

Rainbow Falls is a major tourist attraction in Devils Postpile National Monument.

This hike follows the Middle Fork of the San Joaquin River. Thousands of years ago the river changed course to meander down this valley (which is what you walk along in Devils Postpile) only to reunite with its old course—sculpting a steep gully of volcanic rock and forming Rainbow Falls.

Take the Devils Postpile shuttle bus to Stop 9, Rainbow Falls. Walk toward the ranger station (where you can pick up a free map) and follow signs toward Rainbow Falls. Your first 0.2 mile is on a wide, sandy, flat trail.

In the right conditions, a rainbow can arch the eponymous falls. The sharp edged nickpoint and geology of the area around the falls is evident. ISTOCK

Lower Falls isn't as grand as Rainbow Falls but has plenty of rock area for picnicing or playing in a pool.

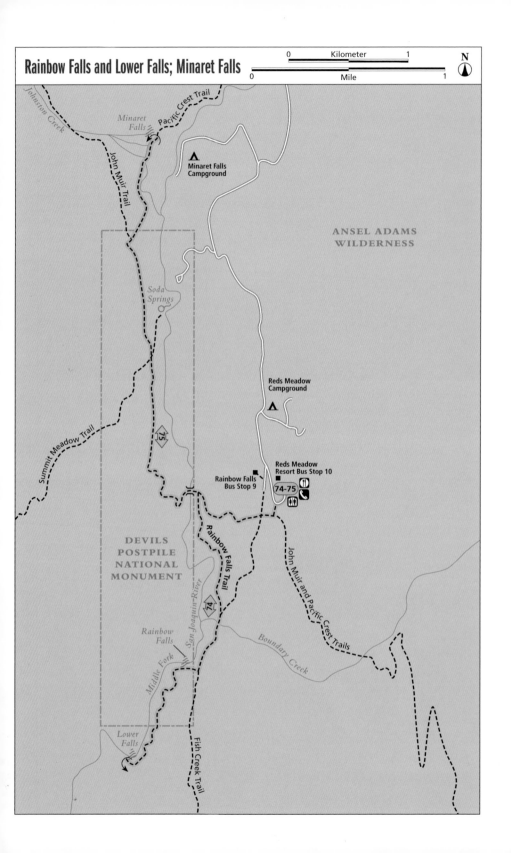

0   Kilometer   1

0   Mile   1

N

Johnston Creek

Minaret Falls

Pacific Crest Trail

John Muir Trail

▲ Minaret Falls
Campground

ANSEL ADAMS
WILDERNESS

Soda Springs

Reds Meadow
Campground
▲

Summit Meadow Trail

◇ 75

Rainbow Falls
Bus Stop 9

Reds Meadow
Resort Bus Stop 10
74-75

DEVILS
POSTPILE
NATIONAL
MONUMENT

Rainbow Falls Trail

John Muir and Pacific Crest Trails

San Joaquin River

74

Rainbow Falls

Middle Fork

Boundary Creek

Lower Falls

Fish Creek Trail

Reach a signed four-way intersection. Devils Postpile is a maze of trails. While trails to Rainbow Falls are well signed, there are at least three different paths that can take you there. At this intersection you *can* head straight, following signs for the most direct route to Rainbow Falls. However, we suggest turning right and downhill, taking the iconic John Muir Trail and Pacific Crest Trail toward the Middle Fork of the San Joaquin River. Why? A wildfire burned this area in 1992. While it is regenerating into a pine forest, this route keeps you more in the shade—something you'll appreciate when climbing this hill on the way back.

Take the JMT/PCT north and in 0.5 mile, reach another signed four-way junction. Here, leave the JMT/PCT and turn left, following signs toward Rainbow Falls. This route has you hiking closer to the Middle Fork of the San Joaquin River, which looks slow and gentle at this point.

After a pleasant 0.7 mile paralleling the river, reach a signed intersection indicating Rainbow Falls is 0.5 mile away (my GPS shows it's a little farther). On the left, the trail is joined by one of the many trails tourists take from the bus stop to Rainbow Falls. Immediately after, cross a bridge over Boundary Creek and then see a sign for Ansel Adams Wilderness.

A little more than 0.1 mile later, you reach another three-way signed junction (see what we mean about the maze of trails?). Follow signs, making a right toward Rainbow Falls (upper platform is 0.2 mile away). In 0.1 mile another sign says you're reentering Devils Postpile.

Keep walking and you may hear the falls (or at least start seeing other waterfall viewers). As the trail comes closer to the falls, the edge of the cliff is roped off. Like many falls of its size, Rainbow Falls creates currents and eddies in the pool and river below. These can cause floating objects to become trapped in the churning water at the base. That's why signs warn not to get close to the edge. People have died here.

From the viewing platform you can see the two layers of the rock that support the falls. The upper layer of the falls is made of volcanic andesite, a hard and slowly eroding rock layer. It forms a "nickpoint" where the falls goes over the edge. The andesite erodes slower than the underlying rock, a volcanic rhyodacite. Because the upper layer "protects" the lower layer from beveling away, the falls maintains its height over geologic time.

However, while erosion isn't impacting the falls' height, it is causing the falls to move upstream! Geologists estimate the falls is 500 feet upstream from its original location. Notice how the lower layer looks like a chunk has been carved out in the area behind the falls? This process is called undercutting. Over geologic time the water erodes away the exact spot where the river goes over the edge.

From the upper viewpoint, take the trail downhill for 0.1 mile to a four-way junction. To your right is the middle viewing platform, often considered the best viewpoint. Straight ahead are a set of more than one hundred stairs that lead to the waterfall's base and the lower viewing platform toward the base and pool (no swimming allowed) below.

If you choose to continue to Lower Falls, instead make a left, following signs to Lower Falls. Before you go, know there is a climb back on the return. In 0.3 mile you pass a sign indicating you're leaving Devils Postpile (again!). The path parallels the river, which returns to being calm. The trail goes downhill until you're near the top of the falls. Here it takes a shorter, steeper grade to curl around to the falls' base and the pool below.

Lower Falls drops through a narrow, rocky chute. You may spot small trout in the pool at its base. The area around the pool is sandy and nice for picnicking, away from the crowds of Rainbow Falls.

Miles and Directions

0.0 Start at Bus Stop 9, Rainbow Falls.

0.2 Turn right onto JMT/PCT north at four-way intersection.

0.7 Stay straight on JMT/PCT north at four-way intersection.

1.4 Three-way junction (a trail joins on the left). Follow signs to Rainbow Falls, then cross a bridge.

1.5 Sign for Ansel Adams Wilderness.

1.6 Signed three-way junction. Turn right, following signs to Rainbow Falls.

1.7 Sign indicates you are reentering Devils Postpile National Monument.

1.8 Upper Falls viewing platform.

1.9 Four-way junction to middle viewing platform, lower viewing platform, and Lower Falls.

2.2 Sign indicates you are exiting Devils Postpile.

2.5 Base of Lower Falls. Return the way you came.

5.0 Arrive back at the trailhead.

75 Minaret Falls

Follow the iconic Pacific Crest Trail and John Muir Trail on this classic Sierra hike. Along the way you get bird's-eye views of the Devils Postpile volcanic formation while traveling through Devils Postpile National Monument, Ansel Adams Wilderness, and the Middle Fork of the San Joaquin River.

See map on page 289.
Height: 150–200 feet
Beauty rating: ★★★★★
Distance: 6.2 miles out and back
Elevation gain: 300 feet ascent/400 feet descent one-way
Difficulty: Easy to moderate (due to distance)
Best season: Summer, early fall
County: Madera and Inyo
Trailhead amenities: Reds Meadow Bus Stop 10 has a store, restaurant, showers, camping, and cabins (reservations required). Reds Meadow Bus Stop 9 has a ranger station.
Land status: Devils Postpile National Monument; Inyo National Forest, Ansel Adams Wilderness

Maps: Free Devils Postpile maps at ranger station or www.nps.gov/depo; Tom Harrison Mammoth High Country; USGS Mammoth Mountain
Trail contact: Devils Postpile National Monument, PO Box 3999, Mammoth Lakes 93546; (760) 934-2289; www.nps.gov/depo. Inyo National Forest Mammoth Lakes Welcome Center, 2500 Main St., Mammoth Lakes 93546; (760) 924-5500; www.fs.usda.gov/main/inyo/home.
Fees and permits: With very limited exceptions, all visitors must buy a round-trip shuttle ticket; longer and annual passes are available.

Finding the trailhead: Google Maps: Mammoth Mountain Ski Area. In the town of Mammoth Lakes, turn right (uphill) on Minaret Road (which is still CA 203) past the bottom of the ski resort to the Devils Postpile entrance kiosk. Between 7 a.m. and 7:30 p.m. daily during the summer, purchase an access pass from the Mammoth Mountain Adventure Center. The bus stops throughout the Devils Postpile National Monument. Get off at Bus Stop 9 (Rainbow Falls trailhead). Note that Devils Postpile closes around October 15 as the road is not plowed during the winter. It's still possible to hike into Reds Meadow, but involves adding 4 miles (8 miles round-trip) of hiking over Mammoth Pass from Horseshoe Lake.
GPS: N37 39.030' / W119 02.129'

The Hike

When it comes to hiking in the Sierra, Devils Postpile is a great place to start a hike because a bus takes you up and over the first crest, saving you some climbing. You can start the Minaret Falls hike from several bus stops, but we suggest starting at Reds Meadow Bus Stop 9. Why? This area is crisscrossed with trails, and despite the park service's best intentions to sign, it can be confusing to stay on the route. By taking the superbly marked PCT almost the entire way, you can follow the wooden PCT confidence markers placed 15 feet up on the trunks of trees near the trail.

From Bus Stop 9 (Rainbow Falls trailhead), follow a wide trail for 0.2 mile to a four-way signed junction. Make a sharp right onto the JMT/PCT north. Follow the JMT/PCT downhill through lodgepole pine forest toward the Middle Fork of the San Joaquin River for 0.5 mile until you reach another signed intersection (see what we mean about this place being a maze of trails?). Stay straight/right, following the JMT/PCT north to cross a bridge over the Middle Fork of the San Joaquin River.

The JMT/PCT twists gently uphill, sneaking between two large boulders, before starting a serious climb up switchbacks 0.5 mile after the bridge. Luckily, it's shady here. After a short set of switchbacks, you keep climbing, but more gently, contouring on the ridge high above the river. Top out at 7,678 feet, about a mile after crossing the river.

Across the valley are a series of hexagonal columns of basalt created by lava flows from 100,000 years ago. That's the Devils Postpile. From here you can enjoy one of the best views of the formation without having to battle the crowds.

At 1.9 miles in, reach a signed four-way junction. Stay straight on the JMT/PCT, staying around an elevation of 7,650 feet.

There is an important intersection 0.6 mile away. The JMT and PCT share a lot of miles together, but at this point, they go their separate ways. For your adventure, stay straight on the PCT, heading downhill toward the Middle Fork. If you're early in the season or if there has been a good snowpack, you may have to ford or rock-hop over creeks, like the outlet from Lost Dog Lake.

At 3 miles in you can hear Minaret Falls before shortly finding the trail and yourself at its base. Above to the left, Minaret Creek drops 300 feet and 100 feet wide down a series of side-by-side streams. Its water originates as snowmelt off the Minarets, a sawtooth-spiky mountain range of almost 12,000 feet. A short side trail with scrambling to the left can get you closer to the falls, but take care among wet and slippery rocks.

Miles and Directions

0.0 Start at Bus Stop 9, Rainbow Falls.

0.2 Turn right onto JMT/PCT north at four-way intersection.

0.7 Stay straight on the JMT/PCT north at four-way intersection, then cross a bridge.

1.3 Switchbacks up a shady hillside.

1.7 High point with views across valley to Devils Postpile.

1.9 Four-way signed junction; stay straight on JMT/PCT north.

2.5 Four-way signed junction; stay straight on PCT north.

3.1 Base of falls. Return the way you came.

6.2 Arrive back at the trailhead.

Option: When you get to the four-way intersection to return to Bus Stop 9, consider staying straight and uphill on the JMT/PCT to a sign marked "Resort." In 0.3 mile you arrive at a restaurant, store, and bus stop.

76 Horsetail Falls

Nestled in a colorful Sierra valley, Horsetail Falls gets its name from a distinctive braided tail.

Height: At least 50 feet visible, more hidden
Beauty rating: ★★★★ (for the area more than the falls)
Distance: 3.7+ miles out and back
Elevation gain: 700 feet
Difficulty: Moderate
Best season: Late spring, summer, fall
County: Mono
Trailhead amenities: 50+ parking spots in a paved lot, privy, food storage lockers to prevent bears

Land status: Inyo National Forest White Mountain Ranger District, John Muir Wilderness
Maps: Tom Harrison Mammoth High Country; USGS Convict Lake
Trail contact: Inyo National Forest White Mountain Public Lands Information Center, 798 N. Main St., Bishop 93514; (760) 873-2500; www.fs.usda.gov/main/inyo/home
Fees and permits: None

Finding the trailhead: Google Maps: McGee Creek Trailhead. From Bishop, drive 27 miles north on US 395. Turn left onto McGee Creek Road. Stay straight through a stop sign, passing a park. Just 0.2 mile later the road turns into a one-lane paved road. Pass a campground. The road turns to gravel 2.1 miles later.
GPS: N37 33.044' / W118 48.077'

The Hike

Horsetail Falls may be the most common name for a waterfall in California. Much like the falls with which it shares its name, this Horsetail Falls has an inverted V-shape with a narrow flow at the top and a wide flowing tail at the bottom.

Start on a sandy, wide trail at the information sign at an altitude of more than 7,800 feet. You'll generally follow McGee Creek up the wide canyon.

Two things make this hike special: First, you're able to get far into the canyon without thousands of feet of steep climbing or switchbacks—a rarity among Sierra trails. You'll also be exposed to three plant ecosystems. You start the trail among sagebrush (*Artemesia tridentata* after its apparent "three teeth"). Then you pass willows, birches, and aspens as the canyon narrows and the trail draws closer to the riparian zone around the creek. This canyon is beautiful during the autumn when leaves change to gold and the color climbs up the entire valley. When you reach the area around the falls, you're among the cedars.

Pass a picnic area. Red and White Mountain is straight ahead, a massive striped and colorful mountain worthy of its name. Those lucky enough to catch its alpenglow early in the morning or in the golden hour before sunset won't forget it. Mount

Baldwin is to the right and Mount Crocker to the left—although you are so deep in this canyon, you can only see the flanks of these giants.

After 0.8 mile the wide, open trail starts switchbacking up the canyon. Cross a small, year-round stream. You can rock-hop across it unless the water is quite high.

Enter the John Muir Wilderness at 0.9 mile marked with a wooden sign. For the next 0.7 mile, the trail heads up the canyon curving to the left (south). The canyon walls are narrower now.

Your major crossing—the outflow from the falls—happens 1.6 miles from your car. In low water or late in the season, it's possible to rock-hop across without getting your feet wet. Before crossing, look up and you may see the falls. This view may be enough for your hiking group, especially if the creek is raging.

If not, continue across the creek. After the major crossing, there's a smaller crossing. In high water after a snowmelt, they may even meld together into one giant creek.

Stay on the trail for 0.1 mile longer as it ascends away from the creek. Turn right on an obvious use trail near a large cedar tree. There are less obvious use trails before you reach the correct one. Keep going if unsure. Once on the correct use trail, you climb for about 0.15 mile. It starts fading the farther back you go, but the view of Horsetail Falls gets better.

Unfortunately, thick willows and vegetation make it nearly impossible to get right under the falls. Several open slabs and boulders work as nice vantage points for getting better views of the creek. You also have incredible views of the valley around you.

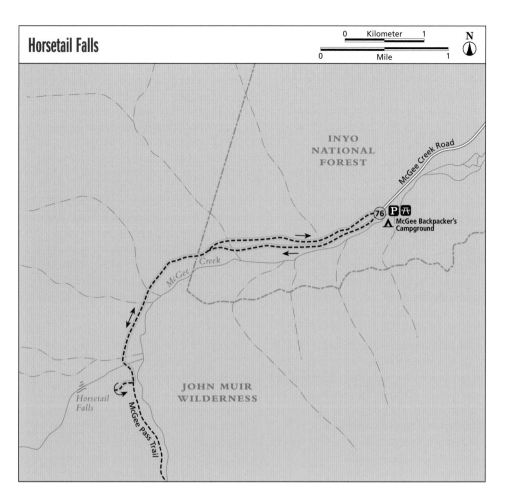

Horsetail Falls

Kilometer
Mile

INYO
NATIONAL
FOREST

McGee Creek Road

76 P

▲ McGee Backpacker's
Campground

McGee Creek

Horsetail
Falls

McGee Pass Trail

JOHN MUIR
WILDERNESS

Miles and Directions

0.0 Start at the parking lot.

0.9 Enter John Muir Wilderness.

1.6 Cross creek outflow below falls.

1.7 Junction to take use trail on the right.

1.85 Pick an end point along the use trail with a good view of falls. Return the way you came.

3.7 Arrive back at the trailhead.

77 Tuolumne Falls and White Cascade Falls

One of the most classic hikes and backpacking trips in Yosemite, this relatively gentle hike (by Sierra standards) through Tuolumne Meadows gives you the taste of all the things to love about Yosemite: water, rock, forest, wildlife, history, and, of course, waterfalls.

Height: Tuolumne: 100 feet; White Cascade: around 50 feet

Beauty rating: ★★★★★

Distance: 11 miles out and back

Elevation gain: 400 feet gain/1,130 loss (total of 1,265 gain over the trip)

Difficulty: Moderate

Best season: Summer, early fall

County: Tuolumne

Trailhead amenities: Free Tuolumne Meadows bus stop near trailhead; limited parking along side of road. Bear boxes, trash/recycle bins. If camping at Glen Aulin High Sierra Camp, composting toilets and potable water are available.

Land status: Yosemite National Park

Maps: Tom Harrison Yosemite Tuolumne Meadows; USGS Tioga Pass, Falls Ridge

Trail contact: Yosemite National Park, PO Box 577, Yosemite National Park, 95389; (209) 372-0200; www.nps.gov/yose

Fees and permits: Vehicle pass required to enter the park, valid 1–7 days; annual passes available. Day hikes do not require a permit. If you intend to visit these falls as a backpacking trip, book your reservations for the Glen Aulin High Sierra Camp well before your trip at www.nps.gov/yose/planyourvisit/wildpermits .htm. You may also be able to get a first-come, first-served backpacking permit by visiting the ranger station no sooner than 11 a.m. the day prior to your backpacking trip (if you score a permit for the following day, you can stay in the frontcountry at the backpackers' campground in the Tuolumne Meadows Campground). As of 2019 there are two permit options: Camp at Glen Aulin (22A) or Glen Aulin pass through to Waterwheel Falls (22B). If you made a reservation, you can pick up your permit at the wilderness permit station the day prior or the day of your hike. You can check whether permits are available for your desired date by visiting www.nps.gov/yose/planyourvisit/fulltrailheads .htm. The system can change, so check with a wilderness ranger by calling (209) 372-0826 (9 a.m. to noon and 1 to 4:30 p.m., Mon through Fri, Mar through early Oct).

Finding the trailhead: Google Maps: Glen Aulin Trailhead. (**Note:** Tioga Pass Road is only open when free of snow—usually June through Oct. Check road conditions before you go.) From the town of Lee Vining, take Tioga Pass Road (CA 120 West) for 12 miles toward Yosemite's Tioga Pass entrance station (vehicle fee). Continue for 6.9 miles toward Lembert Dome in Tuolumne Meadows. The free Tuolumne Meadows shuttle runs every 15 minutes with numerous stops in the area. The closest stop to the trailhead is Stop 4: Lembert Dome. At Lembert Dome (either by bus or car), turn right onto a dirt road, following signs for the Soda Springs trailhead and stables. The trailhead is at the end of this road before it makes a right turn. Store your food, trash, and toiletries in the bear boxes before starting this hike. There are numerous No Parking signs around the trailhead, so you may need to park at the stables.

GPS: N37 52.443' / W119 22.013'

The Hike

When I lived in the Eastern Sierra, hiking to and from Glen Aulin was my intro-duction to walking more than 10 miles in a day. This hike is so lovely, I've walked it dozens of times as day hikes and on backpacking trips on the Pacific Crest Trail.

Not only is the hike to the falls beautiful, but it holds an important place in the history of the conservation movement. Your trail starts on the Old Tioga Road to Tuolumne Meadows where John Muir (1838–1914) first talked with friends about establishing Yosemite National Park. The park was designated in 1890. Some envi-ronmental historians believe every national park in the United States and across the world exists in part because of that conversation.

This is the ancestral summer grounds of the Sierra Miwok (who lived in the west) and Mono Lake Paiute (who lived in the east). In the 1800s the Mono Trail trade route crossed Tuolumne Meadow, allowing exchanges of acorns and shell beads (from the west) with obsidian and pine nuts (from the east). Archaeologists found acorn grinding mortars near Lembert Dome (where you parked or where the bus dropped you off).

As you walk the wide, sandy trail, you'll have expansive views of the meadows and Cathedral and Unicorn Peaks (the jagged ones in the distance). Information boards along the way explain the park's natural history. As recently as 2 million years ago, glaciers flowed down the canyon to the west of where you are, carving this land-scape. Only 20,000 years ago, ice covered all but the highest peaks here. You can see

Tuolumne Falls is the first major waterfall you'll discover on the way to Glen Aulin Camp.
iSTOCK

Follow the Tuolumne River downhill toward Glen Aulin as it passes multiple waterfalls. iSTOCK

evidence of the glaciers all around you in striations in the bedrock and the glacial polish that gives granite a shiny look. Boulders that seem to be in "random" places were moved there by glaciers—hence their name, glacial erratics.

You'll likely see Belding's ground squirrels, marmots, chickarees, or Clark's nutcrackers on your hike. The meadows themselves are made of perennial grasses and shorthair sedge. Winter lasts eight months here, so annuals don't have enough time to sprout, flower, and seed in the short growing season at this high altitude.

At 0.2 mile in, a rusted metal sign indicates a trail to the right to the stables. (*Note:* These ancient signs are notoriously off in their mileage.) Continue straight. In 0.2 mile, ignore a trail on the left over the river. Shortly after, look for a signed Y junction, where either trail works. On the left, you can reach the official trailhead via a detour to Soda Springs (the wooden shack surrounded by reddish soil) and Parsons Lodge (a cabin of historic importance) or via a detour road/trail (to the right). Either way, 0.5 mile in, there's a large trailhead/wilderness sign kiosk area where the path to Glen Aulin starts.

The sandy flat trail travels through forest. At 1.25 miles, stay straight at a signed junction for a trail to the right leading to the stables. Soon after, ford Delaney Creek. Early in the season, you may get your feet wet; later in the season, it's a rock-hop. Gently climb, staying left at a signed junction at 1.65 miles, ignoring the path to the right to Young Lake. At 2.6 miles you reach possible crossings of the branches of Dingley Creek before the trail bends left in 0.2 mile, bringing you close to the Tuolumne River. This is a good place to cool off and snack before heading on.

At 3.5 miles the trail crosses a long, granite slab, and it can be confusing to know where the trail goes. Rock cairns (stacks of rocks) or rocks line the trail. As a rule of thumb, head straight across the slab in the same direction the dirt trail was headed downstream along the creek.

Tuolumne Falls and White Cascade Falls; California, LeConte, and Waterwheel Falls

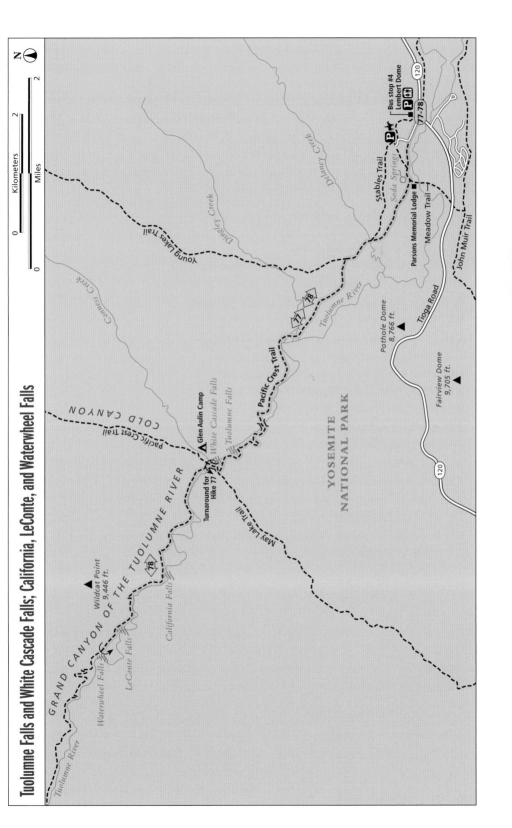

Cross a bridge at 4 miles with open views of the Tuolumne River. You're close. Ascend and then descend via beautifully crafted rock stairs to Tuolumne Falls at 4.9 miles.

Continue descending toward a signed junction 0.25 mile later, staying right toward Glen Aulin for another 0.2 mile. From the bridge over the Tuolumne River, you can see White Cascade Falls tumbling into a gentle, deep pool. There's a sandy beach to better view and enjoy the falls. Linger here. If you brought your backpacking gear and have a permit (or are a strong day hiker), continue to the California, LeConte, and Waterwheel Falls hike (Hike 78 in this book).

Miles and Directions

0.0   Start at trailhead at end of road.
0.2   Stay left/straight at signed junction with stables trail.
0.4   Stay right at signed junction.
0.45 Signed Y junction near Soda Springs; either trail works.
0.5   Wilderness trailhead for Glen Aulin.
1.25 Stay left/straight at signed junction with stables trail.
1.3   Delaney Creek crossing.
1.65 Stay left at signed junction with Young Lake Trail.
2.6   Dingley Creek branch crossings.
2.8   Trail close to Tuolumne River.
3.5   Granite slab crossing.
4.0   Cross bridge over Tuolumne River.
4.9   Tuolumne Falls.
5.15 Stay right at junction with May Lake Trail.
5.35 Bridge over Tuolumne River near White Cascade Falls.
5.4   Stay right toward Tuolumne Falls.
5.5   Bridge and sandy beach below Tuolumne Falls. Return the way you came.
10.7 Arrive back at the trailhead.

78 California, LeConte, and Waterwheel Falls

This backpacking trip or long day hike takes you away from the crowds to the less-visited valley of Yosemite, the Grand Canyon of the Tuolumne, which leads to one of Yosemite's most unique waterfalls.

See map on page 300.

Height: California: about 120 feet; LeConte: over 200 feet; Waterwheel: over 300 feet

Beauty rating: ★★★★★

Distance: 18.2 miles out and back (can be done as a backpacking trip)

Elevation gain: 250 feet ascent/1,900 feet descent (which means climbing on the return)

Difficulty: Moderate backpacking trip; strenuous day hike

Best season: Summer

County: Tuolumne

Trailhead amenities: Free Tuolumne Meadows bus stop near trailhead; limited parking along side of road. Bear boxes, trash/recycle bins. If camping at Glen Aulin High Sierra Camp, composting toilets and potable water are available.

Land status: Yosemite National Park

Maps: Tom Harrison Yosemite Tuolumne Meadows; USGS Falls Ridge, Tioga Pass

Trail contact: Yosemite National Park, PO Box 577, Yosemite National Park 95389; (209) 372-0200; www.nps.gov/yose

Fees and permits: Vehicle pass required to enter the park, valid 1-7 days; annual passes available. Day hikes do not require a permit. If you intend to visit these falls as a backpacking trip, book your reservations for the Glen Aulin High Sierra Camp well before your trip at www.nps.gov/yose/planyourvisit/wildpermits .htm. You may also be able to get a first-come, first-served backpacking permit by visiting the ranger station no sooner than 11 a.m. the day prior to your backpacking trip (if you score a permit for the following day, you can stay in the frontcountry at the backpackers' campground in the Tuolumne Meadows Campground). As of 2019 there are two permit options: Camp at Glen Aulin (22A) or Glen Aulin pass through to Waterwheel Falls (22B). If you made a reservation, you can pick up your permit at the wilderness permit station the day prior or the day of your hike. You can check whether permits are available for your desired date by visiting www.nps.gov/yose/planyourvisit/fulltrailheads .htm. The system can change, so check with a wilderness ranger by calling (209) 372-0826 (9 a.m. to noon and 1 to 4:30 p.m., Mon through Fri, Mar through early Oct).

Finding the trailhead: Google Maps: Glen Aulin Trailhead. (**Note:** Tioga Pass Road is only open when free of snow—usually June through Oct. Check road conditions before you go.) From the town of Lee Vining, take Tioga Pass Road (CA 120 West) toward Yosemite's Tioga Pass entrance station (vehicle fee). Continue for 12 miles toward Lembert Dome in Tuolumne Meadows. The free Tuolumne Meadows shuttle runs every 15 minutes with numerous stops in the area. The closest stop to the trailhead is Stop 4: Lembert Dome. At Lembert Dome (either by bus or car), turn right onto a dirt road, following signs for the Soda Springs trailhead and stables. The trailhead is at the end of this road before it makes a right turn. Store your food, trash, and toiletries in the bear boxes before starting this hike. There are numerous No Parking signs around the trailhead, so you may need to park at the stables.

GPS: N37 52.443' / W119 22.013'

The Hike

California, LeConte, and Waterwheel Falls are the most remote falls in this book. This is an extension of the popular (and crowded) Tuolumne Falls and White Cascade Falls hike and gets you farther into the backcountry.

From Glen Aulin High Sierra Camp, follow signs for Waterwheel Falls. Immediately climb up a rock ledge to your left. There are also signs near Glen Aulin Camp for Virginia Canyon heading northeast on the Pacific Crest Trail, and it's easy to accidentally end up on that route.

After climbing above the river and out of Glen Aulin, go back down to a forested, flat meadow. On your left is the now peaceful river. On your right are towering granite domes.

Continue downhill for 1.5 miles. As you are in the wilderness, there's not much signage indicating where the falls are along the river, so you need to pay attention. There are numerous cascades along the Tuolumne River, and in low water it's easy to miss the falls for the rapids. The trail draws away from the river for about 0.5 mile. When the trail gets closer to the water, you should start paying attention. You're at the top of California Falls right as the water starts to become calmer.

Continue downhill until you see an unmarked use trail that goes to the left down toward the river. It's about 0.1 mile to the base of California Falls, a wide, blocky falls. A slab nearby makes a good lunch spot, but beware the slippery rocks below.

Waterwheels occur when there is enough force in the flow that water hits potholes and bounces upwards. ISTOCK

As you work your way down the valley, you'll see numerous impressive cascades. But LeConte Falls can be trickier to find, especially during low water years or seasons. From California Falls, continue downhill on the trail for 1.1 miles. Above and to the right is Wildcat Point, a distinctive granite dome. Again, watch for an open, flat section of water. Right after, the trail descends on a short series of switchbacks. A use trail that is less distinct than the one to California Falls, on the left, goes to the falls.

LeConte Falls also has waterwheels, so don't confuse it with Waterwheel Falls. Pockets formed in the granite cause the falling water to splash back upward, creating the illusion of "wheels" of water tumbling down the rock.

You descend more steeply on stone steps toward Waterwheel Falls. There isn't a sign or indicator that you're at the falls, but the signed footbridge over Return Creek (a tributary that feeds into the Tuolumne River from the right) is a good indicator you've reached the bottom of the Tuolumne River's falls until it reaches Hetch Hetchy Reservoir.

Waterwheel Falls cascades at a low angle down a tall granite slope. It's technically not a falls but a steep cascade. Instead, the throwing up and back of water (waterwheels) is what makes this falls incredible. It's a sight to behold in early summer, when snowmelt makes the wheels quite distinctive. I've seen photos of rainbows formed over the mist from the falls. Visitors in the autumn or during dry years may view the falls with remorse—the return trip requires 2,000 feet of climbing back to Tuolumne Meadows.

Miles and Directions

0.0 Start at trailhead at end of road.

5.5 Glen Aulin High Sierra Camp (route described in Tuolomne and White Cascade Falls Hike 77).

6.5 Use trail to California Falls.

7.7 Use trail to Le Conte Falls.

8.2 Views of Waterwheel Falls.

9.1 Return Creek footbridge.

18.2 Arrive back at the trailhead.

79 Lundy Canyon Falls

Lundy Canyon Falls is one of the most beautiful, hidden canyons in the Eastern Sierra. Wildflowers, golden aspens, numerous cascades, and red mountains against blue sky are among the many reasons to visit the area.

Height: Several cascades along the hike, ranging from 20–40 feet.
Beauty rating: ★★★★★
Distance: 1.6+ miles out and back
Elevation gain: 250 feet gain/300 feet loss
Difficulty: Easy to moderate
Best season: Summer, fall
County: Mono
Trailhead amenities: 5 parking spots, more spots farther back; outhouse, picnic tables nearby with their own parking

Land status: Inyo National Forest, Mono Lake Ranger District; Hoover Wilderness
Maps: Tom Harrison Hoover Wilderness; USGS Dunderberg Peak
Trail contact: Inyo National Forest Mono Basin Scenic Area Visitor Center, 1 Visitor Center Dr., Lee Vining 93541; (760) 647-3044; www.fs .usda.gov/main/inyo/home
Fees and permits: None

Finding the trailhead: Google Maps: Lundy Canyon Trailhead. From Lee Vining, take US 395 north for 6.7 miles. Turn left on Lundy Lake Road. Five miles from US 395, the road becomes dirt/gravel. Stay straight, ignoring a sign showing a trailer park and campsites to the right. In 0.7 mile, pass a sign that you are entering Inyo National Forest and, 0.6 mile later, enter the one-way loop for parking.
GPS: N38 01.158' / W119 15.565'

The Hike

When I lived in the Eastern Sierra, Lundy Canyon was one of my favorite places to visit. The problem is, the 5 miles of driving a one-lane dirt road can be daunting, especially if it's muddy. The parking lot has but five spots (with options farther out). Nonetheless, if you make it here on a weekday, early in the morning, or off-season, you'll be rewarded.

From the parking lot, take the path behind the trail information signs. Pass through an aspen grove so incredible in the autumn, folks get married there. The trail is rocky and climbs into the narrow canyon with views of red, striped-rock mountains on either side. In summer the lupine, mule's ear, paintbrush, and other wildflowers explode on the hillsides, turning this canyon into a fantasyland.

You climb to a rocky outcrop about half a mile in, where you get your first views of the falls. There are incredible canyon views upstream and downstream of here. The northern flanks of Mount Scowden (11,106 feet) loom over you to the south. A blue-green pond lies below. The hillside lights up with golden aspen in autumn. After taking photos, descend on rocky trail again. Reach a wilderness sign and, 100 feet past it, turn left on a rocky side trail going down toward the falls.

One of many waterfalls in Lundy Canyon during the late season.

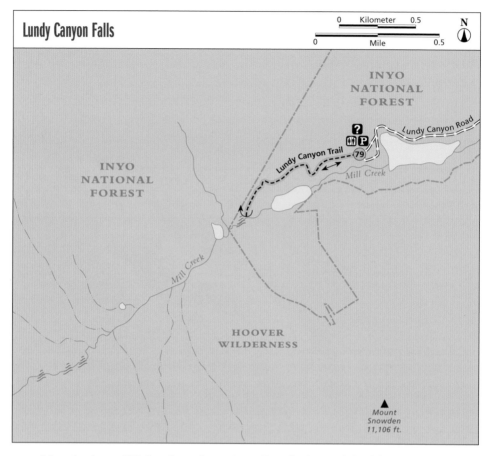

Lundy Canyon Falls

0   Kilometer   0.5

0   Mile   0.5

N

INYO
NATIONAL
FOREST

Lundy Canyon Road

Lundy Canyon Trail

79

INYO
NATIONAL
FOREST

Mill Creek

Mill Creek

HOOVER
WILDERNESS

▲
Mount
Snowden
11,106 ft.

It's only about 400 feet from the main trail to the base of the falls. You may have to crawl through willows. In lower water levels you can cross the water below the first falls, then follow its outflow on what looks like eternally flooded trail. If visiting after snowmelt or in high water years, the falls may not be accessible.

Miles and Directions

0.0 Start at the trailhead and parking.

0.75 Wilderness sign; shortly after, turn left on use trail down to base of first falls.

0.8 Base of first falls. Return the way you came.

1.6 Arrive back at the trailhead.

Option: For those with more time and energy, you can continue on the main trail deeper into Lundy Canyon. There are more rapids and cascades the higher you go, most notably around 2 miles from the trailhead, before the trail starts to switchback upward and south toward Lake Helen, the 20 Lakes Basin, and beyond that, Lundy Pass. This trip makes a wonderful longer day hike or backpacking trip (get your permit at the Inyo National Forest ranger station in Lee Vining before you go).

80 Horse Creek Falls

This hike in the Twin Lakes area of the northern Yosemite region never enters the park, but it's an almost equally popular and scenic area.

Height: About 80 feet with numerous smaller cascades
Beauty rating: ★★★★★
Distance: 3.4 miles out and back (with numerous cascades visible along the way for a shorter trip)
Elevation gain: 680 feet ascent/10 feet descent (total of 690 feet round-trip)
Difficulty: Easy
Best season: Summer, fall
County: Mono

Trailhead amenities: Parking lot for 40+ cars. Do not park on the street; numerous signs say you'll be ticketed or towed. Port-o-potty.
Land status: Humboldt-Toiyabe National Forest, Bridgeport Ranger District; Hoover Wilderness
Maps: Tom Harrison Hoover Wilderness; USGS Buckeye Ridge, Twin Lakes
Trail contact: Humboldt-Toiyabe National Forest, Bridgeport Ranger Station, HC62, Box 1000, Bridgeport 93517; (760) 932-7070; www.fs.usda.gov/main/htnf/home
Fees and permits: None for day-use parking

Finding the trailhead: Google maps: Annett's Mono Village. From the town of Bridgeport, California, take Twin Lakes Road south for 13.4 mile. You'll pass junctions with campgrounds but keep going until the road dead-ends at Annett's Mono Village on the east side of the southeastern lake.
GPS: N38 08.566' / W119 22.367'

The Hike

The trickiest part of this trip is getting out of the campground. Start at the entrance station for the campground. If it is staffed, they can often direct you. Otherwise, take the road to the left through the campground. Turn left onto an old dirt road near a tree signed "1D." This path leads to a wide wooden bridge about 200 feet later. Cross it.

After the bridge, on the south side of the creek, take the second trail on your right (the first curls back toward the creek). The trail forks again. Two hundred feet from the initial footbridge, reach a "hiking trail" sign. Follow its instruction, taking the path to the left. Continue on this path for about 400 feet to cross the stream on a smaller footbridge. Continue for about another 100 feet until you reach an intersection. Turn right on a wide, sandy trail to the large Hoover Wilderness sign.

Take the Horse Creek Trail, which starts behind the sign. It ascends through pine and aspen forest, which is golden and beautiful in the autumn. At 0.2 mile from the sign, you come near Horse Creek, the easiest access to cascades. This is a good place to linger and a turnaround point for most folks.

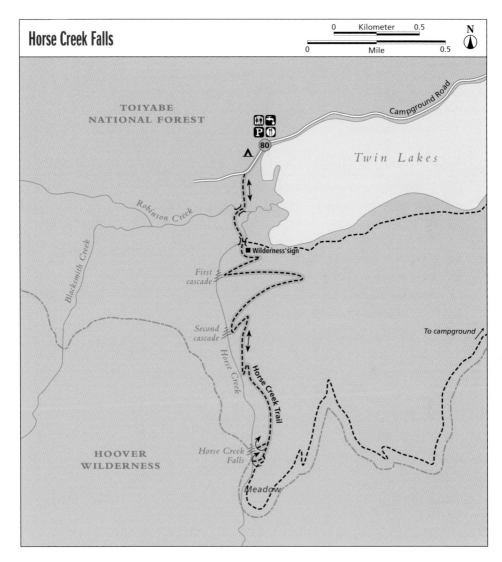

Horse Creek Falls

TOIYABE
NATIONAL FOREST

Campground Road

80

Twin Lakes

Robinson Creek

Blacksmith Creek

Wilderness sign

First
cascade

To campground

Second
cascade

Horse Creek

Horse Creek Trail

HOOVER
WILDERNESS

Horse Creek
Falls

Meadow

If you're feeling energetic and have plenty of water in your bottle, climb on switchbacks through classic Sierra sagebrush. There are incredible views of Twin Lakes below and the Sawtooth Range farther out. Because it isn't shady, the climb through this section can get hot. We were in T-shirts through here in November.

About 0.6 mile and 375 feet of gain since you last saw the creek, reach a side trail down to the water. Otherwise, continue through sagebrush on a switchback to your left, climbing about 200 feet over the next 0.2 mile. The trail contours along the left side of a sunken valley. In an open area you may get your first view of Matterhorn Peak towering over a larger falls of Horse Creek. Unfortunately, there isn't a great

The first cascade of Horse Creek Falls in autumn with golden aspen leaves.
Many hikers choose to turn around here after the first half mile.

place to picnic or an easy way to hang out by the creek here, except a small spot under a large pine near the trail.

If a better picnic spot is what you have in mind, take the trail up a short switchback to the top of this cascade. It's not a great vantage point for the falls, but it is a good sitting spot. Otherwise, continue farther into the wilderness for the next 0.3 mile to reach a hanging valley where the creek looks more mellow (and has great picnic spots with views).

Miles and Directions

0.0   Start at day-use parking by the lake.
0.2   Cross creek on wide wooden bridge and turn right.
0.3   Hoover Wilderness sign.
0.5   First cascade by a switchback.
1.2   Side trail to water and cascade.
1.4   Valley with view of falls at Matterhorn Peak.
1.7   Hanging valley above the falls.
3.4   Arrive back at the trailhead.

81 Leavitt Falls

A waterfall worthy of its own picnic area, Leavitt Falls is one of the grandest water-falls in the book—and it's enjoyable for those with limited mobility.

Height: 200 feet multi-tiered
Beauty rating: ★★★★★
Distance: 0.2 mile out and back
Elevation gain: Less than 20 feet
Difficulty: Easy
Best season: Late spring, summer, early fall
County: Mono
Trailhead amenities: About 20 parking spots, outhouse, picnic tables, shade

Land status: Humboldt-Toiyabe National Forest, Bridgeport Ranger District
Maps: Tom Harrison Hoover Wilderness; USGS Pickel Meadow
Trail contact: Humboldt-Toiyabe National Forest, Bridgeport Ranger Station, HC62, Box 1000, Bridgeport 93517; (760) 932-7070; www.fs.usda.gov/main/htnf/home
Fees and permits: None for day-use parking

Finding the trailhead: Google Maps: Leavitt Falls Vista Point. From Sonora Junction (the intersection of US 395 and CA 108), turn west onto CA 108 toward Sonora Pass for 9.2 miles. Along the way, you pass Leavitt Meadows Pack Station (8 miles in). From there, continue another 1.2 miles on CA 108 and turn left (south) into signed Leavitt Falls Vista Picnic Area. Continue on the gravel road. In 0.1 mile you reach a parking and picnic area. If you're coming from Sonora Pass, it's 6 miles east on CA 108 on your right side.
GPS: N38 19.214' / W119 33.402'

The Hike

Leavitt Falls is one of the bigger waterfalls in this book. Unlike the grand falls of Yosemite, Leavitt can be visited without paying an entrance fee. As it's located off the less frequently traveled CA 108, crowds are fewer here than may be found elsewhere during peak waterfall season.

From the parking lot the falls are visible from a clever railed wooden viewing platform, which includes a picnic table and even is built around a tree for shade.

Leavitt Falls is formed from Leavitt Creek dropping off a hanging valley into the scenic Leavitt Meadow below. It's trapped in a box canyon formed by Leavitt Creek, a tributary of the West Walker River, so is best viewed from a distance instead of walking closer to it. From here you can see it's actually a multi-tiered falls. The upper falls drops into a pool hidden in the chasm, and then it reemerges as a longer, lower falls surrounded by the firs and junipers characteristic of the Sierra at this elevation. From the viewing platform you have the best view of both of these spots.

To the south are panoramic views of the West Walker Valley, which sits hundreds of feet below (literally) the viewing platform. You can see Leavitt Meadow where Leavitt Creek joins the West Walker River. This view lets you appreciate the diversity of this area: the snowy, forested mountains of the Sierra to the west; the dry valley in the middle; and the dry, almost desert-like mountains to the east.

Leavitt Falls originates in a narrow slot canyon visible from above. There are at least two other tiers above it visible from other angles from the viewpoint.

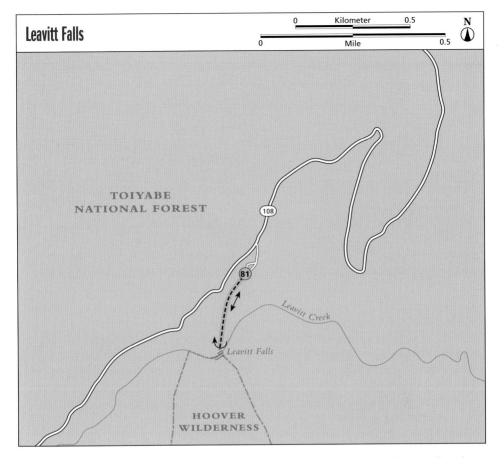

For those looking for more of a walk, carefully follow an informal use trail at the western far end of the parking lot. It parallels CA 108 above and with a big drop-off on a cliff to the left. Although this trail is short, it's one where you want to take special care to stay on the route and watch your kids and pets. Unlike Yosemite, there is no fence or barrier to protect you from the steep cliff drop-off below.

The trail parallels the cliff for 500 feet, branching occasionally. Take care if it appears as if your branch goes off the cliff. That's a good sign it's not actually the trail. Watch for several viewpoints along the way. Be very careful when taking selfies here, especially if there's wind.

Miles and Directions

0.0   Start at parking lot trailhead.

0.1   Closer view of falls. Return the way you came.

0.2   Arrive back at the trailhead.

Option: If you want more of a walk, head up CA 108 toward Sonora Pass to experience Sardine Falls or Emigrant Falls.

82 Sardine Falls

This falls is so prominent from the road, you just have to pull over and walk to it. A pleasant short walk through a meadow and forest brings you to this steep-dropping falls, which topples over a rocky cliff. The only downside? You may have to get your feet wet.

Height: About 75 feet
Beauty rating: ★★★★★
Distance: 2.2 miles out and back
Elevation gain: 300 feet one-way
Difficulty: Easy; easy to moderate navigation
Best season: Late spring, summer, early fall
County: Mono
Trailhead amenities: A glorified gravel pullout fits 4 cars

Land status: Humboldt-Toiyabe National Forest, Bridgeport Ranger District
Maps: Tom Harrison Hoover Wilderness; USGS Pickel Meadow
Trail contact: Humboldt-Toiyabe National Forest, Bridgeport Ranger Station, HC62, Box 1000, Bridgeport 93517; (760) 932-7070; www.fs.usda.gov/main/htnf/home
Fees and permits: None for day-use parking

Finding the trailhead: Google Maps: No Google Maps location. From Bridgeport, drive 17 miles north to Sonora Junction, the intersection of US 395 and CA 108. Turn left onto CA 108, taking it west for 12.6 miles (2.6 miles east of Sonora Pass). Along the way, you enter Toiyabe National Forest. The pullout is 0.4 mile after you cross a bridge signed "Sardine Creek." Pull over to the left (south) side of the road, where you'll find a boulder-lined gravel lot fitting 4 cars. It may have a sign saying No Motorized Vehicles. If you start switching back up toward Sonora Pass, you've gone too far.
GPS: N38 18.523' / W119 36.210'

The Hike

We hadn't planned on visiting this falls, but on a trip in the area, we saw the waterfall tumbling down the valley and had to pull over to get a closer look. Sardine Falls is impressive from the highway, even at the end of the season.

From the four-car lot/pullout, follow the old two-track dirt jeep trail (on which the Forest Service is trying hard to prohibit motorized vehicles) southwest. There are several pullouts, though it's clear the Forest Service is trying to reduce impact to the alpine meadow by keeping foot traffic on the old jeep trail. Having scouted out several of the other use trails, we can attest the walking is much easier if you opt for the main route leaving from the boulder-lined "lot."

In 0.2 mile you have to ford Sardine Creek, which parallels CA 108. Early in the season and in big snow years, it can be knee-deep. At other times it's possible to hop across the creek without getting your feet wet by using the strategically placed rocks found right where the path meets the creek.

Sardine Falls is prominent from the road and set against a backdrop of the Hoover Wilderness it's a peaceful, short, and relatively flat hike.

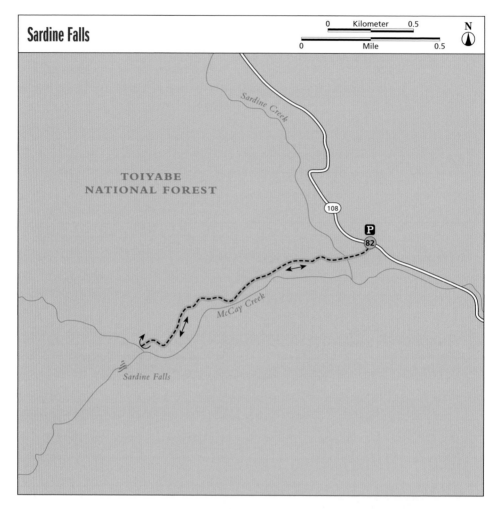

Continue following the jeep track through a pleasant meadow with a view of Sardine Falls. After about 0.5 mile, you enter lodgepole forest and then parallel McKay Creek, the origin and outflow of the waterfall. (McKay Creek feeds into Sardine Creek.) Here the trail tunnels through an aspen grove that's glorious in the fall. While the path here is clear, it can be brushy depending on the time of year.

At 0.7 mile, ascend short switchbacks. At 1 mile the trail comes within 10 feet of a feeder creek. You can hear Sardine Falls. A use trail leaves the main trail and crosses the creek (at this point the main trail takes a sharp turn right, headed up). Within 100 yards you are at the base of Sardine Falls.

Miles and Directions

0.0 Start at four-car gravel lot lined with boulders. A "No Motorized Vehicles" sign may still be standing.

0.2 Ford Sardine Creek.

0.5 Reach forest.

0.7 Switchbacks.

1.0 Leave main trail.

1.1 Reach base of falls. Return the way you came.

2.2 Arrive back at the trailhead.

Sardine Falls from its base viewed on a warm November day.

83 Falls of Emigrant Wilderness

From a grand footbridge over a gorge of granite, you can see two year-round waterfalls in a less-visited part of the Sierra.

Height: About 40 feet on Kennedy Creek, 30 feet on Summit Creek
Beauty rating: ★★★★
Distance: 3.6 miles round-trip
Elevation gain: 550 feet up/150 feet down (one-way)
Difficulty: Moderate
Best season: Summer, early fall
County: Tuolumne
Trailhead amenities: Lodge, restaurant, restrooms, showers, campstore, water, trash cans

Land status: Stanislaus National Forest, Summit Ranger District; Emigrant Wilderness
Maps: Tom Harrison Emigrant Wilderness; USGS Sonora Pass
Trail contact: Stanislaus National Forest, Summit District Ranger Station, #1 Pinecrest Lake Rd., Pinecrest 95364; (209) 965-3434 (note that this is on the western side of the Sierra, which is not the fastest route to visit if coming from Southern California); www.fs.usda.gov/main/stanislaus/home
Fees and permits: None

Finding the trailhead: Google Maps: Kennedy Meadows Trailhead Parking Lot. From Bridgeport, drive 17 miles north to Sonora Junction, the intersection of US 395 and CA 108. Turn left onto CA 108, taking it west over Sonora Pass. Continue on the narrow, paved road until its end at the Kennedy Meadows lodge. There's day-use parking here, but no overnight parking is allowed. For those who are camping overnight, there is a backpacker's parking area at Deadman Campground 0.6 mile from the lodge, which requires you walk the paved road to the lodge. **GPS:** N38 19.027' / W119 44.516'

The Hike

The Relief Dam was built in 1906–1912 as a storage facility for hydroelectric power. Up to 325 people worked through the Sierra's harsh winters. Generator-lit lighting allowed laborers to work night and day. Conditions were so poor that many quit, leaving the site on foot. It's called Relief Dam because the valley was a place of relief to early emigrants who came over Sonora Pass, not because it was a place of relief for laborers here.

Start on a dirt road by the lodge with a sign indicating no cars, bikes, or motorcycles. This is a conifer forest full of Jeffrey pines. Climb to a hill with a gate near a water tank before descending on the road to follow the Middle Fork of the Stanislaus River. There's a meadow (often with horses) on the right. You pass numerous information boards for the next 0.7 mile until the road ends and you officially start the hiking trail at a sign. Pass a wilderness sign 500 feet later. However, maps show the wilderness line is when you cross the Middle Fork of the Stanislaus River 0.15 uphill mile later.

The unnamed falls on Kennedy Creek before it joins Summit Creek (also with a waterfall) here to turn into the Middle Fork of Stanislaus River. Both falls are visible from the footbridge.

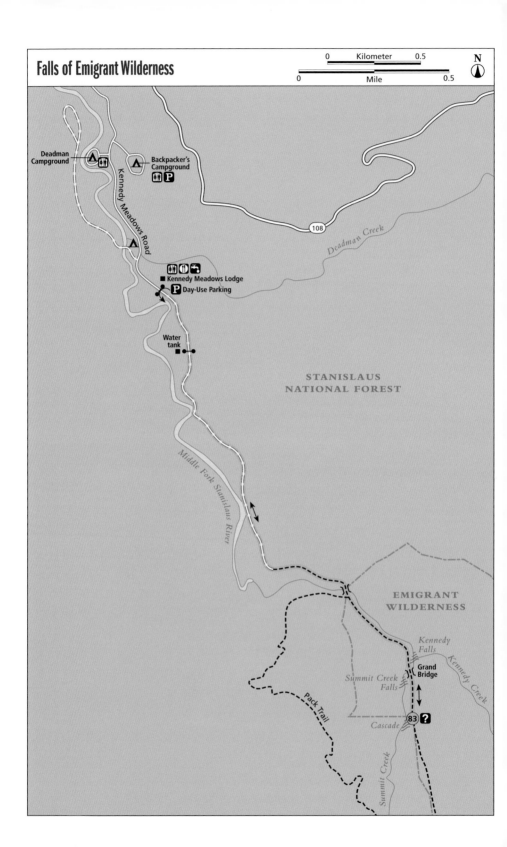

Falls of Emigrant Wilderness

0   Kilometer   0.5

0   Mile   0.5

N

Deadman
Campground

Backpacker's
Campground

Kennedy Meadows Road

Kennedy Meadows Lodge

Day-Use Parking

Water
tank

STANISLAUS
NATIONAL FOREST

Deadman Creek

Middle Fork Stanislaus River

EMIGRANT
WILDERNESS

*Kennedy
Falls*

Grand
Bridge

*Summit Creek
Falls*

Kennedy Creek

Pack Trail

Cascade

83

Summit Creek

108

After the bridge, stay left on the trail following the Middle Fork, ignoring a signed pack trail to your right. In the next 0.3 mile, you climb more than 200 feet. As you climb, you may start seeing more lodgepole and red fir. You are partially on rock stairs along a wide ledge blasted out of the granite. This is classic Sierra trail-building technique, although rarely as dramatic as the overhanging granite ledge along this trail.

You get a view of the first falls—Summit Creek Falls multi-tiered year-round falls on Kennedy Creek before the confluence with Summit Creek, where it turns into the Middle Fork of the Stanislaus. Continue 500 more feet on the trail uphill to a grand bridge near the confluence of Kennedy Creek and Summit Creek.

You're at the only place in this book where there are waterfalls on your left and right. On your right (west), there's a granite gorge with Kennedy Falls, a year-round waterfall on Summit Creek. On your left (east) are the falls on Kennedy Creek. Enjoy views from this long and beautiful footbridge. A short ascent farther up the trail takes you to a "pass" with views of Relief Dam and more rapids on Summit Creek.

Miles and Directions

0.0 Start at lodge parking lot, through a gate to a dirt road, following signs for "Wilderness 1.25 miles."

0.2 Climb hill on dirt road with water tank and gate nearby.

0.4 Road comes close to river and passes meadow for next 0.5 mile.

0.9 Trail kiosk signs; trail becomes singletrack soon after.

1.25 Footbridge.

1.3 Stay straight/right at trail junction.

1.65 View of two waterfalls from footbridge.

1.8 Cascade on left and views of Relief Lake. Return the way you came.

3.6 Arrive back at the trailhead.

Resources

This book is only the beginning of a lifetime of chasing waterfalls. These guidebooks and websites can point you to more falls and quality hikes in the area, as well as give you an appreciation for the history of this land.

Waterfall-Specific Resources

Ann Marie Brown. *California Waterfalls*, 4th ed. Berkeley, CA: Moon Outdoors, 2011.

Tracy Salcedo-Chourré. *Hiking Waterfalls in Northern California*. Guilford, CT: FalconGuides, 2017.

Suzanne Swedo. *Hiking Waterfalls Yosemite National Park: A Guide to the Park's Greatest Waterfalls*. Guilford, CT: FalconGuides, 2017.

Cultural and Natural History

William Bright. *1500 California Place Names: Their Origin and Meaning*. Berkeley, CA: University of California Press, 1998.

James Halfpenny. *Scat and Tracks of the Pacific Coast: A Field Guide to the Signs of 70 Wildlife Species*, 2nd ed. Guilford, CT: FalconGuides, 2015.

Philip A. Munz. *California Spring Wildflowers: From the Base of the Sierra Nevada and Southern Mountains to the Sea*. Berkeley, CA: University of California Press, 1961.

Ann Olander and Farley Olander. *Call of the Mountains: The Beauty and Legacy of Southern California's San Jacinto, San Bernardino and San Gabriel Mountains*. Las Vegas, NV: Stephens Press, 2005.

John W. Robinson. *The San Bernardinos: The Mountain Country from Cajon Pass to Oak Glen, Two Centuries of Changing Use*, 5th ed. Arcadia, CA: Big Santa Anita Historical Society, 2001.

John W. Robinson. *The San Gabriels: Southern California Mountain Country*. San Marino, CA: Golden West Books, 1977.

Philip W. Rundel and John Robert Gustafson. *Introduction to the Plant Life of Southern California*. Berkeley, CA: University of California Press, 2005.

Allan A. Schoenherr. *A Natural History of California*, 2nd ed. Berkeley, CA: University of California Press, 2017.

Hiking Resources

Mike Clelland. *Ultralight Backpackin' Tips*. Guilford, CT: FalconGuides, 2011.

Colin Fletcher and Chip Rawlins. *The Complete Walker IV*. New York: Alfred A. Knopf, 2002.

Ray Jardine. *Trail Life: Ray Jardine's Lightweight Backpacking*. Adventurelore Press, 2009.

Mountaineering: The Freedom of the Hills, 8th ed. Seattle, WA: The Mountaineers, 2010.

Allen O'Bannon and Mike Clelland. *Allen and Mike's Really Cool Backpackin' Book: Traveling and Camping Skills for a Wilderness Environment.* Guilford, CT: FalconGuides, 2001.

Jennifer Pharr Davis and Brew Davis. *Families on Foot: Urban Hikes to Backyard Treks and National Park Adventures.* Guilford, CT: FalconGuides, 2017.

Southern California Hiking Resources

Craig R. Carey. *Santa Barbara and Ventura: A Complete Guide to the Trails of the Southern Los Padres National Forest.* Berkeley, CA: Wilderness Press, 2012.

David Harris. *Afoot and Afield: Inland Empire.* Berkeley, CA: Wilderness Press, 2018.

Bob Lorentzen and Richard Nichols. *Hiking the California Coastal Trail, Volume Two: Monterey to Mexico.* Mendocino, CA: Bored Feet Publications. 2000.

John McKinney. *Hike Southern California: A Day Hiker's Guide.* Santa Barbara, CA: The Trailmaster, Inc., 2007.

Laura Randall. *60 Hikes within 60 miles: Los Angeles.* Birmingham, AL: Menasha Ridge Press, 2006.

John W. Robinson with David M. Harris. *San Bernardino Mountain Trails: 100 Hikes in Southern California*, 6th ed. Berkeley, CA: Wilderness Press, 2016.

John W. Robinson with Doug Christiansen. *Trails of the Angeles: 100 Hikes in the San Gabriels*, 9th ed. Berkeley, CA: Wilderness Press, 2015.

Shawnté Salabert. *Hiking the Pacific Crest Trail: Southern California.* Seattle, WA: Mountaineers Books, 2017.

Jerry Schad. *101 Hikes in Southern California*, 2nd ed. Berkeley, CA: Wilderness Press, 2005.

Jerry Schad and David M. Harris. *Afoot & Afield: Los Angeles County*, 4th ed. Berkeley, CA: Wilderness Press, 2019.

Jerry Schad and Scott Turner. *Afoot & Afield: San Diego County*, 5th ed. Berkeley, CA: Wilderness Press, 2017.

Casey Schreiner. *Day Hiking Los Angeles.* Seattle, WA: Mountaineers Books, 2016.

Robert Stone. *Day Hikes around Santa Barbara*, 3rd ed. Red Lodge, MT: Day Hike Books, Inc., 2010.

Robert Stone. *Day Hikes around Ventura County*, 3rd ed. Red Lodge, MT: Day Hike Books, Inc., 2016.

Websites

worldwaterfalldatabase.com

waterfallswest.com

www.world-of-waterfalls.com/california.html

Outdoor Conservation and Volunteer Groups

Anyone who enjoys spending time in the outdoors should consider donating money or time to these local nonprofits that work hard to build, maintain, and preserve the trails we love and secure the conservation of the land where trails are found. These organizations also improve access and work with willing landowners on mutually agreeable public access easements to ensure historically used trails will be open to hikers forever.

Ventana Wilderness Association: www.ventanawild.org
Montecito Trails Foundation: www.montecitotrailsfoundation.info
Los Padres Forest Association: http://lpforest.org
Los Padres Forest Watch: https://lpfw.org

Wildlands Conservancy: www.wildlandsconservancy.org

Forest Service Volunteer Association: www.fsva.org
Friends of the Desert Mountains: www.desertmountains.org
San Gabriel Mountains Trailbuilders: www.sgmtrailbuilders.org
San Gorgonio Wilderness Association: www.sgwa.org
Laguna Mountain Volunteer Association: www.lmva.net
Cuyamaca Rancho State Park Interpretive Association: www.crspia.org
Cleveland National Forest Foundation: www.cnff.org
Anza Borrego Foundation: www.theabf.org
Santa Monica Mountains Fund: www.samofund.org
San Gabriel Mountains Forever: www.sangabrielmountains.org
Santa Monica Mountains Trail Council: www.smmtc.org
Angeles Volunteer Association: www.angelesvolunteers.org
Arroyos and Foothills Conservancy: www.arroyosfoothills.org
Eaton Canyon Nature Center: www.ecnca.org

About the Authors

Liz Thomas is a professional hiker, adventure conservationist, and outdoor writer who broke the women's self-supported speed record on the 2,181-mile-long Appalachian Trail. She's hiked 20-plus long-distance trails including the Triple Crown of Hiking (AT, PCT, and CDT) and pioneering traverses of the Wasatch Range (Utah) and Chinook Trail (Washington/Oregon). She's also created and hiked twelve urban thru-hiking routes in ten different cities (including to all the breweries in Denver, Bend, and Grand Rapids, Michigan) and is affectionately known as the "Queen of Urban Hiking." Liz is the author of *Long Trails: Mastering the Art of the Thru-Hike* (published by FalconGuides). It received the 2017 National Outdoor Book Award for Best Instructional book, with judges calling it destined to become the "Bible of the Sport."

A former outdoor staff writer at the *New York Times*'s product review site, Wirecutter, Liz is currently editor-in-chief at Treeline Review, an outdoor gear meta-review website. She's also been guest editor at *Backpacker Magazine*, where she's currently the columnist of "Ask a Thru-Hiker" and instructor of the magazine's online class, Thru-Hiking 101.

For more on Liz, visit www.eathomas.com or, on Instagram and Facebook, @lizthomashiking.

Justin Lichter, also known as Trauma, has hiked over 40,000 miles and completed the first winter thru-hike of the Pacific Crest Trail. He has hiked many of the major long trails in the United States and worldwide. He has written articles for *Backpacker Magazine*, *Trail Runner Magazine*, SectionHiker.com, and *Adventure Journal* and has helped design products that have won *Backpacker Magazine* Editors' Choice Awards and *Outside Magazine* Gear of the Year Awards. He is the author of FalconGuide's *Trail Tested*, *Ultralight Survival Kit*, and *Ultralight Winter Travel*. Lichter lives in the heart of the Sierra Nevada in Truckee, California, and works as a ski patroller during the winter.